Stalin's Slave Ships

Jess

Stalin's Slave Ships
Kolyma, the Gulag Fleet, and the Role of the West

MARTIN J. BOLLINGER

NAVAL INSTITUTE PRESS
Annapolis, Maryland

Naval Institute Press
291 Wood Road
Annapolis, MD 21402

First Naval Institute Press paperback edition published in 2008.

Library of Congress Cataloging-in-Publication Data

Bollinger, Martin J., 1958–
    Stalin's slave ships : Kolyma, the Gulag fleet, and the role of the West / Martin J. Bollinger.
— 1st Naval Institute Press paperback ed.
        p. cm.
    Includes bibliographical references and index.
    ISBN 978-1-59114-046-7 (alk. paper)
        1. Convict ships—Soviet Union—History.   2. Prisoners, Transportation of—
Soviet Union.   3. Political prisoners—Soviet Union.   4. Concentration camps—
Soviet Union.   5. Penal colonies—Soviet Union.   I. Title.
HV8959.S65B65 2008
365—dc22

                                                                    2008005118

Printed in the United States of America on acid-free paper

14 13 12 11 10 09 08   9 8 7 6 5 4 3 2
First printing

To James and Elizabeth

Contents

viii

Preface:
A Horrible Secret

One evening in 1999, I settled with my wife in our Sydney, Australia, home and flipped channels on Australian cable TV. We began to half-watch a program about a Russian explorer by the name of Otto Shmidt and his attempt in 1933 to traverse the Arctic Ocean along the northern border of the Soviet Union in the merchant ship *Chelyuskin*.[1]

The program relayed how the ship became stuck fast in the Arctic ice just as it approached the end of its trek, almost within sight of the open waters of the Bering Strait. The world watched helplessly as the Artic ice pack embraced *Chelyuskin* and dragged it back away from open water, almost as a predator might retrieve its escaping prey. The world listened through vivid radio accounts from the scene as the ship was crushed by the massive ice packs. As the ship slipped beneath the ice, over a hundred passengers and crew were forced into tents on the frozen ocean's surface.

The television program described how Soviet aviators were dispatched from Moscow to rescue the stranded survivors and (in ironic testimony to the state of development of the Soviet Union at that time) how they reached the scene—by traveling by boat and train *westward* from Moscow over Europe, across the Atlantic, through the United States, across Canada and Alaska—finally reaching the *Chelyuskin* survivors after almost circumnavigating the world. This was easier than trying to travel eastward from Moscow across their own country.

While watching the program, we began to wonder why the Soviets would undertake this heroic rescue effort when the United States, with personnel and aircraft in nearby Alaska, had offered its assistance, in the spirit of Arctic cooperation. After all, in other emergencies in earlier years, Arctic rescues were the scene of impressive international cooperation between the Soviet Union and other countries.[2] The television program provided an answer. Evidently Stalin was afraid that any personnel from the United States sent to the scene might witness a horrible secret: there was *another* ship stranded in the ice. According to the television program, this second ship—named *Dzhurma*—held imprisoned in its holds some twelve thousand Gulag prisoners who were slowly starving and freezing to death in the icy wastes of the Siberian Arctic. It was said that the guards aboard *Dzhurma* survived that winter by using prisoners as the primary source of food, and that most of the surviving guards went insane from the experience. What is clear is that when *Dzhurma* was freed from the ice the following spring and made its way to port, no prisoners remained on board.

I was astounded to hear this. Surely, if twelve thousand people perished, it must rank as the greatest maritime disaster of all time. Why was so little known about it? What happened to the people on board? Did they all starve, go mad, and die? Were there other incidents similar to this one involving Gulag prisoner transports? Where did these ships come? How were they used? How many people were taken to their fate on these ships?

This book arose from my efforts to answer those questions and satisfy my personal curiosity about *Dzhurma*. Initially, my aspirations were far more modest, in particular since my only previous exposure to Russian history involved frequent viewing of the film *Dr. Zhivago*. First, having learned long ago that healthy skepticism should be applied in these cases, I set myself the objective of confirming *Dzhurma*'s existence as a real ship; that took several weeks. With that task accomplished, I decided to somehow find a photograph; that took several months. Finally, after two years of effort, I was able to obtain copies of the original plans for *Dzhurma*—and my emotional journey was nearly completed.

But while on that journey I learned more about the ships employed on the Gulag run and the misery inflicted upon their passengers. I also learned that while Gulag transport was an internal Soviet operation, there had been strong connections with the United States and Europe, as unwitting but vital accomplices. I concluded that although the history of the Kolyma camps has been at least partially documented, the full history of the transports that brought the victims to these camps remained untold. Moreover, the little bit that had been reported over the years has turned out, unfortunately, to be to a large extent wrong. What follows is the most complete story prepared to date on Stalin's slave ships—the transports fleet of the Kolyma Gulag.

Today the United States, Europe, and Russia all condemn the horrors of the Gulag, including the widespread death in the Kolyma camps, the most infamous of them all. Yet this condemnation is somewhat ironic, since in the 1930s companies and governments in the United States and Europe built most of Stalin's slave ships and sold them to the Soviet Union, in some cases negotiating the deals personally with the commander of the Kolyma Gulag and in others selling ships to agents working for the Soviet Union. The United States and Canada welcomed these same ships into their West Coast ports at the midpoints of their Gulag careers, during World War II. These two countries even helped maintain and improve the Gulag fleet by providing extensive repair and overhaul services for these ships from 1942 to 1945. Finally, several of the ships used in Gulag service were provided free to the Soviet Union by the United States in the 1940s. One of these may have carried American military personnel to the Kolyma Gulag.

Some fifty years after Stalin's death, we are now only untangling the full history of that era. What is interesting is the extent to which the history of ships can yield insight into these topics and reveal truths not previously appreciated. This should not be surprising, because ships are big, expensive, and slow, and their activities are therefore often noticed and recorded. In short, ships leave wakes.

Acknowledgments

I did not intend to write a book—I just wanted to get some answers to basic questions. That my curiosity has yielded this manuscript is evidence of the tremendous support I have received from, quite literally, all over the world.

I am indebted to many hard-working staff members at research institutes and museums across the globe, including Shirley Sawtell of the Scott Polar Research Institute in Cambridge, Cees van Romburgh of the Nederlands Scheepvaartmuseum Amsterdam, Kees van Putten of the Maritiem Museum Rotterdam, Elizabeth Verity of the National Maritime Museum (Greenwich), Carl-Gunnar Olsson of the Sjöhistoriska Museet, Peter Hasling of the Søfartens Bibliotek, Lisbeth Ehlers of the Søfartsmuseet på Kronborg, Dr. Lorraine C. McConaghy and Phyllis Kelly of the Seattle Museum of History and Industry, Aigars Miklāvs of the Museum of the History of Riga and Navigation, Susan Wheeler of the University of Baltimore Langsdale Library, Francis Mansbridge of the North Vancouver Museum and Archives, David Cantrill of the Kirkland Heritage Society, Molly Biddle of the Wisconsin Maritime Museum, Matthew L. Daley of the University of Detroit Mercy Libraries, Elizabeth Rees of the Tyne and Wear Archives Service, Raymond Teichman of the Franklin D. Roosevelt Library, the staff at the U.S. National Archives and Records Administration in College Park, William Kooiman of the San Francisco Maritime National Historical Park, Dr. Richard Osborne of the World Ship Society, and the Slavic Reference Service of the University of Illinois at Urbana-Champaign.

Sergey Myagkov, who runs a maritime bookstore in Moscow, helped me identify and obtain obscure Russian books on maritime and naval history. Invaluable assistance was also provided by Julia Iastrebova Sidorova of Sovfracht and by Victor Volkov of the *Russian Maritime Register of Shipping*. Oleg Delev, who in the early 1990s served aboard *Odessa*, by that time a floating workshop, was kind enough to share his personal observations and to organize research efforts in Vladivostok on my behalf. Akiko Jackson took time away from a busy workplace, demanding husband, and even more demanding twins to assist me in tracking down Japanese writings on *Indigirka*. Ryoichi Nishiguchi of the town of Sarafutsu in far northern Hokkaido lent critical assistance in securing copyright permission to use photographs of *Indigirka*. Molly Pyle provided encouragement along the way and while in Vladivostok helped me make contact with Russian historians and research material relevant to this project.

Maritime history is well served by a global band of enthusiasts, and many of these assisted me in my efforts. The gang at the Internet-based Maritime History Exchange answered a number of incredibly obscure questions, and thanks are owed to Ron Mapplebeck, George Robinson, Roger Jordan, Mike Ridgard, Andreas von Mach, Syd Heal, and Gilbert Provest. It is simply not possible to stump this group. Special thanks to Roel Zwama for obtaining copies of the *Brielle*'s plans from the Maritiem Museum Rotterdam (saving me a long trip from Australia) and for sharing his impressive collection of photos of Dutch merchant ships. Thanks also to Karl Osterman for digging into Swedish archives, and to David Asprey for his invaluable research skills and hospitality in London.

At a time when corporations are accused of putting profits ahead of all else, it is good to know that a researcher can still look to companies for assistance in projects of this kind. In that connection, I wish to thank Steve Turner for rummaging through the corporate attic of Telcon Ltd., Charlotte Beasdale for providing access to the Swire Group archives, and Rollie Webb for personally sourcing old photos from the Todd Pacific Shipyards Corporation. (It was not until later that I learned that Rollie was at the time president of Todd shipyard.)

Dr. Ataullah Bogdan Kopanski was willing to answer questions on his Gulag writings. Igor Samarin of the Sakhalin Regional Museum was kind enough to search his archives for photos of *Indigirka*, several of which appear in this book.

Professional Russian historians Dr. David Nordlander, Prof. Jonathan Bone, Prof. John McCannon, Linda Trautman, Dr. Ilya Vinkovetsky, and Prof. Stephan John helped supplement my limited understanding of Russian history. Their fellowship and courtesy for an amateur intruding upon their professional space was moving. Dr. David Schimmelpenninck van der Oye, in addition to providing a useful review of the original manuscript, provided very helpful assistance in restructuring and editing the material. In particular, Prof. Richard Hellie of the University of Chicago has my deep gratitude. He went out on a limb to publish in *Russian History*, his highly regarded academic journal, a paper about *Dzhurma* from this unknown and previously unpublished amateur historian. That act provided me with the confidence to continue with my research efforts, and it created the aspiration to produce a book on this subject. Perhaps it was a small gesture on his part, but it is one that will likely cement my long-held aspirations to be a writer of history.

I have also benefited from the transmission of personal history, in this case from father to son. Walter Kowalski put me in touch with his father, Stanislaw Kowalski, who provided me with firsthand experience of a voyage aboard *Dzhurma*. Likewise, Robert E. McCabe, Jr., put me in touch with his father, a member of the U.S. mission to Moscow during World War II, who had direct contact with escaping American internees. Chuck McPartlin was kind enough to share photographs taken by his father, Marine lieutenant colonel Charles E. McPartlin, Jr., during a historical visit to Vladivostok in 1937. (His father was an amazing man: he went ashore on the beaches both at Guadalcanal and Da Nang.) Vladimir Chumak, Kathleen Luft, and Chisato Morohashi provided translation services, and Barrie Collits assisted greatly with editing and preparation of early drafts of the manuscript. Anne Doremus provided honest, if at times painful, reviews of these early drafts and contributed significantly to the final product. Along the way, she provided highly valued encouragement and counsel.

Special mention is required of two individuals without whom this work would never have been completed. Declan Murphy, one of the few remaining Renaissance men, evolved into my mentor for this project. Among other things, he is a professionally trained Russian historian. His counsel, connections, and support were invaluable, and I owe him a deep debt. The hope that one day I shall write as elegantly as he does has been a source of great inspiration—and continuing humility.

Finally, my wife, Maura, deserves great credit for humoring me when I came up with this insane idea, for serving as a sounding board for my ideas and hypotheses, and for breaking out her rusty Russian language skills to help me sift through mounds of material, including on one occasion when she was just recovering from anesthesia in the hospital. (Come to think of it, perhaps I should double-check that translation.) I find it much easier to develop my thoughts through conversation with others, and Maura was typically the other party for this discourse. For that—and everything else she brings to my life—I am eternally grateful.

Despite the extensive assistance, the author remains fully responsible for any errors.

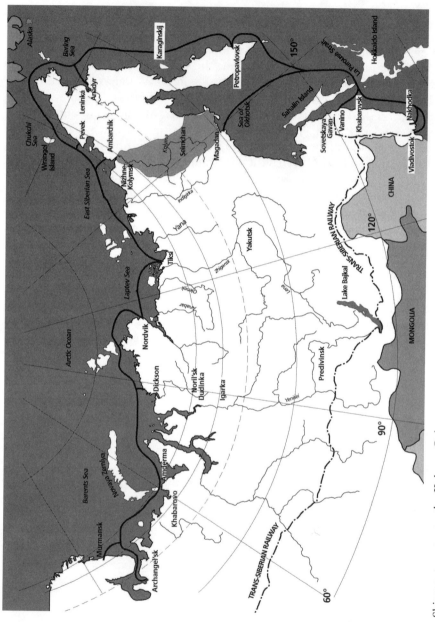

Shipment routes to the Kolyma Gulag

Chapter 1

Here Stones Cry

Ships are the best means of carrying items that have a low value per unit of weight.
—Abraham Resnick and Armand Hammer,
Siberia and the Soviet Far East: Unmasking the Myths

The small steamship *Indigirka* passed through the Okhotsk Sea on the cold night of December 12, 1939, tossed by high winds and heavy seas. It had been a difficult day for the passengers and crew.[1]

It had been a difficult day for most of the world. That day the Nazis, still celebrating their victories in the opening months of World War II, announced compulsory forced labor for all Jewish men aged fourteen to sixty. It was a sign of things to come. Farther north, Finnish forces launched a desperate counterattack against Soviet invaders at Suomussalmi. In the South Atlantic, British cruisers closed in on the German pocket battleship *Admiral Graf Spee*, the crews readying themselves for a dawn confrontation, the first major sea battle of the war. In the United States, which was still at peace, newspapers eulogized Douglas Fairbanks, Sr., who had died earlier that day with the last words, "I've never felt better." In Atlanta, final preparations were under way for the premiere of *Gone with the Wind*.

"Gone with the wind" had a different meaning for the occupants of *Indigirka*, driven through the heavy seas by a strong northwesterly gale. Capt. Nikolai Lavrentevich Lapshin guided *Indigirka* through this gale toward his destination, the Pacific port of Vladivostok. Almost 1,200 people were aboard. It was a mixed group that included 144 fisherman and 105 members of their families, all on their way home from a long tour of duty in the Far East fishing fleet. But the largest group of passengers, 835 in total, was special. These were some of the finest and most imaginative engineers in the Soviet Union, on their way to help prepare Soviet industry for its anticipated war with Germany. They represented critical resources for defense, rocketry, and aircraft establishments, and their talents were being placed at the disposal of these industries by order of the Soviet premier, Joseph Stalin himself.

Earlier that week several thousand people had crowded a dock at Nagaevo Bay, the harbor serving the Siberian town of Magadan, expecting to board a ship for a journey south to Vladivostok. Originally some 2,500 special passengers were to have been transported, but *Indigirka* was a smaller ship than normal for this route. A much larger ship had been scheduled to make the journey but had been detained in Vladivostok by regional administrative personnel during a routine inspection. Officials in Magadan feared that the special passengers might be stranded and were terrified of the consequences to themselves—Stalin's order was explicit, and he was not known for an understanding and forgiving nature. With a Siberian winter on its way, Nagaevo Bay would soon be blocked by ice; it was therefore critical to make this journey immediately. Scanning the available ships and seeing no other choice, the chief of the harbor, a man named Smirnov, commandeered *Indigirka*, which had arrived with cargo on November 23. He ordered its officers to pack into the ship as many passengers as possible for the voyage to Vladivostok.

It must have disappointed officials that despite best efforts there was room for only a third of those who required transport. Many had to be left behind, which in effect meant waiting until new ships could arrive the following spring. One of those left behind was a brilliant engineer by the name Sergei P. Korolev. The Soviet Union would have to wait a bit longer for his contribution, which proved considerable—Korolev was ultimately to become the father of the Soviet rocket and space programs, though his identity was to be a state secret until years after his death in 1966.

The passengers and crew were loaded, along with a small security detachment, and *Indigirka* departed Magadan on December 8 for the ten-day journey to Vladivostok. All proceeded normally until early in the morning of December 13. The previous day *Indigirka* had been approaching the La Perouse Strait, a difficult passage that separates the Japanese island of Hokkaido from the island of Sakhalin, at that time divided between the Soviet Union and Japan. Once past the Aniva Lighthouse, which marks the eastern entry to the passage, the ship followed a heading westward to the beacon on the Stone of Danger, a rock outcropping. Having recently arrived from the Baltic Sea, the captain was not familiar with the area, and he steered by compass alone on this bleak night filled with wind and snow. Fatefully, Lapshin allowed the senior navigator to leave the bridge, assigning navigational duties to the most junior officer, who had only recently completed his training.

The wind was blowing hard from the northwest; conditions were atrocious. As a passenger aboard the ship later recalled, "At times the ship lay almost on her side, and the men rolled over on the bunks. Now and then the straps by which they tied themselves to the posts broke and someone would tumble down to the dirty floor. The air in the tightly shut holds became stifling. Human voices could not be heard over the battering of the waves that shook the whole body of the ancient little ship."[2]

Though crowded with people, *Indigirka* had been designed as a bulk cargo ship, and therefore its load on this voyage was lighter than normal. This meant it rode high in the water and presented considerable surface area to the wind, which slowly pushed the ship off course. Rather than heading west, as indicated by the compass, *Indigirka* was actually drifting to the south, toward Hokkaido. The inexperienced junior navigator did not correct for this offset.

After a while, strange lights appeared to starboard. The captain and his first officer, V.L. Peskovsky, assuming they were in the middle of the strait following the desired track to the west, dismissed the lights as of no concern, merely a ship on an opposite course. In fact, the lights were from Japanese settlements on the northern tip of Hokkaido. Then, at 2:15 in the morning, strange "white stains" appeared on the water directly ahead, and these the captain and first officer could not dismiss.[3] Such "stains" were all too familiar to seafarers—they signified shallow seas and underwater hazards. At this point the officers realized their error and knew they had drifted far off course toward the south.

The captain ordered the helm hard to the right in an attempt to head back north to the safety of the La Perouse Strait. It was too late. At 2:20 *Indigirka* shuddered as it ran hard aground on Todo Reef, about a mile off the coast of Hokkaido, near the small fishing and farming village of Sarufutsu. The hull was punctured, and water began to flood the ship. Then waves pushed the damaged ship off the rocks and into slightly deeper water. Hammered by the waves and encumbered with tons of water, the ship took on a dangerous list to starboard and gradually settled to the bottom of the shallow sea, its decks still above water. The radio officer immediately issued an "SOS," which was picked up by both Japanese and Soviet units.

On board there was chaos. In a scene that has been played out innumerable times during the seafaring era, all scrambled to seek safety on deck and to prepare to abandon ship. As soon as it was apparent the ship was doomed, passengers below decks began to open the hatches leading from the forwardmost hold in hopes of reaching the relative safety of the ship's weather decks. A member of *Indigirka*'s security detachment standing nearby witnessed this struggle and, responding either according to his training or instinct, immediately sprang into action.

He grabbed his rifle, aimed, and fired five shots.

The passengers abandoned their attempt at escape and returned to the hold from which they had come. In hindsight, they would have had greater success if they had rushed into the gunfire and overwhelmed the guard, for within minutes the ship rolled onto its starboard side and the steel hatch covers, by this time under water, could not be opened. The passengers were trapped below decks, a mass of human beings collapsing upon each other, those at the bottom drowning in dark frigid water, those in the middle suffocating in the jumbled pile of bodies, and those at the top clawing at the steel plates trying to get out.

Though the action by this member of the security detachment may seem unusual it was fully in keeping with his duties. For *Indigirka* was a slave ship, serving in the Gulag fleet, and the 835 special passengers, the engineering "brains," were in fact prisoners being transferred from the Kolyma Gulag in eastern Siberia to special forced-labor assignments in the defense industry. Another fifty passengers, also prisoners, were en route to Vladivostok for other purposes, including hearings related to their sentences. Everyone else on board was either in the thirty-nine-member crew and security detachment or one of the 249 fishermen and their families.

Those able to escape from below decks began to abandon ship or were swept into the sea. Only two lifeboats were aboard—not the four required by Soviet maritime regulations—and members of the crew and security detachment commandeered one of them and set off for safety. The attempt to lower the other lifeboat failed; it was crushed against the ship's hull, killing four members of the crew.

The wreck of the *Indigirka* upon Toda Reef in 1939. Almost 750 prisoners died in this wreck, which ocurred a short distance from shore. *Source*: Sarufutsu Village Japan-Soviet Union Friendship Memorial Museum.

Eventually five survivors reached shore and stumbled into the humble house of fisherman Dzin Genitiro. The poor fisherman initially believed that his country was being invaded by Soviet forces. This was not unreasonable. The massive but little known Soviet-Japanese battle of Khalkin-Gol (referred to as Nomonhan by the Japanese) had taken place only four months before, and the 18,500 Soviet and up to sixty-one thousand Japanese casualties inflicted there bore tragic testimony to the risk of full-scale war between the Soviet Union and Japan.[4] Genitiro ran to put on his uniform—he happened, coincidently and appropriately, to be a sailor in the maritime rescue service. Revived with vodka, the Soviet invaders were finally able to explain the reasons for their unexpected arrival. The situation thus clarified and tensions thus reduced, the alarm went out.

A rescue operation was quickly and efficiently organized, using the Japanese ferry *Karafuto Maru* and later the schooner *Sosui Maru* and whaling ship *Sanei Maru*. The rescue was impressive; many hundreds who had managed to escape from the holds were rescued from the sea or the wreckage of the ship. By the next morning 395 people had been saved—twenty-seven crew members (including all of the senior officers) and 368 passengers, including fifty-seven women and children. Few of the rescued passengers were prisoners; most were fishermen or members of their families. Over the next few days another eight members of the crew and a few more passengers turned up alive.

The Soviets, seeking to keep the mission of the ship secret, were slow to reveal the true nature of the loss to Japanese authorities. It was not until three days later that the Japanese learned that there will still hundreds of people aboard the ship, trapped in the holds. The Japanese authorities pressed the Soviet captain for an exact accounting of his passengers and were amazed when he was able to supply only vague estimates.[5] A second rescue attempt was made, this time using acetylene torches to cut holes through steel plates to reach the prisoners still trapped below decks.

The rescuers gained access to the holds, but upon entering the rescuers were horrified at the sight before them. There was a mass of corpses in the dark cold space, half submerged in the frigid water. Many of the prisoners on top of the pile had taken their own lives, slicing their throats in order to end their agony. Incredibly, rescuers were able to pull only twenty-eight living prisoners from the mound of over six hundred bodies, and one of those died after reaching land. In all, 741 prisoners had perished, in addition to the four members of the ship's crew killed while attempting to flee the ship.

One wonders whether the rescuers were able to gain access to the ship's bridge. If they did, they might have noticed a small plaque declaring that the slave ship *Indigirka* had been constructed in Manitowoc, Wisconsin, in 1920 and had originally been named after the nearby college town of Ripon. Perhaps they would also have found papers indicating that the ship, now lying at the southern shore of the Okhotsk Sea, had been built in the heartland

Japanese rescue personnel working aboard *Indigirka* to free hundreds of entombed prisoners. *Source*: Sarufutsu Village Japan–Soviet Union Friendship Memorial Museum.

of America for the U.S. government and had been sold by an American operator just one year earlier to the Soviet Union's infamous security force, the NKVD—Narodnii Komissariat Vnutrennikh Del (Народный Комиссариат Внутренних Дел), or People's Commissariat of Internal Affairs. The NKVD is perhaps better known by its subsequent acronym, KGB.

Today the coast of Sarufutsu is unmarred by *Indigirka's* wreckage, removed in a salvage operation by the Mitsubishi Trading Company in June 1941.[6] Only a small monument appears at the site, inviting observers to look across the sea to where the ship was lost. As a poem inscribed on the monument declares, "Here Stones Cry."[7] Not many people visit the *Indigirka* memorial at Sarufutsu. It is a quiet, empty place.

This silence may be fitting, for the Sea of Okhotsk itself is a quiet and empty place, unfamiliar to most people. This large body of water fills a basin bordered by Kamchatka, eastern Siberia, and Sakhalin Island, some of the most barren and inhospitable lands on the earth. The sea resides at the very northern edge of Asia, north of Japan, well outside the major trade routes of the Pacific Ocean. There are no major cities along its border—the largest has perhaps 150,000 inhabitants. Today, the surface of the Sea of Okhotsk carries only the occasional freighter transporting fish, minerals, timber, or other raw materials from Siberian ports to Japanese or other markets.

But it was not always so undisturbed and lifeless. From 1932 to 1953, these waters were churned by fleets of steamships carrying massive amounts of cargo from south to north—human cargo. About one million people were transported across this sea to the infamous Kolyma Gulag camps in eastern Siberia; fewer made the return journey. It was one of the largest seaborne movements of people in history. To put it in perspective, almost the same number of people crossed the Sea of Okhotsk into exile in Kolyma during these years as emigrated to the United States on all ships across all oceans during the same period.[8] The wreck of *Indigirka* at Sarufutsu provided only a glimpse into what was in fact a massive undertaking hidden from the West for over a decade.

Unlike the immigrants to the United States during these years, the passengers to Kolyma were not voluntary migrants in search of a better future. Instead, for the most part they were political prisoners arrested in Stalin's purges and forcibly relocated as convict laborers to the camps in northeastern Siberia. Some were Polish or Japanese prisoners of war, captured in World War II. A few of the captives may have been U.S. military personnel, rescued from German POW camps or captured during intelligence-gathering flights but never returned to the United States, imprisoned instead in the Gulag.

Today, with one exception, the steamships of the Sea of Okhotsk have long vanished—their hulls and propellers no longer disturb the water's surface. But their wakes remain, and the ripples from these wakes extend far. They reach deep into the corridors of power in the former Soviet Union and across the breadth of Russia and its surrounding nations. They extend across oceans to the shipyards in Europe and the United States. They reach back in time to touch the Roosevelt administration during World War II. And at the center of it all is gold.

Chapter 2

The Labor Camps at the End of the World

Колыма, Колыма
Чудная планета!
Двенадцать месяцев зима,
Остальное лето.

Kolyma, Kolyma
Wonderful planet!
Twelve months of winter,
The rest summer.

          —From a song sung by Gulag prisoners in Kolyma

The Kolyma region is vast, more than four times the size of France. It occupies the most northeasterly portion of Siberia. Few people spend much time thinking about this part of the world, and for good reason. It is a cold, windswept, barren land of ice, snow, and carcass-devouring mosquitoes. The few visitors to the region are stunned by its size and its remoteness, but above all by the brutal, relentless, penetrating, and murderous cold.

How cold does it get? The northeastern parts of this region have recorded the lowest winter temperatures in the Northern Hemisphere, colder than the North Pole itself or the summit of Mount Everest. Only in Antarctica at the height of winter is the cold of northeastern Siberia exceeded. Oymyakon, a Yakut village in this region, is often identified as the coldest inhabited place on earth; there temperatures in winter can plunge to minus ninety-four degrees Fahrenheit (–70°C).[1] By comparison, after one minute of exposure to temperatures below minus forty Fahrenheit (–40°C), human skin freezes.

Gulag historians and Russian émigrés David Y. Dallin and Boris I. Nicolaevsky described life in this part of the world in their 1947 book *Forced Labor in Soviet Russia:*

> The Kolyma region is a desolate land at the very edge of the world, in the coldest wastes of the Arctic. Its rivers are ice-bound eight to nine months a year, and the continuous polar night covers it for from six to ten weeks in the winter. When a blizzard sweeps over the land, usually lasting for several days, even the hardened inhabitants never go out without first tying themselves to their cabins with a rope. In the blinding gale they might never find their way back and lose their lives within a few steps of their homes. The temperature of the region sometimes drops to –92° F or –93° F, so that mercury becomes as malleable as lead, and iron as brittle as glass. The soil of the region is a solid frozen mass— only a thin upper crust thaws out in the short summer. Underneath, reaching down for hundreds and thousands of feet is "geological ice" or permafrost (perennial frost). Scientists view the geological ice with the liveliest interest, regarding it as the guardian of many secrets of the long history of the earth, but to the local population, frozen in not only from above but also from below, it is a curse.[2]

The Kolyma region is defined by the valleys and hills around its namesake river. The Kolyma River forms in the Verkhoyansk and Cherskii Mountains of eastern Siberia north of the Okhotsk Sea, winds its way through these cold and desolate lands, and empties into the Arctic Ocean about 2,500 kilometers later. Some 275 tributaries (each more than ten kilometers long) branch off through hundreds of small valleys.

The climatic challenges of northeastern Siberia apply specifically to the Kolyma River basin as well. The town of Magadan, at the southern end of Kolyma region, is at about the same latitude as Seward, Alaska. Almost half the region lies above the Arctic Circle and thus is plunged into continual twilight or darkness during the long winter.

The climate also contributes to the isolation of the region from the rest of the world. The harbor of Nagaevo, on which Magadan is located, is ice free only six or seven months of the year. Farther north, the small town of Ambarchik, near where the Kolyma River meets the Arctic Ocean, is ice bound except for two or three months of the year. Warm ocean currents join with Arctic air masses to create immense winter storms and fog banks that make sea transport especially challenging. Surface transport is even more difficult. Even today, the region is unserved by railroads, and truck access to Kolyma—over a rough road impassable in winter—is a recent phenomenon. For most of the twentieth century the region was accessible only by sea or air.

There is little in the region to attract outsiders, yet in the mid-1930s about one million people were transported to this part of the world, mostly from cities thousands of miles away. The reason has to do with another exceptional characteristic of the frozen hills above the Kolyma River—they are filled with valuable minerals, including gold, tin, and uranium.

KOLYMA BEFORE THE GULAG

Before the development of the Gulag, the Kolyma region was virtually unpopulated, with perhaps only twenty thousand inhabitants in the whole vast territory.[3] While nominally part of the tsar's realm, the influence of Moscow and St. Petersburg over Kolyma—Russia's "Wild East"—was limited at best. Over the years, Russian leaders in Moscow and St. Petersburg employed forced relocation as a means to populate the region and exert control over this peripheral territory. The first use of the region for purposes of large-scale exile likely involved the Dekabrists, former army officers who attempted a revolt in 1825. Some of them were sentenced to exile in eastern Siberia.

The tsars' interest in the broad area of eastern Siberia increased further with the discovery of gold in the 1850s, but the logistical difficulties of supplying mine sites deep in the interior made large-scale operations impossible. Additional gold strikes in the 1910s and 1920s, however, led to even greater determination on the part of the new communist leaders to exploit this mineral wealth to help build the socialist economy of the Soviet Union.

Soviet mining on a large scale was first attempted in 1927, under the auspices of Soiuzzoloto, or the Soviet Gold Trust (Союз-Золотое), a pseudo–free enterprise organization that allowed prospectors to stake claims and then mine and sell gold to the government, acting as a monopoly buyer.[4] Interest in the region increased even further with documentation of large gold reserves by the First Kolyma Geological Expedition in 1928 and 1929, a survey organized by NarkomPut', the People's Commissariat of Communication Means (i.e., transport).[5]

Around that same time, in June 1929, the city of Magadan was founded on the bluffs overlooking Nagaevo Harbor, not by Gulag administrators or gold prospectors but by the Far Eastern Committee for Peoples of the North, an agency responsible for bringing the cultural and economic benefits of communism to the indigenous Even people of the Kolyma region. Some very limited infrastructure was created, but after two years the population had barely reached five hundred people.[6]

All in all, these initial efforts at developing the Kolyma region were only modestly successful at best. The KGPU—Kolyma Main Mining Administration, or Kolymskoe Gornopromyshlennoe Upravlenie (Колымское Горнопромышленное Управление)—tried in earnest to develop the reserves in the pre-Gulag years. But the lack of infrastructure made it very difficult to supply the remote sites, and in some years there was considerable starvation within the Soiuzzoloto workforce. Since corpses cannot dig for gold, it became clear that a much more ambitious effort was required if these resources were to be exploited for the benefit of Soviet communism.

THE FORMATION OF DAL'STROI

But the Soviet Union faced a difficult paradox. Using free enterprise to exploit the mineral potential—by selling mineral rights to Western companies—would limit the up-front capital requirements but would also undermine the moral position of the communist government. If instead the Soviets were to employ large-scale mechanized mining, massive amounts of Western equipment would be required, taxing the capital resources of the government, which were limited at that time. What to do?

The Soviets had faced this dilemma the decade before, during the construction of the Baltic–White Sea Canal. The answer in that case had been an army of prisoners operating as a slave labor force. Given the success (as it seemed at the time) of that venture, the Soviet authorities decided to exploit the mineral resources of Kolyma in the same way—with forced labor.[7]

The plan was put into action with a series of decrees in late 1931. On November 11 of that year, the Central Committee of the Communist Party issued instructions under Stalin's signature to an array of Soviet organizations for the economic development of the Kolyma region. NarkomVodTrans (Ministry of Transport), under Nikolai Mikhailovich Ianson, was ordered to make available the icebreaker *Feodor Litke* to assist in the transport of people and cargo from Vladivostok to Nagaevo Bay. It was also ordered to provide additional support from the Pacific Fleet (with the steamship *Dobrynia Nikitich* mentioned specifically) and to investigate the transfer of the icebreaker *Lenin* from Archangel'sk to Vladivostok. Other organizations were ordered to provide equipment, trucks, horses, and other support. A man identified in this initial decree only as "Comrade Berzin" was directed to report back in three days with a detailed plan.[8]

Further action was taken two days later, on November 13, when the Central Committee formally created Dal'stroi, a special industrial organization chartered to exploit the mineral resources of eastern Siberia; it was to report, officially at least, to the Council of Labor and Defense.[9] The November 13 decree identified "Dal'stroi" as an acronym of the actual name of the organization but not what it stood for. It has been commonly identified as standing for "Far Northern Construction Trust," though this is a matter of some disagreement.[10]

On November 14, 1931, the Politburo formally appointed Eduard Petrovich Berzin as head of this new organization.[11] Berzin—"a tall, powerfully-built man with clear-cut features and hard, steely eyes"—had a long record of accomplishments that predated the rise to power of Joseph Stalin.[12] A former Latvian military commander, Berzin was a bit of an intellectual, having studied art in Berlin and mixed in Bolshevik intellectual circles at the time of the October Revolution. Berzin's prior experience included a prime role in thwarting the Lockhart-Reilly, or "envoys," plot in 1918, in which British intelligence services attempted to overthrow Lenin by bribing some of the Kremlin's Latvian guards. Berzin, who headed a Latvian regiment, played along with the conspirators but was in reality a double agent for the Cheka, Lenin's secret police.[13] But Berzin also had considerable experience in running industrial enterprises within the Gulag system. His skills made him a logical choice for this important mission.[14] Moreover, as Berzin had risen to power under Lenin and did not owe his status to Stalin personally, the fact that Berzin's posting was about as far from Moscow as one can get in the Soviet Union may have been viewed as convenient by the Soviet leader.

With understandably less public fanfare, the Politburo formed a second organization alongside Dal'stroi. The Northeastern Corrective Labor Camp system—Upravlenia Severo-Vostochnogo Ispravitel'no-Trudovogo Lagerya (Управления Северо-Восточного Исправительно-Трудового Лагеря), also known as USVITL, or Sevvostlag—was created to manage the dozens of labor camps that supplied workers for Dal'stroi, thus maintaining the fiction that Dal'stroi was purely an industrial enterprise without direct links to forced labor.

Sevvostlag operated formally as an arm of the vast network of forced labor camps developed by the Soviet Union in the 1920s and 1930s. The primary operator of the camp system, and the source of its infamous name, was the Main Administration of Corrective Labor Camps and Labor Settlements, established in 1930 under the acronym GUITLTP but later known by the acronym Gulag (Main Administration of Camps). Gulag reported to the Unified State Prison Administration, or OGPU, itself subsumed in July 1934 into the NKVD, the internal security organization and precursor of the KGB.[15]

In reality, however, the Dal'stroi/Sevvostlag distinction was true more in name than fact. Berzin, while head of Dal'stroi, actually reported directly to the head of the NKVD, bypassing the Gulag organization itself and observing only nominal links to the Council of Labor and Defense. Also, despite appearances, the head of the Sevvostlag camp empire reported directly to Berzin.[16]

Once the organizational work was largely completed, Berzin set out to create the industrial infrastructure of the Kolyma Gulag. He personally arrived on the scene in February 1932, forcing his way through the frozen Okhotsk Sea aboard the Arctic transport ship *Sakhalin*. He brought with him a small number of prisoners, mostly trained engineers who had been accused of "wrecking" other Soviet industrial endeavors, though the charges may have been designed more to fulfill Dal'stroi quotas for trained engineers than to punish actual crimes against the state.[17]

Sakhalin, after being renamed *Krasnoyarsk*. It was aboard this ship that Berzin and 150 others arrived in bleak Nagaevo Bay to launch Dal'stroi. *Source*: U.S. Navy.

THE SOVIETS' LOGISTICAL NIGHTMARE

Berzin faced major difficulties in organizing the shipments of prisoners to the newly formed camps. The prisoners and supplies for Kolyma all had to be transported over long distances, often from the far west of the Soviet Union. The rough terrain and brutal climate precluded significant overland travel, and the available air transport resources were very slight, totally unsuited to the massive numbers of people to be moved.

Therefore, almost all prisoners and supplies arrived by sea, principally from Vladivostok (and later its neighboring ports of Nakhodka and Vanino) to Magadan. Some took the much longer and more perilous sea journey from Vladivostok through the Bering Strait and then westward along the Northern Sea Route to the Arctic ports of Nizhnekolymsk and Ambarchik, at the mouth of the Kolyma River. A lesser number traveled eastward by sea along the Northern Sea Route from Archangel'sk and Murmansk to the Kolyma ports, along the same route that sealed the fate of *Chelyuskin*.

This meant that the Kolyma camps were almost totally dependent on sea-based transportation. Ships were required—and were duly provided. A fleet of freighters, mostly built in American, Dutch, and British shipyards, supplied Berzin with the resources needed to move vast numbers of prisoners to these remote locations. These transports—Stalin's slave ships—became the backbone of the Kolyma transport system.

Prisoner transport began almost immediately. By the summer of 1932, fleets of Soviet transports had begun discharging forced laborers, mostly at

Magadan. These initial arrivals began work on preparing the infrastructure of port facilities, workshops, agricultural stations, and roads to support the waves of additional prisoners that would arrive over the succeeding years.

Activity accelerated, and by 1937 Dal'stroi had become a massive industrial enterprise. Sevvostlag supported this expansion with dozens of forced labor camps. The Kolyma highway had been built to connect Magadan with the major gold mining sites farther north along the Kolyma River. By this point, almost eighty thousand forced laborers worked within the Dal'stroi empire, often under incredibly harsh and dangerous conditions. Many died from exposure, overwork, or diets that were kept below sustenance levels for all but the most productive of workers.

Yet prisoners in later years would look back upon this time with envy. For while conditions in the Kolyma region were difficult, the mass brutality and killings of later years had not yet made their presence felt. In his history of Stalin's Great Terror, the Soviet dissident Roy Medvedev reports, "Harsh as nature was in the Kolyma region, few people died in the Dal'stroi camps in the years 1932–1937. There existed a system of examinations which allowed ten-year sentences to be reduced to two or three years, excellent food and clothing, a workday of four to six hours in winter and ten in summer, and good pay, which enabled prisoners to help their families and to return home with funds."[18]

The author Varlam Shalamov was a prisoner in the Gulag system from 1929 to 1932 and again from 1937 to 1951, this latter period in Kolyma. He comments on the relative ease of conditions up to 1937:

> Under Berzin there was excellent food, a workday of four to six hours in winter and ten in the summer, and colossal salaries for convicts, which permitted them to help their families and return to the mainland as well-to-do men when their sentences were up. . . . The cemeteries dating back to those days are so few in number that the early residents of Kolyma seemed immortal to those who came later. No one attempted to escape from Kolyma at that time; it would have been insane. . . . Those few years are the golden age of Kolyma.[19]

Thomas Sgovio, an American sentenced to forced labor in Kolyma, describes rumors about expected conditions in the Dal'stroi camps, relaying a highly optimistic view likely extrapolated from the relative ease of conditions prior to 1938:

> Fabulous stories about Kolyma circulated among us. Most of them originated in the Vladivostok Camp. Prisoners there had the best of conditions and received high wages—upon being freed, prisoners returned home with piles of rubles. Yes it was true the climatic conditions were very severe. Woe to those who had heart diseases. On the other hand, the air in Kolyma was very beneficial for respiratory ailments. Tuberculosis was cured overnight.[20]

THE GREAT TERROR REACHES KOLYMA

Everything changed after 1937, a peak year of the Great Terror. In mid-1937, Stalin ordered the Berzin organization purged. Berzin was arrested in December 1937 and ordered to Moscow for interrogation. He never made it. Before reaching Moscow he was executed, ostensibly for excessive independence from Moscow and for plotting to create seditious relationships with Japan. Today this may seem unlikely, but in the 1930s, just three decades after Russia's humiliating defeat at the hands of the Japanese in the Pacific, just fifteen years after Japan landed seventy-two thousand soldiers in Siberia, and amid aggressive Japanese expansion in Manchuria, such claims, even if untrue, were plausible to many. In fact, less than two years after Berzin's arrest, Russian and Japanese forces were to be engaged in one of the largest battles in Asia in the twentieth century, World War II notwithstanding.

The purges affected the Kolyma camps in at least two ways, both of which increased the demands for transport resources in the region. First, they led to a major increase in the supply of convicts, the number of people arrested and sentenced to forced labor. Second, they led to an explicit decision by Nikolai Ezhov, the new head of the NKVD, presumably with the authority of Stalin himself, to stop the "coddling" of inmates, greatly increasing the rate of fatalities and therefore generating additional demand for replacement labor. As Roy Medvedev points out, "In 1937, all of these liberal systems were abolished by Ezhov and Stalin. . . . The regime in most Kolyma and northern camps was deliberately calculated to destroy people. Stalin and his circle did not want their victims to return; better that they should disappear forever."[21]

A new team arrived in 1937 to replace Berzin's organization. Berzin's replacement as head of Dal'stroi was Karp Aleksandrovich Pavlov. Maj. Stepan N. Garanin assumed responsibility for the Sevvostlag camp empire within Dal'stroi, reporting to Pavlov. Dal'stroi's nominal link to the Council of Labor and Defense was severed—the former now reported officially to the head of the Gulag within the NKVD. While the Dal'stroi acronym remained the same, its formal name became Main Administration for Construction in the Far North.

Major Garanin, almost certainly as a condition of his orders, and very possibly as a result of his character, created a new, more brutal, and far more deadly environment in the Kolyma camps. The death rate rose considerably—by some estimates a third of all prisoners died or were executed each year as conditions became increasingly unbearable.[22] The primary purpose of the Kolyma Gulag shifted from industrial output to punishment of presumed traitors and other undesirables. A special death camp was created in Serpantinka for the purpose of prisoner extermination.

As the great terror rolled through Kolyma, the operation became infamous even within the Gulag community. Silvester Mora, a Pole sentenced to five years in a different camp, writes:

In prison people talked about Kolyma in whispers. It was some mythical land of dread and death. Even in Kharkov, a thousand miles away from the mysterious "island," a legend was forming around those prisoners who were slated to go there for their "re-education," and who would probably remain there until the end of their days. To those who were shipped out to Kolyma we said goodbye in a different way, more discreetly though more cordially too. None of us believed we would ever see these people again.[23]

The turmoil unleashed on the Kolyma camps predictably disrupted industrial production. Trained engineers were assigned to purely manual labor, while heavy equipment was ruined by untrained operators. Disorganization reigned, and production fell. By 1938, the productivity of the labor force had declined to such an extent that it took seventeen new arrivals to eke an additional kilogram of gold each year from the Kolyma deposits.[24]

Ironically, the Great Terror led eventually to much greater awareness of the conditions in Kolyma, since the purge reached deep into the Soviet Union's literary class; a number of future authors spent a decade or more in the Dal'stroi camps. Previously, the inmates had been drawn largely from the class of kulaks—affluent peasants and rural merchants—purged by Stalin in the early 1930s. While there are very few published accounts from prisoners arrested before 1936—few peasants draft autobiographies—one can find many works by victims of the great purges of 1937.

THE ONSET OF WORLD WAR II

Perhaps as a result of declining industrial productivity in the Kolyma camps, and concurrent with an overall campaign to correct the excesses of the Great Terror, the Soviet leadership made another round of changes to Dal'stroi in late 1939. Ivan Fedorovich Nikishov was placed in charge of the Dal'stroi organization, relieving Pavlov, who was assigned to other duties in Moscow. Garanin was not so fortunate—he was convicted of crimes against the state and sentenced to a long prison term in the Pechora Gulag, where he died after a few years "from exhaustion."[25]

The population of the Kolyma Gulag changed as well. A major new influx of foreign prisoners arrived in Kolyma in 1940, when following the 1939 takeover of eastern Poland by the Soviet Union large numbers of Polish prisoners of war and civilians were shipped to Dal'stroi camps. Two transports, almost certainly *Dalstroi* and *Dekabrist,* left Nakhodka on July 5, 1940, carrying approximately eight thousand prisoners to the camps. Another 2,600 prisoners arrived the following year, most likely on *Dzhurma.* An amnesty was declared after the Nazi invasion of the Soviet Union, and the surviving prisoners, only 583 of the original eleven thousand, were released between October 1941 and July 1942.[26] This period is significant because these freed Polish prisoners created the first literature in the West describing in detail the Dal'stroi Kolyma operations.[27]

Conditions in the Kolyma camps deteriorated further following Nazi Germany's invasion of the Soviet Union in June 1941, though for reasons beyond the immediate control of the camp administration. The population of the camps fell considerably, both as starvation gripped the Dal'stroi empire and as demands for military personnel led to the transfer of a large number of prisoners, voluntary or otherwise, to the front lines. Another contributing factor was the diversion of the transport fleet to other duties, including movement of military and industrial aid from the United States to the Soviet Union under the Lend-Lease military assistance program.

The end of the war restored the Kolyma system to its previous levels of activity. The camps' population was transformed again in 1945, this time after Russian soldiers formerly held as prisoners of war by Germany were released to the authority of the Soviet Union. As is well documented, many of these former POWs—viewed by Stalin as traitors and potential enemies of the state—were sentenced to terms in the Gulag. With this new influx, and with a continued inflow of political prisoners, many from Eastern Europe, the population of the Kolyma camps rose gradually through the late 1940s and into the early 1950s, peaking just before Stalin's death in 1953.

Starting in 1953, the Dal'stroi system was rapidly disassembled, and large numbers of the surviving prisoners were released over the next two years. Dal'stroi was moved in March 1953 from the Ministry of Internal Affairs to the Ministry of Metallurgy. In February 1954 it was again realigned, this time within the Ministry of Non-Ferrous Metallurgy, one of two ministries created from the Ministry of Metallurgy.[28] The camps slowly emptied, and the ships moved on to other tasks. Today, the Kolyma Gulag camps are abandoned, and the physical remnants are slowly decaying. Some mining operations continue, but now the region is more likely to harbor eco-tourists than miners.

GULAG GOLD

The Dal'stroi camps in the Kolyma were vital contributors to the Soviet economy during the 1930s and 1940s; they probably fueled a large portion of the Soviet growth during that time. The prisoners produced timber, coal, and agricultural products, but above all, they scratched gold and other minerals out of the frozen earth. In the final analysis, the economic raison d'être for Kolyma was gold. By the early 1940s, almost two hundred metric tons of gold were mined each year, approximately 15 percent of the world's annual production.[29]

Given the price of gold during those ten years, the cumulative market value in "then-year" U.S. dollars of the first decade's production was almost exactly a billion dollars. Given today's value of gold, the first decade's production would be worth almost ten times that amount or roughly ten billion dollars in today's currency. Production in the second decade of the camps' existence would have added considerably to that amount. Of the one million prisoners transported during the life of the camps, about 373,000 were shipped to Kolyma from 1932 through 1941.[30] In today's currency, then, each of these prisoners was worth approximately thirty thousand dollars in gold production.

In summary, it seems that vast numbers of forced laborers were transported to the Kolyma camp system during the years 1932 through 1953—the precise number is a subject of a later chapter. Their forced labor generated significant wealth for the Soviet economy, probably on the order of several billions of dollars in the currency of the time, when factoring in the complete set of mineral ouputs across the full period of operation. But the camps and wealth could not have been created without an infrastructure of shipping to move prisoners and supplies to this distant and hostile region. At a time when the Soviet merchant marine had been devastated by war and neglect, Gulag authorities managed to develop a dedicated fleet and establish a massive transport operation in the Soviet Union's most remote region.

Chapter 3

Development of the Gulag Fleet

> The Central Committee of the Communist Party . . . orders Narkomvod
> . . . to allocate to Dal'stroi steamships such as *Sakhalin* and to send them
> to Nagaevo Bay between 6 and 10 November.
> —Decision of Political Bureau of the Central Committee
> of the Communist Party, October 26, 1932

Where did the ships of the Kolyma Gulag fleet come from? How were they
assembled at a time when Soviet merchant shipping was in tatters following
years of political unrest and civil war? Who controlled them and how were
they used? To what extent can information on the Gulag fleet be used to
understand better the dynamics of Gulag administration during this period?

GROWTH IN THE SOVIET MERCHANT FLEET

The Soviet Revolution and Civil War largely destroyed whatever Russian
merchant capability existed in 1918, and the new communist government
found itself without an effective fleet of ships to support its own trade requirements. By 1931, the situation had reached its nadir, as foreign hulls
carried 96 percent of all exports from the Soviet Union. Something had to
be done. To Soviet authorities the situation was intolerable; not only was it
an insult to nationhood, but it also raised the possibility of economic stran-
gulation should a foreign government cut off the supply of transport ships.

Soviet authorities responded with a concerted effort to rebuild the merchant fleet in the first half of the 1930s.[1] The few obsolete ships inherited
from the tsarist government were supplemented by new vessels built in the
Soviet Union and in overseas shipyards, as well as by large numbers of ships
acquired secondhand from overseas operators suffering the ravages of the

Great Depression. (Even good communists understand the benefits of timing purchases at the bottom of the cycle.) During this period a new or secondhand ship was added to the merchant fleet on average about once every
two weeks.[2] By 1937, about half of the Soviet Union's exports were being
carried in Soviet ships.[3] By 1940 the merchant fleet numbered approximately
375 ships of varying sizes and ages.[4] These vessels carried cargo within the
Soviet Union and between the Soviet Union and its trading partners—and
some of the ships carried prisoners for the Dal'stroi organization.

DAL'STROI, GLAVSEVMORPUT, AND
NARKOMVODTRANS: A COMPLEX TRIANGLE

Dal'stroi itself "owned" few of the ships that moved these prisoners,
especially in the early years. Most were provided through two other organizations, NarkomVodTrans and, to a lesser extent, Glavsevmorput. The relationship of these two organizations with Dal'stroi and with each other varied
considerably during the 1930s and helps explain the evolution of the Gulag
fleet.

The Main Administration of the Northern Sea Route (Glavnaya Upravlenia
Severnoi Morskoi Puti, or Ãëàâíàÿ Óïðàâëåíèÿ Ñåâåðíîé Ìîðñêîé Ïóòè—
also known as Glavsevmorput, or GUSMP) was created in 1932 as the organization responsible for economic development in Soviet Far North, in
effect the Arctic region. Glavsevmorput was the successor to the Committee
of the Northern Sea Route, or Komseveroput (Komitet Severnoi Morskoi
Puti, or Êîìèòåò Ñåâåðíîé Ìîðñêîé Ïóòè). Under the charismatic leadership of Professor Otto Shmidt, hero of the *Chelyuskin* expedition,
Glavsevmorput created a vast organization of research stations, industries and
infrastructure across the Soviet Far North, roughly analogous to that portion
of the Soviet Union above the Arctic Circle.[5] Like Dal'stroi, Glavsevmorput
faced considerable logistical hurdles in supporting its far-flung network of
arctic science stations, nascent cities, and industrial operations.

Glavsevmorput and Dal'stroi did not always work well together. Conflict
between the two entities was likely to emerge from two sources. First, there
was overlap in the geographic zones of responsibility, as the eastern portion
of the Northern Sea Route operated across the region under Dal'stroi's responsibility. Second, both were major consumers of scarce transport resources
operating in the region most distant geographically from the Soviet industrial base and transport network.

Dal'stroi also had to rely on the People's Commissariat for Water Transport or NarkomVodTrans (Narodnyi Komissariat Vodnogo Transporta, or
Íàðîäíûé Êîìèññàðèàò Âîäíîãî Òðàíñïîðòà), which had responsibility for
maritime and river transport operations, including in the Soviet Far North
and Far East regions administered by Glavsevmorput and Dal'stroi. Created
on January 30, 1931, NarkomVodTrans replaced a series of joint-stock ship-

ping companies and foreign-capital mixed shipping companies organized under NarkomPut' (Narodnyi Komissariat Puti Soobshchenia, or íàðîäíûé Êîìèññàðèàò Ïóòè Ñîîáùåíèÿ), the People's Commisariat of Communications, itself part of Sovnarkom (Sovet Narodnykh Komissarom, or Ñîâåò íàðîäíûõ Êîìèññàðîì), the Soviet Union's Council of People's Commissars.[6] In April 1931, five geographically oriented directorates were created under NarkomVodTrans covering specific operations in the Baltic, Northern, Black, Azov, and Caspian Seas.[7] At the time of Dal'stroi's creation in late 1931, NarkomVodTrans was headed by Nikolai Mikhailovich Ianson.

Organizationally, NarkomVodTrans owned most the ships that Dal'stroi and Glavsevmorput would require to support their missions in the Far North and, in the case of Dal'stroi, in the Sea of Okhotsk. At least for a time, both Glavsevmorput and Dal'stroi borrowed or contracted for maritime transport services from NarkomVodTrans, which was forced to allocate the scarce shipping resources between the competing needs of the two organizations.

The relative position of Glavsevmorput and NarkomVodTrans changed repeatedly in the 1930s, and this indirectly affected Dal'stroi. From 1930 until 1934, NarkomVodTrans had responsibility for maritime transport operations across Dal'stroi's and Glavsevmorput's (or before 1932, Komseveroput's) regions. But major changes occurred in this relationship in 1934. On March 13 of that year, Ianson, the head of NarkomVodTrans, resigned to become the deputy chief of Glavsevmorput, while still retaining deputy minister responsibilities within NarkomVodTrans under its new minister, N.I. Pakhomov.[8] This created a tighter alignment between NarkomVodTrans (the owner of the ships) and Glavsevmorput than between NarkomVodTrans and Dal'stroi. Historian John McCannon goes farther, suggesting that Glavsevmorput achieved a "great triumph over Narkomvod," in particular regarding control of the icebreaker fleet.[9] Certainly, by this date, Glavsevmorput was sole operator of the Soviet Union's fleet of four icebreakers (*Krasin, Yermak, Lenin, Litke*) and five modified merchant ships with strengthened bows used as "ice-forcers" (*Sibiriakov, Rusanov, Sedov, Malygin, Sadko*) and thus would play an instrumental role in any winter or springtime operations in the Arctic Ocean and Okhotsk Sea.[10]

From Dal'stroi's perspective the situation after 1934 must have seemed threatening. In many ways Dal'stroi and Glavsevmorput were inevitable rivals for resources in the Far North region, and Dal'stroi possibly feared that Glavsevmorput's closer alignment with NarkomVodTrans would put Gulag needs secondary to those of Glavsevmorput. Certainly the relationship between the NKVD, operator of the Kolyma system, and Glavsevmorput was strained in these years. Historian Linda Trautman reports that the Soviet archives reveal numerous "acrimonious exchanges between GUSMP and NKVD/GUGB over administrative matters, such as the transporting of prisoners, [and] the movement and housing of labor in the Far North."[11] This situation could very well have served as an impetus behind Dal'stroi's decision to acquire for itself a dedicated fleet of highly specialized slave ships that carried the bulk of forced laborers to their fate in Kolyma.

But Dal'stroi's vulnerable position relative to Glavsevmorput did not last long. Starting in 1938, the special relationship between Glavsevmorput and NarkomVodTrans was diminished with another series of major changes that dismembered Glavsevmorput and increased the alignment of NarkomVodTrans with the Gulag authorities. In April of that year, Nikolai Ezhov, the head of the NKVD, also assumed responsibility for NarkomVodTrans. Shortly afterward, with Ezhov's final removal from power in April 1939, NarkomVodTrans was split into two organizations, NarkomMorFlot (Narodnyi Komissariat Morskogo Flota), the People's Commisariat for Marine Transport and NarkomRechFlot (Narodnyi Komissariat Rechnogo Flota), the People's Commisariat for River Transport.[12]

As part of this change, the sea transport operations of Glavsevmorput were subsumed into the NarkomMorFlot, while many other Glavsevmorput activities were taken over directly by Dal'stroi.[13] In effect, Dal'stroi's parent organization, the NKVD, assumed indirect control over the total fleet of oceangoing ships, which meant that the former could now secure scarce transport resources from NarkomMorFlot on at least an equal basis with other users, and probably better. Glavsevmorput was purged by the Soviet government; its leadership was shifted from Otto Shmidt to Ivan Papanin, a Soviet hero of Arctic exploration and probably the first man to actually stand at the North Pole.

Later, during World War II, control over all merchant ships passed to the Soviet military.[14] Once the war ended, the ships were returned to civilian operation, but further changes took place following the death of Stalin in 1953 with the formation of the Ministry of Merchant and River Fleets, which subsumed the Directorate of the Northern Sea Route.

From an organizational standpoint, the control and operation of the Gulag ships can be separated into five distinct periods:

- The early years from 1932 to 1935, when Dal'stroi contracted its shipping needs from an independent NarkomVodTrans.
- The period from 1935 to 1938, when Glavsevmorput was linked with Narkom-VodTrans, a situation that likely drove Dal'stroi to acquire its own core fleet of ships and minimize the use of ships from NarkomVodTrans.
- The years 1938 to 1940, when influence over NarkomMorFlot shifted from Glavsevmorput to the NKVD and, simultaneously, shipment demands surged. During this period Dal'stroi continued to operate its own fleet but also contracted shipping services from NarkomMorFlot.
- World War II, when control passed to the Soviet military and when the Gulag fleet was used heavily in support of Lend-Lease operations.

- The postwar period, including the final years before Stalin's death, from 1946 to the early 1950s and the post-Stalin period, when the ships transferred to general cargo duties and were gradually retired and scrapped.

With this understanding, the evolution of the Dal'stroi shipping operations becomes clearer, and it becomes easier to understand why specific ships were engaged in prisoner transport operations at specific times.

Chapter 4

Prisoner Transport Operations

> The expedition would also transport a large number of "passengers" who would build the settlement, port and other components of the infrastructure; one can assume that few of these were volunteers.
> —William Barr, describing a 1932 expedition to Ambarchik

Information on the Kolyma transport operation is hard to obtain and is usually limited to indirect references to ships, dates, names, and numbers. For decades, and with considerable success, Moscow hid this operation from the West.[1] However, half a century after the last ship of prisoners departed Vladivostok, it is now possible to understand how massive numbers of political prisoners and common criminals were transported to this desolate region. This requires triangulation from firsthand prisoner testimony, limited Gulag archives data, and records of Soviet merchant shipping operations.

THE EARLY YEARS: 1932–34

The development of the Kolyma Gulag system began within a few months of Dal'stroi's formation. By the following spring, forced laborers were already being ferried to Kolyma to create the infrastructure for follow-on shipments. Activity began at both Magadan and Ambarchik, a small outpost at the northern terminus of the Kolyma River high above the Arctic Circle.[2]

In all, it was a formidable task to organize the shipment of tens of thousand of prisoners to these very remote sites, which generally lacked established port infrastructure, let alone access by road or rail. The nearest ground transport site was Vladivostok, about a thousand miles by sea from Nagaevo and 3,826 miles by sea from Ambarchik.

Operations in the south, at Magadan, began on February 4, 1932, with the arrival of the *Sakhalin*, carrying Berzin, camp administrative staff, guards, and about 150 specially chosen forced laborers.[3] Over the rest of the year, the population of inmates gradually increased each month to reach 10,004 at year's end, suggesting a steady arrival of ships. These unenviable prisoners had the arduous duty of constructing the port facilities at Magadan, and then attempting to survive a harsh winter without adequate shelter. Many did not survive.[4]

Soviet archives indicate that *Kashirstroi* and *Dneprostroi* were the first transport ships to bring large numbers of prisoners to the new camps in 1932.[5] In addition, there exists firsthand evidence that *Svirstroi, Shaturstroi,* and *Volkhovstroi* were employed as well in 1932.[6] Most likely each of these five ships made two or more trips during the year, carrying a thousand to 1,500 prisoners each per trip.[7] According to Stanford University historian Robert Conquest, *Svirstroi, Shaturstroi,* and *Volkhovstroi* were used in 1932 but not thereafter.[8] However, it is clear that *Svirstroi* was making trips to Magadan as late as 1934, though there exists no direct evidence that there were convicts aboard during these trips.

Shipments continued in 1933. About twenty-two thousand new prisoners were brought to the region, more than double the ten thousand delivered the previous year. In the years 1934 and 1935 activities continued, with population in the camps rising to a total of almost forty-five thousand by the end of 1935.[9] Operations at Ambarchik also took place during 1932–35, though at substantially reduced scale. Statistics on these Far North shipments are more widely available, since missions along the Northern Sea Route were considered adventurous and received broad coverage in the Soviet media, though without reference to the Gulag operations supported on these journeys.

Dneprostroi was one of the first two ships to bring prisoners to Magadan in 1932. This ship, constructed just a short distance from the Statue of Liberty in New York, was owned by the U.S. government until 1930. *Source*: U.S. Navy.

Kashirstroi was the other ship in the first wave of prisoner shipments. It was one of the ships sold by the U.S. government to an agent of the Soviet Union in 1930. *Source*: U.S. Navy.

In 1932, the first shipment of prisoners to the far-northern Kolyma camps took place as part of the first-ever large-scale transport operation to Kolyma. In that year, Capt. N.I. Evgenov commanded an eight-ship convoy consisting of the ex-Canadian icebreaker *Feodor Litke*, the schooner *Temp*, three cargo ships (*Uritskii*, *Mikoyan*, and *Krasnyi Partizan*), and three new purpose-built passenger/cargo ships (*Suchan*, *Anadyr*, and *Sever*). Two of these ships, *Suchan* and *Anadyr*, carried approximately one thousand forced laborers on this journey.[10] The following year, in 1933, a new four-ship

Shaturstroi, along with *Svirstroi* and *Volkhovstroi*, ferried prisoners to the new site at Magadan in 1932. All were built for the U.S. government during World War I. *Source*: U.S. Navy.

Anadyr in March 1945. This Soviet-built ship was used to carry forced laborers to Ambarchik at the far north end of the Kolyma River, well above the Arctic Circle. *Source*: U.S. Coast Guard.

convoy left Vladivostok for Ambarchik, including the passenger/cargo ships *Khabarovsk* and *Sverdlovsk*. In 1934, two combined passenger/cargo vessels arrived from Vladivostok, most likely the *Suchan* and *Smolensk*, along with the cargo ship *Uritskii*. It is highly likely at least some of these passenger/ cargo ships carried forced laborers.

Operations expanded considerably in 1935. A fleet of three ships made the usual trip to Ambarchik and back: *Uritskii*, *Smolensk*, and *Tovarishch Krasin*. Two others journeyed from Vladivostok through the Bering Strait to Ambarchik, and then, rather then returning the same way, continued on to Murmansk (*Anadyr*) and London (*Stalingrad*). A first-of-a-kind voyage was made to the Kolyma camps by *Rabochii*, which in an impressive display of Arctic seamanship traveled eastward along the Northern Sea Route from Murmansk to Ambarchik and then returned the same way in the same season. According to Conquest, this ship was carrying Gulag prisoners.[11]

THE DAL'STROI CORE FLEET: 1935–38

Starting in 1935, Dal'stroi began to create its own dedicated Gulag transport fleet. There could have been at least two reasons for this.

First, as has already been seen, in 1934 Glavsevmorput effectively assumed responsibility for NarkomVodTrans shipping operations in the Far North, and it is likely that Dal'stroi, which competed with Glavsevmorput for transport, looked upon this with some concern. In fact, the number of prisoners transported to Kolyma in 1934 was only two-thirds the number in the previous year, when NarkomvodTrans was independent of Glavsevmorput. The number transported in 1935, even with the late addition of the Dal'stroi fleet, was still below the totals from 1933.[12] With huge demands for labor, Dal'stroi needed a high degree of predictability in fleet access, which may have been difficult to achieve through a contracting relationship with a Glavsevmorput-dominated NarkomVodTrans.

Second, Dal'stroi could have invested in its own fleet to develop highly specialized ships for carrying large numbers of prisoners at high speed, in order to make the transport operations as brutally efficient as possible. Ships used until that point were relatively small and slow, and they could probably only carry relatively small numbers of passengers. As Dal'stroi built its own fleet, it acquired relatively large and modern cargo ships that could be converted into vessels carrying large numbers of prisoners, perhaps up to seven thousand per trip, though most estimates from prisoners aboard ship are in the range of three to five thousand.

In any case, in early 1935 Eduard Petrovich Berzin, the Dal'stroi commander, personally traveled to the Netherlands to acquire three ships for Dal'stroi, including the *Yagoda* (later named *Dalstroi*), *Dzhurma*, and *Kulu*. These vessels arrived in Magadan for the first time in autumn 1935.[13] These had all been built in the Netherlands between 1917 and 1921, and were laid up there by the Depression.[14]

Dalstroi, Dzhurma, and *Kulu* were just the start, as additional ships were added to the core Dal'stroi fleet over the following years. Next to be added, in January 1937, was *Felix Dzerzhinsky,* a large British-built cable layer.[15] Shortly afterward the fleet was supplemented with a small freighter *Indigirka* (as a replacement for *Kulu,* which was transferred out of the fleet), and in 1941 it was joined also by the Swedish-built *Sovietskaya Latvia.* It is possible that other ships served as part of the NKVD Dal'stroi fleet. No official

Dzhurma in May 1944, on its way to Portland, Oregon, to pick up Lend-Lease cargo. Just a few months after this voyage, *Dzhurma* transported over six thousand people to the Dal'stroi labor camps on one voyage. *Source*: U.S. Navy.

Dalstroi in August 1944, departing Tacoma, Washington, with Lend Lease cargo. Upon completing this voyage, *Dalstroi* picked up its next load of cargo—almost 4,500 slave laborers—and took them to the Gulag. *Source*: U.S. Navy.

compilation of the Dal'stroi fleet appears to exist in the West, though several authors have addressed this topic.[16]

For example, according to Gulag survivor Nadezhda Surovtseva, *Dzhurma, Dalstroi, Kulu,* and two other ships were operating in 1937 on the Kolyma route.[17] Even with thirty thousand prisoners transported each month, these vessels were insufficient to handle the torrent of new victims of the Great Terror. These new arrivals overwhelmed the facilities in Vladivostok; the crowding led to an outbreak of typhus among the port's citizens.

A sailor from the Soviet Union claimed in a 1945 interview in *Socialist Bulletin* (*Социалистический Вестник*) that the primary Dal'stroi fleet in the years 1937 to 1940 consisted of four ships: *Dalstroi, Dzhurma, Felix Dzerzhinsky,* and *Sovietskaya Latvia.*[18] The inclusion of *Sovietskaya Latvia* is mistaken, as that ship did not come under Soviet control until early 1941.

Kulu on convoy duty during World War II. *Source*: U.S. Navy.

Felix Dzerzhinsky was the largest and fastest ship used in Kolyma transport operations. *Source*: U.S. Navy.

During World War II the U.S. Navy compiled a list of Soviet merchant ships and updated it carefully to assess needs and capabilities regarding military aid shipments. The list as compiled in July 1944 clearly noted that *Dzhurma, Dalstroi, Felix Dzerzhinsky*, and *Sovietskaya Latvia* were under "Dalstroi ownership."[19] They are the only four ships so noted among the over one hundred on the list.

Conquest argues that the core Dal'stroi fleet can be identified because it was uniquely based in Nagaevo Harbor instead of Vladivostok, where the bulk of the Pacific merchant fleet was registered.[20] By these criteria, he contends that five ships served in the Dal'stroi fleet, including the three purchased by Berzin in 1935 (*Dzhurma, Dalstroi*, and *Kulu*) and two others mentioned in the *Sotsialisticheski Vesnik* interview and U.S. Navy reports (*Sovietskaya Latvia* and *Felix Dzerzhinsky*).

The *Indigirka* at sea (as the SS *Commercial Quaker*), shortly before its sale to the Soviet Union. *Source*: Courtesy of the University of Detroit Mercy Special Collections—Fr. Edward J. Dowling, S.J. Marine Historical Collection.

Sovietskaya Latvia was a mainstay of Kolyma Gulag operations in the years after WWII. *Source*: U.S. Navy.

Perhaps the most authoritative descriptions of the Gulag fleet come from Magadan-based historian Aleksandr G. Kozlov, who has written extensively of the Gulag fleet in recent years.[21] Kozlov confirms that the core fleet consisted of *Dalstroi, Dzhurma, Kulu, Felix Dzerzhinsky, Indigirka,* and *Sovietskaya Latvia.* He further writes that *Kulu* was handed over to the Soviet Navy in early 1938 and replaced with *Indigirka. Indigirka*'s participation was limited to the period from August 1938, when it arrived in Vladivostok for the first time, to December 1939, when it was lost off the coast of Japan, a fact that explains its absence from most other compilations.

A final bit of evidence, albeit indirect, comes from the frequency with which these ships are mentioned in firsthand reports by former convict passengers or others. There are many more eyewitness reports for these ships—over a dozen in the case of *Dzhurma*—than for other ships used at times for Gulag prisoner transport (see Table 4.1).[22]

Conquest also speculates that *Kolyma* and *Sovietskaya Gavan* were part of the Gulag fleet, basing this on the fact that their names are associated with the Dal'stroi region, even though their port of registry was Vladivostok, not Magadan.[23] However, this logic does not hold up. *Kolyma* was acquired and given that name during 1911, some twenty years before Dal'stroi was formed. It was one of the ships in regular service on the Northern Sea Route supplying distant Arctic outposts, starting the year it was acquired.[24] It was based out of Vladivostok, not Nagaevo, at least in 1935.[25]

Finally, one other change likely occurred during the mid-1930s—it seems probable that this period also saw a defocusing of shipments of prisoners to the Far North in favor of heavier shipments to Magadan itself. In the mid-1930s, the Seimchan road from Magadan to the Kolyma River was completed. This allowed cargo to be moved directly from Magadan by road to Seimchan and then down the Kolyma River to Ambarchik. This new

Table 4.1
Primary Evidence of Ship Operations: The NKVD Core Fleet (Initials refer to primary date sources.)

ERA

SHIP	Initial	Core		Pre-War Surge			WorldWar II					Post-War Surge						Final
	1932 33 34 35	36	37	38	39	40	41	42	43	44	45	46	47	48	49	50	51	52
Dal'stroi	Acquired in mid 1935	VP	NS	YM KO	VP	KA SL	SL	RL					Exploded in 1946					
Dzhurma	Acquired in mid 1935	VP	NS BD	AS BL YM	AG EG GN	AG EL	SL			SO					MS	LR		
Kulu	Acquired in mid 1935	LS	NS SG	AS					Seconded to military in 1938, returned to civil use in 1939									
Felix Dzerzhinsky	Acquired in early 1937		VP		VP GN	SP				NV								
Sovietskaya Latvia	Seized in late 1940						RL				DA			MS IS				
Indigirka	Acquired in mid 1938			TS	VP				Destroyed in late 1939									

capability reduced the need for arduous and inefficient journeys through the
Bering Strait to Ambarchik.[26]

PREWAR SURGE FLEET: 1938–41

Several major developments in the late 1930s greatly influenced the Gulag
transport operation. First, there was a change in the management of the
Kolyma camps, with the arrest and eventual execution of Berzin, the Dal'stroi
commander from 1932 until 1937.[27] Berzin's replacement, Pavlov, introduced a much more ruthless operating model with tremendous brutality and
a consequent rise in the death rate—which only increased the demand for
new laborers.[28]

Second, corresponding changes were occurring on the supply side, with
the great purges under way under Ezhov, Yagoda's replacement at the
NKVD, and a massive increase in the number of prisoners available for forced
labor in the Far North. The current fleet was simply unable to keep up with
demand, as reported by Solzhenitsyn, quoting an individual involved in the
shipping operation at the time: "The big bottleneck was in the Sea of
Okhotsk, and in Vladivostok. The steamships could transport only thirty
thousand a month, and they kept driving them on and on from Moscow
without taking that into account. Well, and so a hundred thousand [prison-
ers] piled up."[29]

An analysis of annual prisoner movements suggests that shipments to the
camps must have surged in 1938, possibly above the capacity of ships then
in the Dal'stroi core fleet. Annual prisoner shipments may have jumped from
a calculated forty thousand in 1937 to almost double that by 1939. With
this increase, it is not surprising that additional shipping capacity would be
introduced.

Conveniently, it also became easier for Dal'stroi at this time to engage
more vessels, in part because of the troubles of its rival Glavsevmorput. The
latter suffered a disastrous and humiliating Arctic shipping season in 1937,
when eighteen merchant ships and eight of the Soviet Union's nine icebreakers were forced to winter in the ice. Indeed, the *Rabochii*, which pioneered
the Murmansk to Kolyma route in 1935, was crushed in the ice during that
winter.[30] Combined with the poisonous atmosphere of the Great Terror, this
disastrous season led to the downfall of Glavsevmorput, which was dismembered in 1938, its various operations and resources reallocated to
NarkomMorFlot and to Dal'stroi itself, both organizations under the control or influence of the NKVD.[31]

These developments all benefited Dal'stroi and enabled it to exert once
again considerable influence over ship allocations. In addition to the core fleet,
which continued in use (albeit with *Indigirka* replacing *Kulu*) and expanded
with the acquisition of *Sovietskaya Latvia*, Dal'stroi once again engaged cargo
ships from other agencies for use in its Gulag prisoner operations. Before 1940,
these ships included *Nevastroi* and *Dneprostroi*, which do not seem to have

been part of the core Gulag fleet but were nonetheless at least at times in the service of Dal'stroi. From 1940 to 1941, a number of additional ships were used to transport prisoners to Kolyma, mostly likely on a one-off basis in conjunction with the shipment of cargo (see Table 4.2). In their study of Soviet labor camps, Gulag authors Dallin and Nicolaevsky write that five more ships were added to the route in 1940–41, including *Uritskii, Minsk, Kiev, Igarka,* and *Komsomolsk*.[32] Other reports indicate that another ship, *Dekabrist,* was used to transport Gulag prisoners during this period.

The Russian historian Kozlov writes that Dal'stroi used the services of twenty ships in 1940, although some of these perhaps did not carry prisoners.[33] While there are few direct references to these vessels in the Gulag literature, the additional numbers of inmates moved in those years supports this conclusion.

Table 4.2
Primary Evidence of Ship Operations: Other Fleets (Initials refer to primary data sources.)

ERA																					
SHIP	Initial				Core		Pre-War Surge				WorldWar II				Post-War Surge					Final	
	1932	33	34	35	36	37	38	39	40	41	42	43	44	45	46	47	48	49	50	51	52
Sakhalin																					
Svirstroi	IK									Sunk or Captured in 1941											
Shaturstroi	IK																				
Volkhovstroi	IK																				
Kashirstroi																					
Dneprostroi	VN					AS															
Siasstroi						Ran aground and lost in 1936															
Suchan						Foundered in 1938															
Anadyr																					
Khabarovsk																					
Sverdlovsk														Sunk in WWII							
Smolensk														Sunk in WWII							
Rabochii												Sunk in early 1938									
Dneprostroi						AS															
Dekabrist									SL SK				Sunk in 1942								
Minsk									SM										GL		
Uritskii																					
Kiev													Sunk in 1942								
Igarka		Built in 1936																			
Komsomolsk		Built in 1936																			
KIM															VS						
Lvov				Transferred to USSR in 1945																	
Nogin			Transferred to USSR in 1943												ON	TL					
Kamenets-Podolsk			Constructed in 1944																		
Erevan			Constructed in 1943												MI						
Balkhash			Constructed in 1943																		
Vitebsk			Transferred to USSR in 1943																		
Odessa			Constructed in 1943																		

Nevastroi served as swing capacity for the Kolyma operation. *Source*: U.S. Navy.

THE WAR YEARS: 1941–45

The Soviet Union became directly embroiled in combat operations against Nazi Germany in June 1941. While Gulag transport operations continued during World War II, they did so at a reduced rate, as the entire Soviet merchant fleet came under the control of the military and many of the ships were drafted into other duties. In addition, a large number of ships were lost to enemy action during the initial years of the war.[34] The net result was a diversion of the Gulag transport fleet into direct support of the Red Army's supply operations.

One of the primary duties of the Soviet fleet in those years was to support the Lend-Lease program.[35] While the infamous Murmansk run received the most attention due to its very high rate of losses during 1941 and 1942,

Minsk during World War II. It was aboard this ship in 1948 that mass rapes and murders occurred during a prisoner transport operation. *Source*: U.S. Navy.

almost half of all Lend-Lease cargoes were shipped from the American West Coast to Soviet ports in the Far East. Since the Soviet Union and Japan still remained at peace, shipments of nonmilitary supplies in Soviet merchant ships were typically unmolested by Japan, even if the source of the cargo was the United States, and even though the supplies were clearly intended to bolster the Red Army's ability to combat Japan's Axis partner, Germany. Nonetheless, this task put huge demands on the Pacific Fleet. In an operation still little known today, approximately 1,350 sailings were made by Soviet ships on the Pacific Far Eastern route, often in difficult and dangerous conditions. The limited Soviet merchant resources were bolstered by some former U.S. merchant ships transferred to Soviet ownership during the war.

The Gulag fleet seems to have been apportioned into two parts during this period. Drawing the short straw were the crews of *Dekabrist, Kiev,* and *Uritskii,* which were assigned to hazardous North Atlantic convoy service. In fact, the first two ships were lost; only *Uritskii* appears to have survived. *Dneprostroi* also operated in the Atlantic convoys for a short time, but it was primarily used in the Pacific theater.[36]

All four of the surviving NKVD Dal'stroi ships (*Dalstroi, Dzhurma, Felix Dzerzhinsky,* and *Sovietskaya Latvia*) were used in Pacific transport operations for Lend-Lease. Each of these traveled to the United States during this period on numerous occasions. Other Soviet merchant ships used in Gulag operations before the war also saw Lend-Lease service in the Pacific, including

Dekabrist in port. This ship, which once carried Polish POWs to Kolyma, survived the Battle of Tsushima, World War I, and the Russian Civil War only to be sunk by German aircraft in World War II. *Source*: World Ship Society.

Igarka, Komsomolsk, Minsk, Nevastroi, Shaturstroi, and *Volkhovstroi.*[37] The war in the Pacific claimed its own share of Gulag ships. *Svirstroi* and three other Soviet ships were attacked by Japanese and British artillery in Hong Kong harbor in December 1941, years before official hostilities broke out between Japan and the Soviet Union.[38] It is unclear whether *Svirstroi* was sunk in this attack or captured by the Japanese.[39]

Some Gulag vessels also participated in combat operations during the war. On August 13, 1945, a military force under an Admiral Yumashev initiated offensive operations against the Japanese in Korea with amphibious landings at Seishin. According to Russian maritime historian Georgi Alekseevich Rudnev, the amphibious fleet included thirteen ships from the Far East Shipping Company supported by ships from Dal'stroi and Krabotresta (a fishing fleet).[40] Serious resistance was encountered, and the Soviet invasion forces suffered heavy losses; a larger Soviet force, including four transport ships, assembled at Vladivostok and arrived in the area two days later to reinforce the initial Soviet units. On August 16, three of the transport ships in this second fleet—*Dalstroi, Nevastroi,* and *Nogin*—hit mines laid by American submarines or aircraft.[41] Some sources report *Dalstroi* as sunk during this mission, but in fact the ship, though damaged by the mine, survived the explosion and was repaired over a period of many months in Vancouver.[42]

POSTWAR SURGE FLEET: 1946–49

Despite these losses, about two-thirds of the Gulag ships from the 1930s survived the war. *Svirstroi, Kiev, Sverdlovsk, Smolensk,* and *Dekabrist* were victims of war, and *Nevastroi* possibly so. The survivors included three of the original NKVD ships (*Dzhurma, Felix Dzerzhinsky,* and *Sovietskaya Latvia*), a former NKVD ship (*Kulu*) now in regular merchant service, and several other ships used in prewar Gulag service (*Shaturstroi, Volkhovstroi, Anadyr, Dneprostroi, Minsk,* and *Uritskii*).[43]

With the return to normal operations after the war, shipments of prisoners rose rapidly, and the camp populations reached two hundred thousand again. When transport operations were resumed, *Dzhurma, Felix Dzerzhinsky,* and *Sovietskaya Latvia* were again pressed into service. There are firsthand reports for each of these ships, but in general reports from these years are very scarce—which is surprising, given the large number of prisoners moved during these years.

Soviet efforts to develop atomic weapons also spurred the demand for forced labor. Uranium was discovered in Kolyma in 1946, and by 1947 a series of uranium mines were being constructed in the "Coastal Camp" system outside Magadan. At the same time, the Soviet government decided forcibly to relocate "freed" prisoners at the Arzamas-16 atomic city to camps in Kolyma, in part to preclude disclosure of their efforts outside the Soviet

Union. Several thousand people were thus relocated, making the journey across the Sea of Okhotsk on the Gulag fleet.[44]

The demand for prisoner transport almost certainly exceeded the capabilities of *Dzhurma, Felix Dzerzhinsky,* and *Sovietskaya Latvia;* additional ships again supplemented the core fleet. For example, there exists firsthand testimony of *Minsk*'s being used as late as 1951.[45] Additional ships were also deployed on Gulag duties for the first time, including *KIM*.[46] Around this time, the fleet was also expanded by the use of former Lend-Lease ships given by the United States to the Soviet Union. There are unpublished eyewitness reports of prisoners being shipped on *Nogin* and *Kamenets-Podolsk* and other reports on the use of *Lvov, Balkhash, Erevan, Odessa,* and *Vitebsk*.[47] The last three of these, as well as *Kamenets-Podolsk,* were among the famous Liberty ships built by the thousands in the United States during World War II and given to the Soviet Union in 1943 and 1944, with the expectation of their return following the war.

Even more ironic is the real possibility that American personnel were carried aboard these same vessels to the Kolyma Gulag. Rumors persist that a number of U.S. military personnel were imprisoned in the Gulag—men transferred from Axis POW camps in World War II, airmen captured during spying missions during the Cold War, or soldiers captured during the Korean War. A Russian source recently provided the following account to the U.S.-Russian Joint Commission on POWs/MIAs:

> Later, at the very beginning of navigation in the Sea of Okhotsk, I met still another group of Americans in the summer of 1948, at the Magadan transfer point in the Bay of Nagaev. There were 14 of them, and they had just been

KIM during World War II. It was aboard *KIM* in 1947 that prisoners were inundated with freezing water and frozen together in a mass of bodies. *Source*: U.S. Navy.

Balkhash began its career carrying passengers between Hawaii and U.S. West Coast ports. It was given to the Soviets in War II and later used in Gulag operations. *Source*: U.S. Navy.

taken from the holds of a ship transporting slaves: helpless, enfeebled by a week-and-a-half's worth of tossing on the seas, hunger, exhaustion and desperation. . . . One night they were taken off to the depths of Kolyma, into the bottom-less abyss of its vastness.[48]

The special report released in February 2001 cites additional data from a witness in the camps during the late 1940s:

In 1947, a Ukrainian witness from Gribenko was moved from Lvov to the Vanino Bay transitional prison in the Soviet Far East where he remained for about two years, 1948–49. He claimed that there were numerous American prisoners there, awaiting movement of other prisons. He believed the Americans were from WWII. The witness described the layout of the Vanino Bay transitional prison as consisting of 15 separate zones, each zone containing 5000–7000 prisoners, and that the Americans were housed in zone #2. He said that all prisoners were moved to Kolyma by the ships: "Felix Dzerzhinski," "Nagin," "Dyurma," and "Dal'stroi." He said that whenever these ships passed by Hokkaido, the crew put on civilian attire so the Japanese would not know these were prison ships.[49]

This latter report should be treated with some caution, since not all of the details are accurate. For example, the witness includes *Dalstroi* as one of the prison ships, yet it is definite that this ship was destroyed in 1946. Nonetheless, the information is entirely consistent with confirmed reports that *Felix Dzerzhinsky*, *Nogin* ("Nagin"), and *Dzhurma* ("Dyurma") were performing Gulag transport duty in the late 1940s. In light of these reports, it is worth remembering that *Nogin* was also provided to the Soviet authorities free of charge as part of the Lend-Lease program.

Nogin, as *Eldridge* in June 1919. In WWII, *Eldridge* was provided to the Soviet Union and renamed *Nogin*. A joint U.S.-Russian investigation suggested this ship carried American servicemen to Kolyma. *Source*: Puget Sound Maritime Historical Society.

THE FINAL STAGES: 1951–52

The early 1950s was a time of major changes in the camps, starting with a restructuring of the Gulag system in the late 1940s and accelerating with its gradual dissolution following the death of Stalin in 1953. By mid-1953, Dal'stroi had been effectively disbanded. Its economic operations were subsumed into other ministries, while the administration of the penal camps was shifted to the Ministry of Justice. The mass transportation of Gulag prisoners to Kolyma came to an end, and over the next two years the bulk of prisoners still alive were released as the camps gradually closed.

With the reduction in mass prisoner shipments, the Arctic shipping operations under GUSMP were transferred to the Ministry of Merchant and River Fleets, which subsumed the Directorate of the Northern Sea Route. Within a few months, the ministry was divided again into separate ocean and inland (river) ministries, but these were again united in 1956, when a Ministry of the Merchant Marine was formed.[50] In 1957, the ships formerly within Dal'stroi's operation were allocated to new shipping companies, the Far East Shipping Company (FESCO), and the Murmansk Shipping Company, both under the ultimate control of the merchant marine ministry.[51] It was at this point that the surviving Gulag ships became reassigned to general transport duties. Over the next twenty-five years, all were scrapped or otherwise lost, with the known exception of *Odessa*, which remains afloat today in Vladivostok.[52] Even *Odessa* seems destined for the scrapyard; its

Odessa was supplied to the Soviets during WWII. On its third voyage in 1944 it carried three thousand female prisoners to a Gulag mission. It was scrapped some time after 2004. *Source*: Author's Collection.

owner, Dalmoreprodukt, put it up for sale as scrap in early 2002. Aside from *Odessa*, the only parts of a Gulag ship still remaining are to be found in the hills high above Nakhodka Bay—the last remnants of *Dalstroi*, the first ship in the NKVD fleet.

Chapter 5

Below Decks:
The Prisoners' Stories

Я помню тот Ванинский порт
И вид пароходов угрюмый,
Как шли мы по трапу на борт,
В холодные, мрачные трюмы.

I remember the Vanino port
The morose drone of the steamships
As we climbed aboard the gangway,
Into the cold and gloomy ship hold.
—From a song sung by Gulag prisoners

The reputation of the Kolyma camp system was infamous—even in its own time—for harsh conditions, cruelty, and death, especially after 1937. Prisoners in other Gulag camps would go to great lengths—including self-mutilation—to avoid transfer to Kolyma.[1] Gustaw Herling, who was imprisoned for eighteen months in the Kargopol forced-labor camp near Archangel'sk, wrote of the camp's reaction to rumors that prisoners were about to be transferred to Kolyma:

In the first days of April we suddenly heard that a transport for Kolyma was being prepared in our camp. Now that I have read something about German concentration camps, I realize that a transfer to Kolyma was in Soviet labor camps the equivalent of the German "selection for the gas-chamber." . . . Our camp froze in fear and expectation at the news: conversation in the barracks died down, no one grumbled at work, the infirmary was empty of patients. The day of our last judgement was approaching and we faced the countenance of our Lord with humble faces, following the lightning thrusts of his sword with a suppliant gaze.[2]

Even with this reputation, the fear and anxiety of the camps was over-shadowed by the horrors aboard ship. Once at sea, prisoners found condi-tions so unbearable that they eagerly looked forward to a speedy delivery to the notorious Kolyma camps: "In the case of Magadan, prison life was exacerbated by one of the longest Soviet trips that antedated arrival into the arms of Sevvostlag. No trek to any other part of the Gulag was as grueling as the one to this frozen citadel, a fearful adventure noted by former pris-oners as among the most awful aspects of their time in the camps."[3]

Historians have benefited from reliable firsthand reports on the transport experience to Kolyma. Starting in the late 1940s, and continuing to this day, former prisoners have documented their experiences in biographies, both published and unpublished, and many of these contain vivid descriptions of life and death about the Gulag transport fleet. Other firsthand experiences have been recorded in a number of books written over the years on the Gulag system.[4]

The voyage to Kolyma typically began at one of three locations. In the early years, prisoners were transported via the main transit camp in Vladivostok, the original eastern terminus of the Trans-Siberian Railroad. Later, during the height of the Great Terror and then World War II, a sec-ondary transit facility at Nakhodka Harbor was employed, a few hours from Vladivostok. Starting in the early 1940s, another Gulag port was created at Vanino, near Sovetskaya Gavan, farther up the coast from Vladivostok. It had more direct access, via a new spur to the Trans-Siberian Railroad.

Prisoners arrived at the camp after monthlong trips by rail and truck from points farther east, the journeys themselves often following months or years in Soviet prisons. Traveling in very crowded conditions, the inmates fre-quently died from starvation or dehydration. Once in the transit camps them-selves, prisoners faced further risks from frequent outbreaks of typhus or other diseases. After a period of time that might range from a few days to many months, groups of prisoners would be assembled and taken to the Gulag transport ships for final dispatch to Magadan. The luckiest would ar-rive in transit camps late in the year, after the shipping season to Magadan closed for the winter. This would mean a period of several months in which to recover from the arduous ground transport to Vladivostok, Nakhodka, or Vanino before beginning their journeys to Magadan.

Once aboard ship, they found the voyage to Magadan filled with danger. Conditions on the steamers were very harsh and crowded; they threatened the lives of many inmates already weakened by long journeys and periods of imprisonment. Moreover, political prisoners on the ships were frequently terrorized by common criminals being sent to the same destination—abuse overlooked and very possibly encouraged by Gulag officials. At times, this abuse included mass rape of women prisoners. Insurrections by political prisoners—or more typically common criminals—would often lead to harsh reprisals by crew or guards, reprisals that threatened the safety of all prisoners on board, even those who had not participated in the insurrection. Finally, the transport ships were at times used by camp officials as vehicles for intentional atrocities.

SURVIVING THE PASSAGE

The ships used to carry prisoners to the Gulag camps were designed not as passenger ships but as general bulk freighters. Prisoners did not travel in berths or cabins but in cavernous holds specially outfitted for the purpose. The typical merchant steamer in use during the early 1930s was a relatively simple ship. The hull was constructed of riveted plates, secured to a series of transverse frames. Above the main deck, in a classic "three-island" design there would be the forecastle, bridge, and poop in which the crew (and guards) would be housed. Below deck and occupying about 20 percent of the hull would be the engine spaces, built around a single triple-expansion steam engine powered by oil-fired (in some cases coal-fired) boilers and turning a single screw. This propulsion system was able to drive the ship at ten knots, about the same speed as a fast jog. A few of the more modern ships, such as *Sovietskaya Latvia,* had diesel engines.

Holds, cavernous open spaces for the storage of bulk cargo, lay both fore and aft of the machinery spaces. In *Sovietskaya Latvia,* these holds measured from 32,575 cubic feet, or 922 cubic meters (hold number four, farthest aft) to 136,545 cubic feet, or 3,867 cubic meters (hold two, second from the bow).[5] The holds were dark and poorly ventilated, topped by large hatch covers. It was in these spaces that the prisoners ate, slept, and relieved themselves, though mostly the time was spent waiting in fear. It was not uncommon for prisoners to spend the entire voyage below decks under cover and without access to fresh air or light.

Stanislaw Kowalski, a Polish prisoner aboard *Dzhurma* in the early 1940s, explains how these holds were modified for carriage of prisoners:

A typical slave ship was *Dhzurma* [*sic*]. Its internal structure illustrates best how the human cargo was transported northwards within its holds. A wooden structure had been erected around the walls of its cargo holds, and comprised of [*sic*] four tiered bunks, with the floor serving as the fifth. Each of the bunks was divided into sections to accommodate five men in lying position. To take their places the prisoners had to slide in legs first with their heads facing the passages to avoid suffocation. If there were not enough places to accommodate prisoners, men had to use the passageway as they're put up for a sea voyage lasting six to eleven days.

The sanitary arrangements consisted of two 50-gallon barrels, called "parashas," which were emptied periodically into the sea. It was quite common for these barrels to spill over, causing the inside of the holds to smell with the

odor of human waste. An outside latrine was also available, but only few prisoners at a time were allowed to use it. Therefore the queues were always long
and moved slowly. This outside arrangement was fenced with barbed wire to
prevent prisoners from jumping into the sea, especially when the ship was in
Japanese territorial waters.[6]

Michael Solomon, a doctor, was a prisoner aboard several Gulag ships and
describes similar conditions when he visited the women's hold aboard
Sovietskaya Latvia in the late 1940s:

> As I began to see where we were, my eyes beheld a scene which neither Goya
> nor Gustave Doré could ever have imagined. In that immense, cavernous, murky
> hold were crammed more than 2,000 women. From the floor to the ceiling,
> as in a gigantic poultry farm, they were cooped up in open cages, five of them
> in each nine-foot-square space. The floor was covered with more women. Be-
> cause of the heat and humidity, most of them were only scantily dressed; some
> had even stripped down to nothing. The lack of washing facilities and the re-
> lentless heat had covered their bodies with ugly red spots, boils and blisters.
> The majority were suffering from some form of skin disease or other, apart from
> stomach ailments and dysentery.[7]

Evgenia Ginzburg, who drafted a widely read autobiography of her years
in the Gulag, was a prisoner on *Dzhurma* in the late 1930s and wrote of
her experiences on the trip to Magadan: "Finally we found ourselves in the
hold. The air was so think and stifling one could have cut it with a knife.
Packed in our hundreds so tightly that we could not breathe, we sat or lay
on the dirty floor or on one another, spreading our legs to make room for
the person in front of us."[8]

Thomas Sgovio, one of the U.S. citizens caught up in the Great Terror
and sentenced to forced labor in Kolyma, recalls his 1938 voyage to Magadan
aboard *Indigirka:* "As I look back and remember the voyage, I see darkness—
the feeling that I am one of three thousand human bodies lying on plank
tiers; from up above, vomit is trickling on me; someone is groping his way
through the slimy aisle; I see an unending line on the staircase, and I remember the hunger that tormented me[;] . . . I remember the dead bodies
being carried up on deck.[9]

Even return voyages from the Kolyma camps to freedom forced passengers to sustain nearly unbearable conditions. Elinor Lipper, who published
one of the first autobiographical accounts of life in the Kolyma Gulag, describes one such voyage shortly after World War II:

> Here was a hell where people fought with one another for a drink of water. I
> looked around at the gray-faced male prisoners in our locked storeroom, sea-
> sick, vomiting from the planks on the floor, or doubled over the battered pail
> where they must also relieve themselves before the eyes of the two women who

were locked up with them. I looked at them lying above and on top of one another. Their hands had stubs where fingers had been frozen off; their legs were covered with sores.[10]

AT THE MERCY OF CRIMINALS

Inmates at the Kolyma camps included political prisoners as well as common criminals. In the eyes of the Gulag administration, the political sins were the graver, and consequently political prisoners were treated more harshly than the common criminals. The common criminals—called "*urkas*" (урка)—were often better equipped mentally and physically for the violent world of the transport fleet and labor camps and subsequently preyed upon the political prisoners, stealing their few possessions and in some cases engaging in mass violence. Many political prisoners wrote that such behavior was tolerated or overlooked by the Gulag administration, perhaps even encouraged.

For most of the political prisoners, the violence of the *urka* community came as a major shock and a harbinger of life within the Gulag camps themselves. One female prisoner describes her first few minutes at sea aboard a Gulag transport ship:

> We were down under the deck. Bunks rose in tiers. I stood in a corner with my fur in a sack under my feet. The boat moved off to the sound of the mournful singing and dancing and the noise of retching. In the darkness hands reached out towards me from all sides. One tore off the shawl, the Polish shawl I wore on my head. Others tried to drag off my sweater and seize my sack. We fought in the darkness of the night and of my blindness. . . . I could taste blood and I knew that somehow I must get my back against a wall. . . . A brigade leader had gambled and lost the brigade's bread ration at cards. For this he had been tried by the men apaches and found guilty. They literally cut him up with their knives. His brains lay scattered on the decks. . . . In seven days we reached Bukhta Nagaievo. Then Magadan.[11]

A.V. Gorbatov, a Red Army general convicted of political crimes and sentenced to the Gulag, describes his experience on *Dzhurma*:

> While we were in the Sea of Okhotsk misfortune befell me. Early in the morning, when I was lying half awake as many of us did, two "trusties" came up to me and dragged away my boots which I was using as a pillow. One of them hit me hard on the chest and then on the head and said with a leer: "Look at him—sells me his boots days ago, pockets the cash, and then refuses to hand them over!"
>
> Off they went with their loot, laughing for all they were worth and only stopping to beat me up again when, out of sheer despair, I followed them and asked for the boots back.[12]

Evgenia Ginzburg continues her description of life aboard *Dzhurma* and her first contact with the *urkas*.

> But the worst was yet to come: our first meeting with real, hardened, female criminals among whom we were to live at Kolyma. . . . Down through the hatchway poured another few hundred human beings, if that is the right name for those appalling creatures, the dregs of the criminal world: murderers, sadists, and experts of every kind of sexual perversion. . . . The fetid air reverberated to their shrieks, their fantastic obscenities, their caterwauling and peals of laughter. . . . Within five minutes we had a thorough introduction to the law of the jungle. They seized our bits of bread, snatched the last rags out of our bundles, and pushed us out of our places.[13]

While guards manned the transport ships, they rarely attempted to maintain order within the prisoner holds.

> During the entire voyage, which lasted a week, no members of the guard or the ship's crew ever entered the prisoners' hold. They were afraid to, especially when a large number of murderers and bandits were being transported. . . . None of them took any account of what went on below decks. As a result, during all such voyages the criminals put across a reign of terror. If they want the clothing of any of the counterrevolutionaries, they take it from him. If he offers any resistance, he is beaten up. The old and weak are robbed of their bread. On every transport ship a number of prisoners die as a result of such treatment.[14]

In some cases, lack of intervention led to major riots, including one episode reported by Lipper, as told to her by another prisoner:

> In 1944 several hundred young girls came to Kolyma. They were the so-called *ikazniki*, sent out here for unauthorized absences from a war factory, or for some similar minor offense. . . . The criminals, who formed the greater part of the human freight aboard this ship, had an absolutely free hand in the hold. They broke through the wall into the room where the female prisoners were kept and raped all the women who took their fancy. A few male prisoners who tried to protect the women were stabbed to death. . . . One of the criminals, who appropriated a woman whom the leader of the band had marked for his own, had his eyes put out with a needle. When the ship arrived in Magadan and the prisoners were driven out of the hold, fifteen were missing; they had been murdered by the criminals during the voyage and the guards had not lifted a finger.[15]

Janusz Bardach was a prisoner aboard a transport ship to Magadan and describes a similar incident of mass rape:

> I looked down into the passageway. Men were clustered around a hole in the wall, pulling women through the opening like bags of flour and carrying them

away. I didn't know women prisoners were on the ship; they must have been loaded on after we'd been locked in the holds. As soon as the women appeared through the hole, the men tore off their clothing. Several men attacked each woman at once. I could see the victims' white bodies twisting, their legs kicking forcefully, their hands clawing at the men's faces. The women bit, cried, and wailed. The rapists smacked them back.[16]

But sometimes the guards intervened in cases of abuse or mass rape, as described by passenger Solomon in 1949: "I could make out vaguely, as in my sleep, one of the doctors saying that a bunch of ruffians had pushed through the rust-weakened bulkhead and managed to enter the women's hold, and had tried to rape them. I heard him say that soldiers had intervened and that some of the rampaging prisoners had been killed."[17]

One of the most chilling accounts of mass rape and murder is relayed by Elena Glinka, who traveled on *Minsk* to Kolyma sometime in May 1951, toward the end of the Kolyma Gulag era. She describes what it was like to witness the "Big Kolyma Streetcar":

Through the sharp, torn edges of the wall, half-naked male criminals poured in, their tattooed bodies glistening with sweat. With frightening squeals and howls of the sort that medieval hordes must have emitted when attacking a particularly dangerous enemy, the men grabbed the nearest women and dragged them onto the bunks. The overcrowded hold was again filled with the women's plaintive screams and entreaties, which blended with the men's ululations and whoops. . . . And we witnessed the opening scenes of the endless gang rapes, known among convicts as the "Kolyma Streetcar." . . . Women who resisted were killed on the spot. Many of the convicts were armed with knives, razors, and spikes and here and there fights flared up among them. From time to time, to the accompaniment of foul obscenities and cheers, they tossed down corpses from the upper bunks—the women they had tortured to death. . . . If Hell exists, the Kolyma Streetcar must have been its earthly manifestation. . . . In childhood, I read a book about slave trade in America, and how poor black slaves were cruelly treated by white slave-traders as they were transported to the New World. But the atrocities described in that book pale in comparison to the torture these women endured.[18]

INSURRECTIONS AND ATROCITIES

Not surprisingly, conditions aboard ship, and the desperate nature of men and women facing death or years of confinement in the Gulag, created conditions likely to produce insurrection. The Soviet authorities were prepared for this and had adequate, if brutal, means to cope. Insurrections would be met with gunfire or blasts of near-freezing water from fire hoses.

Varlam Shalamov, a prisoner in the Kolyma Gulag for many years, writes of a particular incident in 1947 that illustrated the consequences of rebellion aboard a Gulag ship:

On the fifth of December 1947, the steamship *KIM* entered the port of Nagaevo with human cargo—three thousand convicts. During the trip the convicts had mutinied, and the ship authorities had decided to hose down all of the holds. This was done when the temperature was forty degrees below zero. Kubantsev [a doctor] had come to Kolyma to speed up his pension, and on the fourth day of his Kolyma service he learned what third and fourth-degree frostbite were.[19]

Once aboard ship, prisoners were at the mercy of the crew and guards for the duration of the trip, either a week or two in the case of trips to Magadan, or many weeks in the case of journeys to Ambarchik. Crew members and guards aboard ship at times took advantage of their power, especially over female prisoners, as reported on one such trip during 1939:

For eight days and as many nights, several thousand girls were packed into the holds of a big prison ship sailing north to Kolyma. They had to put up with the foul air, the stench and the lack of hygiene typical of such transports. Whenever they tried to get out on deck to breathe some fresh air, they were assaulted by soldiers and sailors trying to rape them. Some of the girls had better luck and were entertained by the captain, the chief mate, the battalion commander, and other officers who treated themselves to the charms of these unfortunate women on their way to the wastes of Kolyma.[20]

There are several stories, generally unconfirmed, of Gulag ships being used to dispose of prisoners at sea, by the hundreds or thousands. One such account is from a former Polish prisoner of the Kolyma camps:

In September and October 1941 a medical commission from Magadan visited some of the Kolyma mining and lumber camps. A long procession of human phantoms appeared in the town and were put into ships. Those who saw them go aboard could hardly believe they were human. It was a procession not of human beings but of corpses and trunks. The majority had neither noses, lips nor ears; very many were armless or legless. Among these was a handful only of Poles. The rest were all Soviet citizens. The Magadan commission had recognized them as being unfit for work! In Magadan, it was said that, once aboard ship, they were taken out to sea and drowned, but there is not any proof of this.[21]

Nadezhda Mandelstam, wife of Russian poet Osip Mandelstam, reports a similar account of murder that occurred at the Vladivostok transit camp where prisoners destined for Kolyma were prepared for shipment (and where her husband perished):

Narbut's death was incomparably worse. They say that he was employed in the transit camp to clean out the cesspits and that together with other invalids he was taken out to sea in a barge, which was blown up. This was done to clear the camp of people unable to work. I believe that such things did happen. When I later lived in Tarusa, there was an old ex-convict called Pavel who used to get water and firewood for me. Without any prompting from me, he once told me how he had witnessed the blowing up of a barge—first they had heard the explosion and then they had seen the barge sinking.[22]

Another incident is reported to have taken place in 1933 aboard a Gulag transport ship carrying three thousand passengers from Vladivostok to Nagaevo. At least this is the uncorroborated story of Victor Fedonuk, as told to the court during the 1949 Kravchenko hearings in Paris.[23] Fedonuk, identified as a resident of Vladivostok and a twice-decorated hero of Soviet combat operations during World War II, reports that this ship ran aground off the coast of Japan and that the guards machine-gunned prisoners in the water as they sought to flee the damaged ship. It is difficult to corroborate this incident. There are no reports of Soviet ships running aground off Japan in 1933. Moreover, the ships known to have operated on the Gulag route in 1933 carried fewer passengers than the three thousand reported to have been aboard this ship. It was not until Dal'stroi created its own Gulag fleet in 1935 that prisoner transport ships with this capacity operated on the Vladivostok to Nagaevo run.

Moreover, if the ship involved was lost following this incident (it is unclear from Fedonuk's testimony whether this is the case), such a loss in 1933 is uncorroborated by maritime records of the era. Perhaps Fedonuk is re-telling the story of *Indigirka*, which ran aground in 1939 off Japan with just over eight hundred Gulag prisoners. It has been reported that guards fired upon passengers who attempted to flee that ship. Or perhaps Fedonuk is telling the story of *Syasstroi*, which ran aground in 1936 in the Bering Sea with 1,090 laborers, or of the *Suchan*, which foundered in the La Perouse Strait in 1938 with an unknown number of prisoners (if any). Of course, it is entirely possible that Fedonuk's account is correct. Certainly such an incident would fall far short of atrocities known to have been committed in the Kolyma era.

Chapter 6

Shipwrecks in the Far North

Hot water solutions containing more than 50% of ammonium nitrate can decompose explosively, especially if the solution contains catalyzing impurities, such as ammonium chloride or iron chloride (this may be possible during sea transport).

—International Labor Organization,
International Program on Chemical Safety

A fire involving ammonium nitrate in an enclosed space could lead to an explosion. Closed containers may rupture violently when heated. These accidents rarely occur, but when they do, they have high impacts.
—Safety sheet prepared by
the United Nations Environment Program

If the conditions aboard ship were not bad enough, prisoners also faced the inherent hazards of a voyage through dangerous seas, often on ships loaded with hazardous cargo. The passages from Vladivostok and its satellite ports to Magadan and Ambarchik presented unique challenges for ship captains and their crews, and the unforgiving sea inevitably took its share of those who dared to tempt it.

Every type of sea hazard presented itself to the ships running on the Dal'stroi routes. The routes required navigation through difficult passages where a single miscalculation could send ships aground. Storm-tossed seas could wreak havoc aboard ship and even bury transports beneath massive waves. Gulag ships in the Arctic faced the special dangers of ice-filled seas that could either reach out and sink a ship quickly through collision or, worse, hold a ship in an icy embrace for months until the ice pack crushed the hull. Finally, the risk of fire aboard ship was ever present, and in the Okhotsk Sea, hundreds of miles from inhabited land, the odds of rescue could be slim.

For Gulag transports, the dangers of the sea had to be confronted in old and poorly maintained ships. In 1942, for example, many of the Gulag ships were employed on Lend-Lease missions to transport military aid from the United States to the Soviet Union. When American authorities performed routine inspections when the ships first arrived in U.S. waters, they found conditions so poor that extensive upgrades and overhauls—usually lasting months—had to be performed before these ships were allowed to leave port.

DANGEROUS PASSAGE

Voyages from Vladivostok to the Kolyma camps, either to Magadan or Ambarchik, almost inevitably involved a passage through the La Perouse Strait. The strait is named after French explorer Jean-François de Galaup, Comte de la Perouse, the first European to pass through these waters in 1787. The La Perouse Strait is a twenty-five-mile-wide stretch of water dividing the islands of Hokkaido and Sakhalin.

The edges of the strait are strewn with rock hazards, and as if this were not enough, the middle of the strait is punctuated by a large rocky pinnacle named, appropriately, the Stone of Danger. In the 1930s ships had to navigate through this strait, often at night in low visibility, purely through dead reckoning without benefit of modern navigation aids. Only the Kriljon Lighthouse at the southern end of Sakhalin Island marked the way. Constructed by the tsar's convict workforce in 1884, it had an effective range of only fifteen miles in good weather. The Stone of Danger itself was marked only by an automatic beacon and fog bell, installed by the Japanese in 1913.[1]

Before the 1930s relatively few ships passed through these waters, but after the Soviet government committed itself to a massive buildup in Kolyma, the La Perouse Strait became a major passage for ships carrying prisoners and supplies to the new Gulag camps. Freighters laden with human cargo would make dozens of transits every season. The results were predictable.

In June 1938, the *Suchan* foundered in La Perouse Strait after running aground on the Stone of Danger.[2] According to one source, the Japanese switched off their navigation beacon on the Stone of Danger just prior to this accident, thereby in effect leading *Suchan* onto the rocks.[3] It is not known whether the ship carried Gulag prisoners on this voyage, but it has been reported that the *Suchan* had previously carried about five hundred Gulag prisoners on voyages through the La Perouse Strait in 1932 and probably again in 1934. Likewise, no information has surfaced on the number of casualties from this incident. It may be that the loss of *Suchan*, demonstrating as it did both the inherent dangers of the passage and the unreliability of Japanese navigation aids, galvanized the Soviet government into action, because following this accident a decision was taken to put a lighthouse on Sivuchya, a small rock near Cape Aniva, the eastern entry point to La Perouse Strait. But this did not solve the problem, as demonstrated by the foundering of *Indigirka* just eighteen months later, with the loss of almost 750 lives.

The Stone of Danger was to claim another victim in 1941. On June 26 of that year *Snabzhenets-2*, part of the Krabotresta crab fishing fleet, ran aground on this reef while trying to return from fishing fields off the Kamchatka coast. There is no evidence that *Snabzhenets-2* was used in Gulag operations; while the ship was lost, the entire crew was rescued.[4] Other ships used in Gulag service only narrowly missed running aground on voyages to Magadan, including *Sovietskaya Latvia* in 1942 during a Lend-Lease passage to the United States, and *Kashirstroi* in the early to mid-1930s on a return trip from Magadan.[5] While both of these ships are known to have transported prisoners to Kolyma at various times, it is uncertain if prisoners were aboard on these specific trips.

Once through the La Perouse Strait, ships making the run to Magadan had relatively clear sailing. But those heading farther north and hugging the Kamchatka coast faced additional hazards in the form of Karaginski Island in the Bering Sea. The Sovtorgflot steamer *Kamo*, under the command of Captain Snetko, ran aground off the coast of this island in November 1935.[6] It is unknown whether this ship was carrying Gulag prisoners.

Another ship, *Syasstroi*, ran aground in October 1936 in the Bering Sea under the command of Capt. Ivan Georgievich Erixon. The collision was blamed on fog and crew error. The ship was transporting 1,090 workers at the time, almost certainly Gulag prisoners on their way to a northern camp. (*Syasstroi* was one of seven ships acquired by the Soviet government in 1930 from the U.S. government; the other six ships in that group are all confirmed in use as Gulag transport ships in the early and mid-1930s.) *Syasstroi* foundered after this collision, but a rescue operation involving the ships *Suchan* and *Itelman* managed to rescue the crew and passengers.[7]

Storms at sea presented additional dangers to Gulag convicts even if the ships themselves escaped undamaged. For the prisoners locked below decks in the holds, the storms created horrific conditions, as witnessed by passenger Stanislaw Kowalski:

> During my voyage, she was caught by a typhoon in the Japan Sea. As she was doing her crazy dance on the backs of the violent waves, the five-tiered bunks loaded with Polish prisoners fell down, burying hundreds of men under the debris and sending some to a tragic end. The survivors for the rest of the eight day journey had to bear with internal heat, a shortage of water, stinking latrines and thick polluted air.[8]

Richard Lopacki was a prisoner on board a transport ship to Magadan in 1941—almost certainly the same as Kowalski's—and reported similar experiences during a storm:

The compartment had four layers of wooden platforms called *"nary"* on which prisoners could lay [*sic*] down. At the opening to the deck, there was a ladder for people to go to latrines erected at the side of the ship; beside the ladder there were barrels for urine. While the ship was passing by the island of Sakhalin, the southern part of which was then in Japanese hands, a heavy sea storm developed. The wooden platforms meant for laying [*sic*] down collapsed. Many men were caught under it (there were four layers). The men screamed, moaned, yelling in pain—fights broke out, men were trying to get out from under the debris—everyone was fighting for his own life the best he could. The urine barrels near the exit tipped over, spilling out their contents—*bedlam*. This was probably what Hell must be like or close to it.[9]

A number of ships were lost at sea from such conditions. In October 1934 the Sovtorgflot (Soviet state shipping company) schooner *Krestianka* was lost in the Okhotsk Sea, and all aboard perished.[10] In June 1935, *Sibir* foundered in a typhoon in June 1935 while sailing in the Okhotsk Sea.[11] It is not known if either ship carried Gulag prisoners on these voyage. The NKVD ship *Dalstroi* was almost lost to a freak wave during one of its Lend-Lease trips from Seattle to Vladivostok in December 1943.[12]

Travel in the ice-filled waters of the Okhotsk Sea and Arctic Ocean brought additional dangers. In the early years of the Gulag, thousands of prisoners were brought to camps at the mouth of the Kolyma River, high above the Arctic Circle and hard against the Arctic Ocean. Before the completion of a road from Magadan to the Kolyma River at Seimchan, the only practical means of transport to these regions was by ship during the two-month navigation season. This took place either via the dangerous Northern Sea Route from Murmansk eastward across the northern coast of the Soviet Union—a trip completed in one season for the first time only in 1932—or through an equally long and dangerous voyage from Vladivostok through the Bering Strait and westward across the Arctic coast of Siberia to the mouth of the Kolyma River.

It was not uncommon for ships to suffer damage from these voyages in ice-filled waters. The ships *Dalstroi* and *Dzhurma*, the backbone of the Gulag fleet, had to be removed from service in the 1938—at the peak of shipment activity to the camps—to undergo repairs for ice damage.[13] *Kamenets-Podolsk*, another Gulag ship, suffered damage from a collision with ice in 1955, though on this voyage the ship was not carrying prisoners but coal.[14]

Soviet Arctic literature is filled with stories of ships stuck in the ice pack and either crushed or, if the ship was lucky enough to survive that long, carried along by the pack until the late spring thaw brought rescue. The worst incident occurred in 1937 when eighteen freighters and eight of the nine Soviet icebreakers were caught in the ice pack; fortunately, one icebreaker remained available to free the others. One of the cargo transports, *Rabochii*, was crushed.[15] It is not known if *Rabochii* was carrying prisoners on this

A painting of merchant ships being escorted by the icebreaker *Krasin*. The ship in the middle is the *Felix Dzerzhinsky*. *Source*: Magadan Regional Museum.

journey—it is unlikely given its routing on this trip—but there are reports of this ship carrying prisoners on a similar journey in 1935.[16]

In May 1938, according to Solzhenitsyn, a convoy of four ships (*Dzhurma, Kulu, Nevastroi,* and *Dneprostroi*) was caught in the ice on their way to Magadan. After suffering from a week's imprisonment aboard the ship, the prisoners were forced to disembark and walk across the frozen sea to the prison camps.[17]

Richard Lopacki describes an incident in 1941 about fatalities on board *Sovietskaya Latvia* as it was locked in ice:

> At the end of December, Polish ex-prisoners were told they could board the ship *Soviet Latvia* which was anchored several kilometers in a frozen bay. . . . However, on arrival at the ship the crew on deck would not allow anyone to get on the ship. Apparently some people got on board, but the latecomers were refused. . . . Three days later the men who managed to get on board of the ship came back to the transit camp less the few men who died. Two men trying to get warm got into the ship's funnel and got asphyxiated. The ship *Soviet Latvia*, frozen in the bay, could not move out and was frozen for the duration of the winter.[18]

FIRE

Fire was another hazard, both for the direct injury it could cause and for the danger of drowning and frostbite as crew members sought to put out the fires with indiscriminate use of cold seawater. The most famous incident of fire aboard a Gulag ship involved *Dzhurma*.

On August 25, 1939, this steamship departed from Vladivostok on a six-day journey to Magadan to deliver yet another batch of prisoners to the Kolyma Gulag. *Dzhurma* had operated on this route for four years, and such trips were routine for the crew. However, the experience was fearfully novel for the future slave laborers aboard ship. About seventy women, all political prisoners arrested during the Great Terror of 1937 and 1938, were corralled into one of the ship's holds.[19]

But there was something a bit different about this particular journey. Locked away in another area of the ship was an unusual shipment for a slave ship—a large consignment of candies, chocolates, and cookies, intended no doubt for the guards and civilian administration of the Kolyma camps. The prisoners, living on minimal rations, learned that these delicacies were aboard.

The temptation of the treats was too much for a small group of criminals who understood that such delicacies would be distant dreams for slave laborers in the Dal'stroi Gulag. They also knew that they would be valuable currency on a ship abounding with female prisoners in a state of near starvation. On August 27, topside for maintenance work, these prisoners broke into the rooms containing the special provisions and began to help themselves until movement outside the room spooked them. Fearful of discovery—one can imagine the consequences—they set fire to the compartment in hopes of covering their tracks. Unfortunately, the painted wooden partitions in the room made excellent fuel, and the fire spread very quickly.

Smoke penetrated an adjacent hold, which was filled with male prisoners. It remains unknown exactly how many were in this confined space, but based on data from other voyages, the hold probably contained 1,000 to 1,500 men stuffed into a latticework of tiered wooden platforms four layers high. There must have been great apprehension among the prisoners confined in this space when the first veils of smoke became apparent, followed by frantic gasps as they fought to breathe. Not surprisingly, the survival instinct took over, and the men began to crawl out of the crowded and smoke-filled room. Upon seeing the prisoners fleeing the hold, the guards at once opened fired on them.

When he arrived on the scene, the captain dismissed the guards and ordered the crew to lower makeshift ladders into the hold to help the prisoners escape. This action was not born of altruistic motives. It may have reflected a simple fact of self-preservation; a fire on a ship is a serious threat to all aboard and it would be difficult to fight the flames if a thousand or more prisoners barred the way. But progress was slow, and with panic setting in each ladder was attacked by dozens of men. Unable to support the combined weight of the frenzied prisoners, the ladders collapsed. Some prisoners were trampled to death in the rush to escape, others were injured as they fell from the ladders, and still others remained trapped in the hold.

Rescue efforts were suspended, and a concerted effort was made to fight the fire, initially with conventional water hoses. This must have proved inadequate, since the crew resorted to a more desperate measure, releasing compressed hot steam directly from the boilers into the hold in an attempt to smother the fire.

Accounts of what happened vary at this point depending upon the source. According to Nadezhda Grankina, one of the political prisoners aboard ship at the time, some 120 men were killed, either trampled to death or boiled alive by the steam.[20] Others suggest that casualties were larger and the direct result of actions by the guards and crew, who used fire hoses to force prisoners back into the burning hold. Evgenia Ginzburg, a prisoner in Kolyma and one of its most famous chroniclers, writes that her friend Julia, who was a passenger during this very voyage, told her the following:

> A fire broke out on board and some of the male criminals, who had seized the opportunity to try to break loose, were battened down into a corner of the hold. When they went on rioting, the ship's crew turned the hoses on them to keep them quiet and then forgot about them. As the fire was still burning, the water boiled and for a long time afterward the ship was permeated by the sickening stench of boiled human flesh.[21]

On August 30, *Dzhurma* limped into Nagaevo Harbor with the fire still burning, escorted by *Felix Dzerzhinsky*, the flagship of the NKVD Gulag fleet. The dead aboard *Dzhurma* had already been dumped overboard, but the stench proved much harder to eliminate.[22]

On January 31, 1942, two and a half years after this fire, *Dzhurma* steamed into San Francisco Harbor for repairs in support of its new, albeit temporary mission to haul Lend-Lease cargo from the United States to the Soviet Union. The repairs started in San Francisco but for the most part took place in the Seattle area, as was the case with most of the Soviet ships sent to the United States for overhaul. These Soviet ships, including *Dzhurma*, made an impression on the shipyard workers in Seattle. One such impression was reported by the archivist of the Kirkland, Washington, Heritage Society: "Some of our old timers in the area remember Russian ships at the shipyard. They remember the horrible smells that came from them."[23]

EXPLOSIONS

Fire was a particular danger on cargo ships loaded with explosives for use in the Dal'stroi mines. On at least two occasions Gulag ships exploded, with considerable loss of life. The first explosion involved *Dalstroi*, namesake of the Dal'stroi organization and the first of the original ships in the NKVD Gulag fleet.

On July 24, 1946, *Dalstroi* was moored off Cape Astaf'eva in Nakhodka Harbor preparing to sail to Magadan with a cargo of industrial materials.

Preparations were under way for departure, but most members of the crew were still ashore, enjoying the relative comforts of Vladivostok. Gulag prisoners worked on the ship and ashore nearby, loading last-minute cargo and provisions.[24]

Capt. Vsevolod Martinovich Bankovich remained aboard *Dalstroi*. Bankovich was a veteran of the NKVD Gulag fleet, having been *starpom* (second in command) on *Kulu* in 1937 and rising to captain of *Kulu* in 1938, just before the ship was transferred out of the Gulag fleet. He took over responsibility for *Dalstroi* and had steered the ship and its crew through the difficult years of World War II, receiving a Red Star and two awards of the Labor Red Banner for his accomplishments. His *starpom* was Pavel Pavlovich Kuyantsev, another veteran of the NKVD Gulag fleet. Kuyantsev had served on *Kashirstroi* and *Svirstroi* during the initial voyages to Magadan in 1932 and had joined *Dalstroi* in time for service during World War II. (He later went on to command the flagship of the NKVD fleet, *Felix Dzerzhinsky*.)[25]

Dalstroi had just returned from a major repair in Vancouver following damage inflicted during the Soviet invasion of Japanese-held Seishin in Korea in August 1945. With his ship fresh from the repair yard, and with the war now over, Bankovich probably looked forward to this voyage as a period of relative calm and routine operations. Such was not to be the case, for loaded in the forward hold was a pile of loose ammonal, a mixture of ammonium nitrate and powdered aluminum, destined for the mines of Kolyma. On top of the mound of ammonal had been tossed a large number of other packages, most likely miscellaneous cargo for the community in Magadan. Ammonium nitrate is a compound widely used to make fertilizer, but it has another use as well. When mixed with other compounds, such as powdered aluminum and fuel oil, it becomes an explosive material widely used in mining operations. While bulk storage of loose industrial-grade ammonal or ammonium nitrate is not, per se, dangerous, it can become so if the ammonium nitrate comes in contact with other chemicals, especially oil, perhaps from the bilges. When loose, ammonium nitrate is friable and can seep into tight spaces and so this becomes a real possibility. Meanwhile, in the second hold, separated only by a single bulkhead from the hold containing the ammonal, were four hundred tons of TNT encased in rubber bags.

As prisoners continued to load final cargo, one of the crew noticed wisps of smoke coming from the forward hold. Somehow, the ammonal had caught fire. Soon flames were raging out of the forward part of the ship. *Dalstroi*'s crew was highly experienced in these matters and realized the real danger was that the fire in the forward hold might spread to the second hold, containing the TNT. Perhaps they even knew that TNT will boil when its temperature exceeds 464° F (240° C), and self-ignite (explode) at temperatures above 570° F (299° C), but that the risk is reduced if the TNT is diluted with water above 30 percent by mass. In any case, the few crew members remaining aboard started to hose down the second hold while they simultaneously fought the fire in the first hold.

But the fire in the first hold raged out of control. Moreover, the attempts to water down the TNT in the second hold were frustrated because the rubber bags protected the material from water, as designed. Bankovich realized the severity of the situation and issued the order to abandon ship. Following orders, Kuyantsev and others fled to shore. The captain was the last to leave the ship.

Moments thereafter, just eight minutes after the initial fire broke out in the forward hold, a mighty explosion ripped through *Dalstroi*. Captain Bankovich was killed; a fragment pierced his neck. Seven crew members died, along with a large number of prisoners who had been working on the ship. The huge explosion devastated the surrounding area, killing hundreds nearby on shore. The waves kicked up from the explosion raced across the harbor, washing into the sea people even great distances away.

Former Kolyma prisoner Elinor Lipper writes of speculation that the incident had been caused by Lithuanian or Latvian prisoners.[26] It is known that many Latvian nationalists were rounded up and sent to Kolyma in the years immediately after World War II.[27] Independent confirmation has not surfaced, though it is certainly conceivable that one or more of the prisoners initiated the fire that caused the explosion. But it is also entirely possible that the event was an accident—indeed, such explosions were not uncommon in the years after World War II before the properties of ammonium nitrate were fully understood. On April 16, 1947, less than a year after *Dalstroi*'s destruction, the *Grandcamp*, a French freighter loaded with ammonium nitrate, caught fire and exploded in Texas City, Texas, killing almost six hundred people and largely devastating the town. The *Grandcamp*'s 1.5-ton anchor, roughly the same weight as a typical family sedan, was tossed two miles inland by the force of the explosion.

On December 19, 1947, tragedy struck the Dal'stroi operations again. The cargo ship *General Vatutin,* loaded with 8,593 tons of cargo including 3,133 tons of explosives, was moored in Nagaevo Harbor outside Magadan. Nearby was the ship *Vyborg,* which itself contained 193 tons of explosives, mostly high-explosive detonators. Together, the explosive power of the cargo aboard these two ships was about one-third the power of the atomic bombs that had devastated Nagasaki and Hiroshima.

In a repeat of the *Dalstroi* incident, the *General Vatutin* caught fire; despite desperate efforts on the part of the crew to move the ship from the harbor, it exploded in the midst of a fleet of ships delivering supplies and prisoners to the Kolyma Gulag. The *General Vatutin* was obliterated—not even small parts remained. The *Vyborg* was blown apart and settled quickly onto the bottom of the harbor, with only the masts showing. The explosions damaged Gulag transports *KIM, Sovietskaya Latvia,* and *Minsk,* anchored nearby, killing one or two crew members on each and an undetermined number of prisoners.[28]

The loss of life due these explosions aboard *Dalstroi* and *General Vatutin* was not publicized in the West and was largely hidden in the Soviet Union. It had been largely forgotten for many years except within the tightly knit community of Far Eastern seamen. Then in 1998, walkers high in the hills above Nakhodka came across unrecognizable chunks of steel, their jagged edges and burned surfaces providing testimony to the forces that had hurled them into the hills far from the harbor. It was the wreckage of *Dalstroi*, from the explosion fifty-two years earlier.[29]

Chapter 7

Did Twelve Thousand People Starve to Death on *Dzhurma?*

> Many people even in a long life do not experience a hundredth part of
> the delight which I was to experience in the course of a few days.
> —Soviet pilot Ivan Doronin, on his rescue
> of crew members from *Chelyuskin*

Many historians have described a particularly horrific incident involving *Dzhurma* that if true would represent by far the single largest maritime disaster in history, yet one that is virtually unknown.[1] According to these sources, twelve thousand prisoners may have starved or frozen to death when *Dzhurma* was caught in the ice on its way from Vladivostok to Ambarchik in the winter of 1933–34. Upon its return to Vladivostok, according to these reports, most or all of the guards and ship's crew had to be treated for mental illness—reinforcing the image of a journey of unbearable cruelty. Within Russia, the story is imbued with storytelling tradition and now encompasses reports of cannibalism and mass murder. It is said the guards and crew aboard *Dzhurma* survived that winter only by feasting on the corpses of the prisoners.

The *Dzhurma* story takes on a deeper mysterious and political hue when linked to Russian Arctic explorer Otto Shmidt and the voyage of his ship *Chelyuskin*, crushed in the Arctic ice in early 1934 during an attempted traverse of the difficult Northern Sea Route. It is often written that Stalin refused offers of help from nearby Americans in Alaska and in doing so consciously put at risk the crew and passengers of *Chelyuskin*, who were at that point stranded on the ice pack following the loss of their ship. Evidently Stalin wanted to avoid accidental discovery of a horrible secret: *Dzhurma* and its suffering cargo of twelve thousand Gulag laborers, locked in the ice near the camp of the *Chelyuskin*'s survivors.

If this account is true, the winter of 1933–34 aboard *Dzhurma* represents a tragedy of major proportions. To put the *Dzhurma* incident in perspective—twelve thousand would be a toll eight times as great as the loss of passengers on the *Titanic,* and twice the number lost on the *Wilhelm Gustloff,* a German cruise ship crammed with refugees sunk toward the end of the World War II and generally considered to be the worst maritime disaster of all time.[2] The only problem is that it could never have happened. The real mystery in fact is how this story has persisted for so long and been repeated by so many eminent historians, when the evidence needed to dispel the myth has been in the public domain for over sixty years.

ORIGINS OF THE STORY

The first published account and original source for of the *Dzhurma* incident—the "patient zero" of the case—is Dallin and Nicolaevsky's 1947 account in *Forced Labor in Soviet Russia:*

> One of the early—and the most tragic—of the sailings to the Kolyma estuary was that of the steamer *Dzhurma.* The *Dzhurma,* a large ocean liner especially equipped for shipment of Dalstroy prisoners, sailed from Vladivostok in the summer of 1933 on its maiden voyage to Ambarchik . . . and was caught in pack ice in the western part of the Sea of Chukotsk, near Wrangel Island. We are not likely ever to learn what went on in the ship during that terrible Arctic winter, how the doomed prisoners in its hold struggled for life, and how they died. The fully authenticated fact is that the *Dzhurma,* when it finally arrived at Ambarchik, in the summer of 1934, did not land a single prisoner. It is also further reported that on their return to Vladivostok nearly half of the crew of the *Dzhurma* had to be treated for mental disorders. . . . The place where the 104 members of the *Chelyuskin* party were waiting for deliverance was not far (no more than 200 miles) from the wintering place of the *Dzhurma* and its 12,000 prisoners doomed to death from cold and starvation. Moscow feared that in the course of saving the heroes of the *Chelyuskin* American fliers might by accident uncover the terrible secret of the *Dzhurma* martyrs.[3]

Dallin and Nicolaevsky do not provide their source for this specific account.[4] But they are careful to draw an important distinction between a "fully authenticated fact"—that the ship arrived without passengers in 1934—and the conjecture that *Dzhurma* must have wintered in the ice pack with a full complement of prisoners, who, since they were unseen when the ship finally arrived the following spring, must have perished.

In his book *The Great Terror: A Reassessment,* eminent Russian historian Robert Conquest also describes the incident, citing Dallin (1947) as the source:

> The first ship sent [from Vladivostok to Ambarchik], the *Dzhurma,* was caught in the autumn ice and when it arrived in Ambarchik the following year (1934),

none of its 12,000 prisoners remained. This was at a time when the exploring ship *Chelyuskin* was caught in the ice. American and other offers to try to rescue them by air were refused, and it has been suggested that the reason was that their camp was only a couple of hundred miles from the wintering place of the *Dzhurma*, which might have been stumbled upon by foreign fliers.[5]

Historian John McCannon has written of this incident, using Dallin as one source, but also reflecting the conventional wisdom—or more precisely, urban legend—about the incident in present-day Russia. However, McCannon adheres to Dallin's original view that the prisoners' fates remains conjecture or rumor:

> The Kremlin was afraid that American pilots [if engaged to rescue the *Chelyuskin*'s crew] might stumble across yet another stranded ship: the *Dzhurma*, a Dal'stroi prison steamer bound for Magadan. Allegedly, the *Dzhurma* had 12,000 convicts packed into its holds when it became trapped in the ice less than 200 miles from Camp Shmidt. If the rumors are true, the ship's fate was a gruesome one: all of the prisoners were said to have died of hypothermia or starvation, and every member of the crew supposedly went irretrievably insane.[6]

More recently, the *Dzhurma* incident, which has been a part of Russian popular culture for some time, may be starting to reach the same status in the West. For example, Colin Thubron, a widely read travel and fiction writer, described the loss of *Dzhurma* in a recent book on Siberia: "In 1933, the SS *Dzhurma* mistimed her sailing and was locked in pack ice for nine months while her 12,000 prisoners all froze to death, and half the crew went insane."[7] Note how the caveats in the original version by Dallin and Nicolaevsky, echoed by McCannon, no longer appear in this more recent version, where the story is presented as fact rather than conjecture.

Author Martin Amis, in his 2002 book *Koba the Dread: Laughter and the Twenty Million*, presents the most recent Western version of the story, reporting quite simply: "In 1933 the Dzhurma sailed too late in the year and was trapped in the ice near Wrangel Island: all winter. She was carrying 12,000 prisoners. Everyone died."[8] This version of the incident, absent any qualifications or caveats, was subsequently repeated by *Forbes*, the widely read business magazine, in its Fact and Comment section on February 3, 2003.[9]

DISPELLING THE MYTH

What happened in 1933–34? How likely is it that twelve thousand people perished on *Dzhurma* as it wintered off Wrangel Island during the 1933–34 winter? Does this explain Stalin's reluctance to accept aid for the *Chelyuskin* survivors? In fact, the incident as described could not have happened, for the simple reason that *Dzhurma* was not engaged in Gulag transport operations until late 1935, about eighteen months after the incident involving *Chelyuskin*.

The first evidence that *Dzhurma* was not in Soviet hands during 1933 or 1934 comes from *Lloyd's Register of Shipping*, which did not update the registration data to reflect the new owner or name until after the 1935–36 edition was published.[10] (*Lloyd's Register of Shipping* has been an internationally recognized authority on this topic for several hundred years.) Robert Conquest writes accurately that the data in *Lloyd's Register of Shipping* on Soviet ships are often out of date. He cites as evidence examples in which changes to Soviet ship names are not reflected in the *Lloyd's Register of Shipping* for several years after the fact. However, none of his examples refers to errors in recording sales *to* the Soviet Union, just to name changes after ships had already been operated by the Soviet Union.

In fact, the *Lloyd's Register of Shipping* data are verified from two other sources. First, while the Soviet buyers may have been unconcerned about maintaining accurate Western records of their ships, it is almost certain that the Dutch sellers worked to a higher standard of compliance. Official Dutch ship registries as well as published histories of the Dutch shipping line KNSM clearly indicate that the transfer of *Brielle* to the Soviet Union was in April 1935.[11]

Second, there are data from the Soviet side that confirm this timing. A history of the Kolyma camps by Magadan-based historian Aleksandr Kozlov confirms that the transfer of *Dzhurma* took place in 1935 and identifies autumn 1935 for *Dzhurma*'s first arrival in Magadan:

> On July 19, 1935, E.P. Berzin returned to the Kolyma. He was on holiday and official business for several months until he left for Holland, where in Amsterdam the purchase of vessels for the Dal'stroi maritime fleet took place. Familiarizing himself with the already acquired two vessels having received the names *Dzhurma* and *Yagoda*, E.P. Berzin accelerated the purchasing of a third, *Kulu*. In the autumn of 1935 they arrived in Magadan.[12]

This account supports the data from *Lloyd's Register of Shipping* and from Dutch maritime records that the sale of *Dzhurma* did not occur until spring 1935 and that the ship did not arrive in Magadan to begin its duties until autumn 1935—almost two years after the alleged fateful voyage began.

Moreover, the absence of data can also be illuminating, if less compelling. Soviet accomplishments in the Arctic in the 1930s were a source of prestige for the Soviet Union, and trips along the Northern Sea Route to the Kolyma region were often noted, even if the accounts are silent on the relationship of these voyages to the Gulag. Yet there is no record in any of the contemporary journals of *Dzhurma* making such a voyage in the 1933 season or returning in the 1934 season. In fact, there is no record of any ship in the core Dal'stroi fleet (*Dzhurma, Dalstroi, Kulu, Felix Dzerzhinsky,*

Indigirka, and *Sovietskaya Latvia*) ever making the journey through the Bering Strait to the Arctic Kolyma region, at least in the 1930s. This may not be surprising, for by the mid-1930s, with the completion of the Seimchan road from Magadan to the Kolyma River, passengers and cargo could be moved the length of the Kolyma basin without hazardous transits along the Northern Sea Route.[13]

A CASE OF MISTAKEN IDENTITY?

If the ship in question could not have been *Dzhurma*, that still leaves us with at least two unanswered questions. First, if the *Dzhurma* incident did not occur in 1933–34, does this diminish the reasons for Stalin's apparent reluctance to seek aid from America during the *Chelyuskin* disaster? Second, could this be a case of mistaken identity—could another ship have been involved? To attempt an answer to these questions, it is first necessary to review the background of Soviet shipments to the Kolyma region, in particular the impact of the Arctic ice pack on those shipments.

Soviet operations along the eastern portion of the Northern Sea Route, from the Bering Strait to the ports at the Kolyma River (Nizhnekolymsk, and later Ambarchik), Lena River (Tiksi), and Khatanga River (Nordvik) began early last century. From 1911 to 1931, one or two steamships each year, usually the freighters *Kolyma* or *Stavropol* (ex *Kotic*), would make the journey to supply distant outposts along the Arctic coast, including Kolyma. It was a difficult journey, and it was not uncommon for ships to be blocked by ice or even forced to spend the entire winter locked in ice.[14] In 1914, for example, *Kolyma* was forced to winter in the ice. In 1919, *Stavropol* was blocked by ice from delivering its cargo and forced to return to Vladivostok. The 1924 shipment was also blocked by ice. In 1929, the *Stavropol* spent a winter in the ice. In 1931, both ships steaming to Nizhnekolymsk, *Kolyma* and *Lieutenant Shmidt*, were forced to winter in the ice, and the schooner *Chukotka* was stuck and then crushed by the same ice pack.[15]

For two decades the small communities along the Arctic coast had looked forward to the occasional visit of one or perhaps two small ships each year, when ice conditions permitted. This changed in 1932, when the major convoy of six freighters—*Anadyr, Mikoyan, Krasnyi Partizan, Suchan, Uritskii,* and *Sever*—made the journey from Vladivostok to Ambarchik, with *Suchan* and *Anadyr* together carrying about a thousand Gulag laborers. All six ships reached Kolyma, not without difficulty, and the freighters began unloading passengers and cargo. The passenger unloading was completed, but cargo unloading had to be suspended with the onset of winter, and all six of the freighters went back to sea to wait out the winter of 1932–33 in the ice. When conditions improved in the spring of 1933, two of the ships (*Krasnyi Partizan* and *Suchan*) proceeded back to Vladivostok, but four (*Uritskii, Mikoyan, Sever,* and *Anadyr*) returned to Ambarchik to finish unloading cargo. Once completed, these four attempted a return to Vladivostok, though only *Uritskii* and *Mikoyan* escaped the ice in time.[16]

In short, it was not uncommon for shipments to the Kolyma region to be interrupted by ice. In the 1931 and 1932 seasons combined, all eight freighters sent to Kolyma were forced to winter in the ice, and two of these from the 1932 season (*Sever, Anadyr*) were forced to winter in the ice a *second* time in the 1933 season. Based on the 1932 season, there exists a precedent for ships to arrive at Ambarchik, partially unload cargo, leave port to winter in the ice, and then return the following spring to unload any remaining cargo.

This brings us to the 1933–34 season and a scenario that might explain both Stalin's reluctance to involve outsiders in a rescue of *Chelyuskin,* and the alleged *Dzhurma* incident. The year 1933 must have been a busy and confusing time at Ambarchik. The ships *Uritskii, Mikoyan, Sever,* and *Anadyr* returned to finish unloading—this almost certainly had not been originally scheduled. Reports indicate that four other ships arrived from Vladivostok as part of the 1933 fleet, including *Khabarovsk, Sverdlovsk,* and *Lieutenant Shmidt.* These records indicate that at least *Khabarovsk* was forced to winter in the ice after unloading at Ambarchik.[17]

Thus, in the 1933–34 winter, at least three cargo ships—*Sever, Anadyr,* and *Khabarovsk*—were locked in the ice not far from the location of *Chelyuskin.* To the extent Stalin was motivated for reasons beyond national prestige, this fact may provide for a more credible explanation for his reluctance to involve American assistance in rescuing the crew of *Chelyuskin.* Perhaps Stalin feared not the exposure of a single stranded ship with twelve thousand prisoners—who were largely invisible from the air in any case—but the identification of a fleet of cargo ships in an undeveloped and remote region, which could have exposed his newly developed Kolyma Gulag system to the West.[18]

The records of early shipments to the Kolyma also support a different interpretation of Dallin's "fully authenticated facts." It is now known that ships, including those carrying Gulag prisoners, would reach port, unload prisoners and some cargo, winter in the ice, and then return the following spring to complete unloading. An observer might record the arrival of a passenger-carrying ship from its ice-bound wintering position, assume it had been blocked by the ice prior to reaching port (as was often the case), and note that when it finally did arrive it contained no passengers. If this same observer did not record the arrival of the ship the previous season, he might conclude that the prisoners had been lost during the winter. Such rumors might easily become associated with *Dzhurma,* the most infamous of the Gulag ships.

One wonders if the *Khabarovsk,* one of the ships that wintered both in 1932–33 and 1933–34, is linked to the confusion in Dallin's original account. In fact, the history of *Khabarovsk* fits the data offered by Dallin more

Khabarovsk at sea. The widely reported death of 12,000 prisoners aboard *Dzhurma* during the winter of 1933/34 was in error and possibly involved this ship in a case of mistaken identity. *Source*: World Ship Society.

accurately than does *Dzhurma*. While not a "large ocean liner" as described by Dallin, *Khabarovsk* was a cargo/passenger ship of respectable size and certainly fits his description more aptly than bulk freighter *Dzhurma*. *Khabarovsk* "sailed from Vladivostok in the summer of 1933 on its maiden voyage to Ambarchik" since it was part of the 1933 convoy and was completed only in 1932 (and was not part of the 1932 convoy). Moreover, *Khabarovsk* "was caught in pack ice in the western part of the Sea of Chukotsk, near Wrangel Island" and its location was not far from "the place where the 104 members of the *Chelyuskin* party were waiting for deliverance." Also, there is strong reason to believe that when *Khabarovsk* finally reached port in 1934 (although which port is unclear), it contained no passengers—not because they froze or starved but because they were discharged when the ship docked in Ambarchik in 1933.

NEW LEGEND OF THE *PIZHMA*

Related to the story of *Dzhurma* and *Chelyuskin* are new allegations making the rounds in Russia around a ship named *Pizhma*.[19] According to these allegations, *Chelyuskin* did not make its journey along the Northern Sea Route alone. Rather, it was accompanied by *Pizhma*, a recently built ship hastily converted for the carriage of two thousand prisoners to Arctic labor camps. The story suggests that *Pizhma*, like *Chelyuskin*, had been constructed

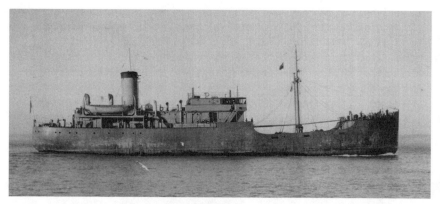

Refrigerator No. 1 in December 1943 in San Francisco. Some have suggested that this ship was destroyed in 1934 as it sailed with *Dzhurma*. *Source*: U.S. Coast Guard.

in 1933 in Denmark and transferred later that year to the Soviet Union. The story goes on to suggest that *Pizhma* was stranded in the ice very close to *Chelyuskin* and that Stalin ultimately ordered the ship and passengers to be dynamited, but not before some of the prisoners were able to contact American authorities by radio and arrange for rescue by U.S. officials. These escapees, fearing for the lives of family back in the Soviet Union, never publicized their experiences; hence this incident has only recently come to light.

There are several difficulties with this account, the main one being the complete absence of any records relating to a ship named *Pizhma* built in 1933 and transferred from Denmark to the Soviet Union. Danish records clearly indicate that only three ships were transferred in 1933 to the Soviet Union, all of them built that year by the Copenhagen-based firm Burmeister & Wain.[20] One was *Lena*, which was renamed *Chelyuskin*, and the other two were imaginatively named *Refrigerator No. 1* and *Refrigerator No. 2*.[21] These last two were the first in a long series of fishing ships with refrigerated holds that eventually extended up to *Refrigerator No. 15*.[22]

These were small ships, about a thousand tons, ill suited for carrying large numbers of passengers and certainly ill equipped for a pioneering voyage along the Northern Sea Route.[23] Unlike *Chelyuskin*, which is recorded as lost in February 1934, the other two ships continue to appear in ship registries after 1934.[24] For example, they are identified—with contemporary photographs—in U.S. naval intelligence records as being active in the Pacific region as late as December 1942, and they appear in similar records throughout the war.[25] They are reported as in operation even in the late 1950s.

In all likelihood, the *Pizhma* story is just another version of the original *Dzhurma* account, which has over time taken on the status of an urban legend in the Soviet Union. If nothing else, the similarity of names in Russian (*Джурма* and *Пижма*) suggests this possibility.

One always takes risks in reporting on historical events based on a partial compilation of the data. In this case, a careful review of the record casts se-rious doubts on the *Dzhurma* story and raises questions around the rigor employed by past writers on this topic. The *Dzhurma* legend has evolved from a hypothesis put forward by Dallin and Nicolaevsky in 1947 to the the definitive declaration that "everyone died" as determined by Martin Amis some 65 years later. All of this happened without, apparently, any of these authors actually testing the original hypothesis against the clearly available data.

Chapter 8

Questions of Numbers: Correcting the Historical Record

> Cruel treatment, inadequate food, frigid cold, and damp working conditions at Kolyma resulted in an extremely high mortality rate—estimated at over 3 million during the 15-to-20-year period of operation.
> —A formerly classified CIA report prepared in 1985

It is clear by all accounts that the Gulag ships carried large numbers of passengers in horribly crowded conditions.[1] Yet no authoritative report has surfaced to help us resolve a long-standing debate: Just how many prisoners were transported to the Kolyma camps, on each voyage and in total? Several historians have attempted to resolve these issues, and the estimates produced vary tremendously. For example, the most commonly held view prior to the release of the Soviet archives was that about 3.5 million forced laborers were transported to the Kolyma Gulag, though the estimates ranged up to eight million. Others insist that the figure must have been much lower. Likewise, scholars have never been able to agree on how many prisoners were crammed aboard each ship on these cruel journeys.

NUMBER OF PASSENGERS PER VOYAGE

Almost all firsthand estimates, from passengers or observers at points of embarkation and disembarkation, place the passenger loads on the Gulag ships at between two thousand and four thousand, though one estimate is five thousand and two others seven thousand. Many writers have taken up this figure of seven thousand and assumed this was indicative of most voyages. Some historians have reported that *Dzhurma* carried up to twelve thousand convict laborers on each voyage. Other Gulag and maritime historians suggest this would have been impossible and believe the numbers to be much lower.

It has been possible for many years to resolve this debate by employing simple analyses, though apparently these calculations have never been performed, or at least never published. The passenger-carrying capacity of the Gulag fleet can be estimated using published statistics on the size of the ships and testimony of passengers on the configuration of the passenger spaces. In both cases, while the results confirm the magnitude of the horror in Kolyma, the analytically derived estimates are substantially below numbers claimed by most authors.

How Big Were the Ships?

It may surprise many to learn that measuring the size of a ship is actually a very complicated task. Four standard definitions of size are employed, each yielding a number expressed in tonnage, though in fact only half of the measures refer to weight; the other two refer to volume. To make things even more complicated, the two tonnage measures that do refer to weight, as opposed to volume, are in fact computed indirectly by measuring volume— and not even of the ship itself but of water. Even when tonnage does refer to weight, there are three different types of tons (short, long, and metric), and they are all slightly different. Unfortunately, many authors use the different measures inappropriately and without explanation. It is important to be precise; the ratio between the various measures for the same ship can exceed three to one. Here is how it works.

The first common measure of a ship's size is *displacement*, which in fact is the only actual measure of a ship's weight. Fortunately, it is not necessary to measure the ship itself on some impossibly giant scale, because one can infer the ship's weight from the volume of water it displaces; this is relatively easy to calculate from the ship's design drawings and by noting the depth of the ship in the water. A floating ship displaces a volume of water that weighs the same as the ship itself. This volume will vary depending upon whether the water in question is fresh water or salt water—ships, like swimmers, float higher in salt water—but there are standard methodologies for conversion for salinity.

Displacement is a useful measure for warships, for indeed, in these classes of ships size does matter: one can infer capability from the weight of the ship itself rather than the weight of what it carries. The functionality of these ships is not directly related to how much cargo they can carry without sinking. However, it is not a very useful measure for merchant ships, since the volume (and hence weight) of water displaced will vary tremendously depending upon whether the ship is loaded or unloaded, and whether the constraint ultimately reached is weight (dense cargo) or space (bulky cargo). In fact, in the case of cargo ships, our primary interest is not in what the ship weighs when empty but in how much it carries—the difference between the empty weight and the weight when fully loaded. One can argue that for the same volume, a light merchant ship (i.e., low empty displacement) is more capable than a heavy merchant ship (i.e., high empty displacement) of identical volume. Everything else being equal, a lightweight ship can carry more weight in cargo. So with cargo ships, unlike battleships, size per se does not always matter.

For these purposes, a second measure is used. This measure, typically employed only for cargo ships, is *deadweight tonnage* (DWT). DWT is a measure of the weight not of the ship but of what the ship can carry—cargo, passengers, crew, fuel, and stores—when it is loaded to its summer load line (deepest safe draft for summer conditions, indicated by a mark on the hull). It is equal to the difference between the ship's displacement when empty and the displacement when fully loaded. Traditionally, displacement tonnage and deadweight tonnage were calculated in *long tons* (2,240 pounds)—the weight of seawater needed to fill the volume occupied by two thousand pounds (a *short ton*) of fresh water. This amount is slightly more than a *metric tonne:* one thousand kilograms equal to about 2,204 pounds. Today, it is common to express displacement and deadweight tonnage in metric tonnes. However, a measure such as DWT, while very helpful in assessing the capacity of a ship to carry cargo, is not very useful in measuring the capacity to carry prisoners, since the limiting factor for carriage of people is space rather than weight.

Fortunately for our purposes, merchant ships are also measured in *gross* and *net tonnage,* which while nominally expressed in units of weight, actually refer to the cubic volume of the ship. In fact, the origin of the word "ton" in this context is probably not the common unit of weight but the older word *tun,* which referred to a wine cask of a certain size (volume).

Gross registered tonnage (GRT) is the internal capacity of a ship, or the total volume of enclosed spaces in the hull and superstructure, in cubic feet divided by one hundred (or in cubic meters divided by 2.83). This somewhat arcane formula is supposedly based on estimates that one hundred cubic feet (or 2.83 cubic meters) of wheat weighed about one ton. Over time, this measure became unreliable as individual countries applied their own standards and definitions to tonnage, in part to circumvent expensive tariff, canal, and port charges that were based on a ship's gross or net tonnage. To correct for these variations, a specific measure of gross tonnage was employed in the first half of the twentieth century that reflected standard definitions and certification processes used by British authorities. This measure of gross tonnage is called *British Registered Tonnage* (BRT), though this term is not commonly used today. For many of the Gulag ships, published data on gross registered tonnage in contemporary literature is expressed as BRT, indicating that it was measured and certified in accordance with international standards.

However, figures on gross tonnage have limitations, in that they include space that is occupied by engines, navigation equipment, other machinery, fuel tanks, and crew accommodations—in other words, space not available for carriage of passengers and freight. To adjust for these factors, the measure of *net registered tonnage* (NRT) was developed, which like gross tonnage is actually a measure of volume rather than weight. Net tonnage refers to the enclosed space available both above and below decks for carriage of cargo and passengers, again divided by one hundred in the case of cubic feet, or 2.83 for cubic meters.

How do these measures compare? The different measures yield very different results. For example, the infamous *Dzhurma* was a ship of 9,960 deadweight tons, 6,908 gross registered tons, and 3,924 net registered tons. In other words, *Dzhurma* could carry 9,960 tons of cargo while remaining seaworthy, and its hull and superstructure enclosed a volume of 19,550 cubic meters, of which 11,100 cubic meters were available for cargo or provisions. As is typical for cargo ships, *Dzhurma*'s displacement is not reported, but a reasonable estimate based on rules of thumb is that the ship itself, apart from any cargo, weighed about four thousand tons.

For our purposes, the net registered tonnage is the most relevant measure, as it identifies the volume of enclosed space of machinery, ship's equipment, fuel, and crew accommodations. Measured this way, the ships in the Gulag fleet varied considerably in size. At the upper end was *Felix Dzerzhinsky*, with almost fourteen thousand cubic meters of space available for people or cargo. At the other extreme, the small *Indigirka* had less than 4,700 cubic meters of space. Most of the ships in the core NKVD fleet (*Dzhurma, Kulu, Dalstroi*) had between eleven and twelve thousand cubic meters of available space.

How Much Space Was Allocated to Each Convict?

The Gulag archives have not yet yielded official standards for space allocations for convict passengers—if any such standards ever existed. But some information is available from firsthand testimony. For example, a convict doctor aboard *Sovietskaya Latvia* reported that there were five prisoners crammed into each nine-foot-by-nine-foot square.[2] This equates to eighty-one square feet, or 7.5 square meters, in total floor space, or about 1.5 square meters in floor space per prisoner. This space, equal to a two-meter-by-0.75-meter rectangle—roughly the "footprint" of a coffin—suggests considerable crowding of prisoners and fits in well with testimony of other prisoners about the conditions on board the ships.

Former Kolyma prisoner Stanislaw Kowalski has described the hold in which he and other passengers were carried aboard *Dzhurma*. Kowalski reports that there were five layers of passengers in this hold, one on the bottom of the ship itself and the other four on tiered wooden platforms (*nary*) constructed in the hold.[3] The depth of the hull on *Dzhurma* was just under ten meters, about the same for all of the larger ships employed on Gulag service. This suggests that each layer of prisoners was about two meters apart, though not all of this was available to the prisoners, as it was also occupied by the deck plates, hull plates, bulkheads, and the wooden *nary* structure itself. Nadezhda Grankina provides information that might, on the surface, imply a more generous allocation of space. She writes that *Dzhurma*'s "hold was packed with bed boards in three tiers."[4] But the hold in which Grankina was confined was above the engine spaces, where there was space for only three rather than four tiers of bunks.

Combining the estimate of 1.5 square meters for average floor space per prisoner and two meters separation for each layer suggests the space allocated to each prisoner (with supporting structures) was about three cubic meters, or the size of a box 1.4 meters in width, height, and depth. Given the likely space used by the ship's structure, the *nary*, and passageways, the actual space available per passenger was probably about the size of an average telephone booth. Clearly, these voyages, lasting anywhere from one to several weeks, imposed great hardships on the convict passengers.

How Many Passengers per Voyage?

Using the three-cubic-meters estimate of space per passenger and published data on net tonnage (expressed in cubic meters), it is a relatively straightforward matter to estimate the passenger-carrying capacity of the Gulag ships. By this method, the largest Gulag ship, *Felix Dzerzhinsky*, would be able to accommodate about 4,600 passengers. *Indigirka*, the smallest ship in the core NKVD fleet, would be able to carry 1,500 passengers. *Sovietskaya Latvia* had a capacity of 2,200 prisoners. The other core NKVD ships (*Dzhurma, Dalstroi, Kulu*) would be able to carry 3,700 to 3,900 passengers each.

These estimates are far below the twelve thousand prisoners historians David Dallin and Boris Nicolaevsky once claimed were aboard *Dzhurma*.[5] It is also substantially less than the six to nine thousand passengers per ship estimated by Robert Conquest.[6] (But, as will be apparent later, these authors also vastly overestimated the total number of Kolyma Gulag prisoners, as is now known from released archival material.)

These analytically based estimates of carrying capacity fit in well with most direct firsthand reports and with the limited data available from archival sources. With only a few exceptions, all of which involve the same ship, all firsthand reports and archival sources fall within 10 percent to 20 percent of the computed values using the methodology described above. For example, when wrecked upon the rocks off Sarufutsu Island in Japan, *Indigirka* was carrying about than 1,200 people, about 75 percent of them prisoners.[7] The rest were fishermen and their families, who were probably accorded slightly more space than the convicts. This fits in well with the analytical estimate that *Indigirka* should have been able to carry about 1,500 prisoners if no other passengers were carried. Likewise, prisoner Varlam Shalamov estimates about three thousand prisoners disembarked from *KIM* in 1947 following a difficult journey to Magadan during which prisoners rebelled.[8] Shalamov's figure fits in well with the analytical calculation that *KIM* could have carried about 2,800 passengers. Meanwhile, *Odessa*, a U.S.-built Liberty ship with a computed capacity of 4,100, carried three thousand women prisoners on a trip to Vanino.[9]

Sovietskaya Latvia, with a computed capacity of 2,200, is reported to have carried 2,370 passengers on a voyage in 1949.[10] Michael Solomon reports that the ship carried five thousand passengers on another voyage, but he may have misidentified the ship.[11] He reports that *Sovietskaya Latvia* was a five-thousand-ton ship constructed in 1939 in Scotland, whereas in fact *Sovietskaya Latvia* was a 4,138-ton ship built in 1926 in Sweden.[12] Solomon also states that two thousand prisoners were confined in one hold on *Sovietskaya Latvia*, which is a very large number for this ship, given that it has four holds and that the estimated total capacity is only 2,200. It is possible that Solomon's number refers to the total number of prisoners aboard rather than those in the single hold, if this is not simply a case of mistaken identity.

Author Aleksandr Solzhenitsyn reports that a convoy of ships including *Nevastroi, Dneprostroi, Dzhurma,* and *Kulu* arrived in Magadan with three to four thousand prisoners per ship.[13] As this was during a peak travel period, it is likely the ships would have been full. Solzhenitsyn's report fits well with computed estimates for *Dneprostroi* (2,800), *Nevastroi* (3,400), *Dzhurma* (3,700), and *Kulu* (3,800). Other reports for *Dzhurma* suggest that at times the ship carried fewer than 3,700 passengers, and certainly far less than the twelve thousand suggested by Dallin and Nicolaevsky. Vladimir Petrov estimates that two thousand men were aboard the ship at a time when the four holds were "packed to the brim with men."[14] Michael Solomon estimates that 2,500 passengers accompanied him on a voyage from Magadan to a point a bit farther along the coast.[15] Petrov also reports that *Felix Dzerzhinsky* carried approximately five thousand prisoners during a voyage in 1937, which fits well with a computed 4,600-passenger capacity for *Felix Dzerzhinsky*.[16]

The Exception: *Dzhurma*

A number of firsthand accounts of passengers and former crewmen suggest that *Dzhurma* at least on a few occasions carried more passengers than our simple analysis might suggest. Two of the reports are from former Kolyma prisoners, Elinor Lipper and Janusz Bardach. Lipper reports that seven thousand prisoners were carried on one journey on *Dalstroi*, a ship with a computed capacity of about 3,900.[17] Bardach reports that on his voyage he overheard a prisoner rumor that there were seven thousand people on his ship, but he does not indicate whether he thought that was accurate.[18]

Information from Vladivostok-based historian Alla Paperno supports these estimates for *Dzhurma*. According to Paperno, seaman Pavel Stepanovich Chigor, who sailed on *Dzhurma* in the prewar years (and *Sovietskaya Latvia* during the war and *Felix Dzerzhinsky* afterward) reported that the ship carried at times up to 6,500 prisoners. Paperno herself reports that archival records indicate *Dzhurma* carried 6,387 passengers on a special voyage in 1944.[19] (*Dalstroi*, which accompanied *Dzhurma* on this special voyage, carried just over 4,400 prisoners, which is just over 10 percent of the computed estimate of *Dalstroi*'s capacity.) It is possible that *Dzhurma* was specially outfitted at a higher density than the other ships. This would be in keeping with its reputation as a ship of horrors for prisoners sentenced to the Dal'stroi Gulag.

Finally, even higher figures are reported by an anonymous sailor interviewed in the New York–based newsletter *Socialist Courier* in 1945.[20] This sailor reported that four of the core NKVD ships carried between six and nine thousand on each voyage during the peak years in the late 1930s. However, this same sailor estimated that 1.5 million prisoners were carried to the Kolyma camps during 1937 to 1940. According to the NKVD Gulag archives, only 227,000 prisoners actually made the journey during that period, which raises questions about the reliability of this source.[21] That reliability is further undermined by this sailor's inclusion of *Sovietskaya Latvia* in the core fleet during those years when it did not even come into the Soviet Union's possession until 1941. In any event, no firsthand reports or analytical models indicate that *Dzhurma* ever carried twelve thousand prisoners on one voyage, as reported by Dallin and Nicolaevsky in 1947 and repeated by Conquest and numerous other authors.

POPULATION OF THE KOLYMA CAMP SYSTEM

Perfect statistics on the number of prisoners transported to Dal'stroi's Kolyma camps are hard to find. In the past, before the opening of the Soviet archives, observers have had to estimate this based on the presumed population of the camps or the availability of transport resources—though these also were traditionally sources of speculation rather than fact.

There are two empirical questions to answer. First, how many prisoners were in the camps at any given time? Second, how many were transported to the camps across the entire period of operation?

Total Population over Time

A number of writers have tried to estimate the population of the camps on the basis largely of indirect evidence and testimony from former inmates.

Conquest, using what he acknowledges were rough methodologies, in 1990 estimated the peak prisoner population in Kolyma at five hundred thousand.[22] In an earlier work he presented a series of estimates ranging from 150,000 in 1937 to 300,000 in 1942, 250,000 in 1944, and 500,000 in the postwar period.[23] The U.S. Central Intelligence Agency arrived at similar estimates. In the early 1950s it informed its consumers that the "slave labor force of Dal'stroi is estimated to be 400,000."[24]

However, information from the recently opened Soviet archives helps clarify the issue, though different sources report different numbers, perhaps reflecting inconsistencies in the archival record. Based on these records, the number of Kolyma prisoners reached as high as two hundred thousand twice—once just before Soviet involvement in World War II, and once in the final years of Stalin's rule (see Table 8.1). [25]

In general, the CIA's and Robert Conquest's estimates were consistently about twice the numbers subsequently revealed by the Soviet archives, an error Conquest at least has subsequently acknowledged. But by no means were these the only observers to overestimate the number of Kolyma prisoners. The continuing debate about the number of Gulag prisoners across a number of academic journals makes very entertaining reading.

This is not surprising—there has been at times a lack of rigor in the analysis. In some cases, data refer to the number of prisoners at a point in time, most commonly January 1 of each year. In other cases, the data reflect the average number of prisoners in a year (though it is unclear if this is a mean across each day in the year, the average of the start and end points in each year, the median, midpoint, or some other calculation). Some estimates include all of the Sevvostlag camps transferred to Dal'stroi in the late 1930s; others exclude some of those camps. Some estimates encompass the total labor force, including those prisoners technically freed but forced to remain in Magadan; others include only prisoners serving sentences. We may never have perfect data.

Total Number of Prisoners Transported: 1932–53

Another question relates to the total number of prisoners transported to the camps over the entire period of operation. Robert Conquest, writing in 1978 without the benefit of access to the Soviet archives, calculated the number of transported prisoners after estimating the number of ships used to transport prisoners, the frequency of trips per year, and the average number of prisoners per trip. He concludes that a total of 3,500,000 prisoners were transported to the camps from 1932 to 1953.[26]

Conquest was by no means alone in estimating the number of prisoners transported as well into the millions. For example, the Central Intelligence Agency was reporting as late as 1985 that over three million prisoners *perished* in Kolyma during this period, which meant of course that well over

Table 8.1
Prisoners of the Dal'stroi System: Competing Estimates

three million were transported: "Large numbers of forced laborers were used in the expanding timber industry in the north and in gold mining operations in the remote Kolyma River area of northeastern Siberia. Cruel treatment, inadequate food, frigid cold, and damp working conditions at Kolyma resulted in an extremely high mortality rate—estimated at over 3 million during the 15-to-20-year period of operation."[27]

It is likely these estimates contain the same error as the earlier estimates of camp population at specific points in time. The archives have yet to yield a definitive number of prisoners transported to the Kolyma camps across the full life of the camps; multiple and somewhat inconsistent data sets are available for the years 1932 to 1941 and for some of the years during World War II. For the remaining years, it is possible to estimate the number of transferred prisoners by building a simple model to fit the known number of prisoners at each point in time and factoring in expected "attrition," or the number of prisoners who transferred out, were released, or, more likely, perished during the year.

The Russian historian I.D. Batsaev has obtained archival data on annual arrivals and departures from Magadan from 1932 to 1941 (in addition to the total camp population at the beginning of each year). These data suggest that attrition during those years ranged from 13 percent to 33 percent and averaged 27 percent.[28] In other words, about 27 percent of the prisoners resident at the start of each year needed to be replaced by new prisoners, in addition to new prisoners brought in to increase the total camp population. This is consistent with estimates from prisoners in the camps that between 20 percent and 35 percent of the camp population died during some years up to 1942.[29] Other attrition would represent prisoners who escaped without being recaptured, were transferred to other facilities, or were freed. Petropavlovsk-Kamchatka-based historian Alla Paperno has obtained archival data for prisoner movements in 1945 that indicate a total of 37,600 prisoners were shipped to Magadan that year.[30]

To estimate the number of prisoners shipped via Magadan in other years after 1942, one must make assumptions about the rate of attrition in those years. The war years were exceptionally difficult for the Kolyma camps, and a reduction in rations ordered by the Soviet government led to much higher death rates.[31] In addition, a large number of prisoners were freed (or more likely compelled) to join the Soviet armed forces, fighting against Germany. An analysis of archival records by researcher Edwin Bacon indicates that the attrition rate for 1942 for the combined Dal'stroi and Osobstroi camps was 47 percent in 1942.[32] For our purposes, one might assume that rate of attrition in Dal'stroi ranged from 40 percent to 60 percent during all of the war years, declining back to 27 percent—the average for the prewar period—following the end of the conflict. These numbers suggest that the average prisoner spent approximately one and a half to two and a half years in the camps before perishing (or, less frequently, being released) during the war

Table 8.2
Estimated Annual Prisoner Shipments to Kolyma

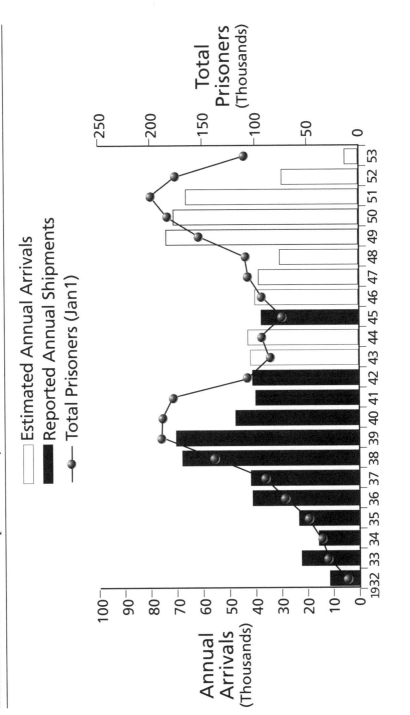

years, and about four years before perishing (or being released) in the years before and after the war. In addition to reinforcing the harsh reality of the Dal'stroi camp system, these estimates are generally in line with anecdotes of former prisoners.

On this basis, one can compute that about 875,00 to 925,000 prisoners were transported to the Kolyma camps through Magadan during their operation from 1932 to 1953. (The precise calculated figure is about 898,000.) There is, of course, much uncertainty in this estimate. Moreover, other prisoners, though probably a much smaller number, arrived via the Arctic port of Ambarchik, so one would not be far off in concluding that about one million forced laborers were transported to Kolyma camps during the twenty-three years of their operation (see Table 8.2).

This estimate is fully consistent with recent analysis of the Soviet-era archives by historian Aleksandr G. Kozlov of Magadan. Based on a careful review of the Dal'stroi and Sevvostlag records, he estimates the total number of prisoners transported to Kolyma at between eight hundred thousand and one million. He further estimates that about 130,000 died before completing their sentences—of famine, cold, or overwork—and that another eleven thousand were executed by Gulag authorities.[33]

While the actual number is a far cry from the earlier estimates of eight million, the hardships imposed on a million slave laborers remain not only a statistic but a tragedy.

Chapter 9

The NKVD's Ships

The steamers acquired by Dal'stroi, in terms of their displacement and technical equipment, are the largest and fastest in the civilian fleet of the Pacific basin.

—Comments on *Dzhurma, Dalstroi,* and *Kulu*
in a 1935 annual report of the Dal'stroi trust

Dominia was sold in 1937 to the Russian government. . . . It is believed that she is still afloat but not employed on cable work.

—K.R. Haigh, author of *Cableships and Submarine Cables,*
describing the ship that became the flagship of the
NKVD Kolyma fleet

After reliving the experiences on the Gulag transport ships, one is tempted to conclude that the entire phenomenon is unbelievable.[1] Indeed, it is hard for many to imagine the reality that a million or more people were transported to remote locations in northeastern Siberia in horrific conditions on steamships largely supplied by the United States or Western Europe. But the experiences were real, just as the names of the freighters described earlier relate not to imaginary vessels but to real ships with real crews—and real histories.

The careers of these merchantmen are windows into many of the most tumultuous events of the first half of the twentieth century. Through these simple merchantmen one might revisit the last stages of the industrial revolution, World War I and its aftermath, the Great Depression, the Spanish Civil War, the rise of the Soviet state, the annexation of the Baltic states, World War II, and the emergence of the Cold War. Their lives span almost a century—the oldest of the ships was built in 1904, and one of the last constructed remains afloat today.

Six of these ships served in the core NKVD transport fleet. These ships deserve special attention, since they were purchased and configured specifically to carry large numbers of prisoners on regular voyages to the Kolyma camps. Previous authors, especially Robert Conquest, have attempted to collect and present basic data on the ships, but what follows is certainly the most complete record of the ships reported to date.[2]

DZHURMA (ДЖУРМА, DJURMA, DYURMA)

Any discussion of the Soviet Gulag ships begins with *Dzhurma*, as it is clearly the most infamous of all.[3] By far, it is the ship cited most frequently in firsthand accounts of Gulag voyages, and it is the ship that emerges most frequently in passengers' tales of horrors and atrocities. If the importance of a ship is measured by the number of lives it has touched, then *Dzhurma* is one of the most significant vessels of the twentieth century and probably the one of which the touch has inflicted the most pain. The full impact of its service may never be known, but it would not be beyond reason to conclude that 225,000 people were taken to Siberian forced labor camps on *Dzhurma* alone.[4]

Dzhurma was built as the *Brielle* in 1921 in Flushing (Vlissingen) Netherlands by shipbuilder Koninklijke Maatschappij "deSchelde," one of many such shipyards producing merchantmen at that time in the Netherlands. The new ship was operated by Vereenigde Nederlandsche Scheepvaartmaatschappij (VNS), a Dutch shipping company formed just after World War I; eventually the firm was absorbed into one of the companies in the consortium that formed it, Koninklijke Nederlandsche Stoomboot-Maatschappij (KNSM). (KNSM survives today as Royal Nedlloyd.)[5] A typical bulk merchant ship of the time, *Brielle* measured 6,908 gross tons and was 403 feet in length. It provided its owners with several years of valued service, during which it circled the world, but it could not circumvent the Great Depression of the 1930s. *Brielle* was laid up, and its owners, facing

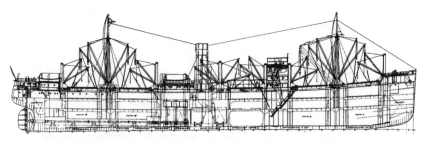

Original arrangements plan of *Dzhurma*, which was constructed as the *Brielle* in the Netherlands. This single ship probably carried over 225,000 prisoners to the camps. *Source*: Maritiem Museum Rotterdam.

severe financial problems, looked for opportunities to sell the freighter in order to raise cash.

VNS found a willing buyer in Dal'stroi. Eduard Berzin, the Dal'stroi commander, personally visited the Netherlands to arrange for the purchase of *Brielle*, perhaps using his fluency in German (from his days as an art student in Berlin) to help negotiate terms in a language more readily accessible to the Dutch than his native Russian language. The ship was renamed *Dzhurma*, which means "shining path" in the language spoken by the indigenous Even people of the Kolyma region.[6] *Dzhurma* arrived in Nagaevo Harbor in 1935 under the command of Capt. N.A. Finjaki.[7] There it was assigned international registration UPKZ[8]

Dzhurma is the Gulag ship most widely reported in firsthand accounts of former passengers. There exist published accounts by passengers of voyages made in 1936, 1939, 1940, and 1949.[9] In addition, there exist unpublished passenger accounts of voyages in 1937, 1938, 1941, 1944, and 1950.[10] Previous authors have reported its use in the Soviet slave trade in 1937, 1938, 1939, from 1937 to 1940, and in 1949, when the ship transferred workers to support atomic weapons development in the Kolyma region.[11] Overall, there is ample evidence that *Dzhurma* was used extensively on Gulag routes from 1936 through 1950.

While *Dzhurma* served as the backbone of the Gulag fleet, it was also used on American Lend-Lease operations in the Pacific during World War II, making about a dozen trips to San Francisco, Portland, and Seattle.[12] The United States performed extensive repairs on *Dzhurma* during these years, with costs totaling over $555,000—roughly equivalent to one-third the cost of a new merchant ship.[13] But even when drafted into Lend-Lease service,

Brielle prior to its sale to the Soviet Union. *Source*: Collection of Roel Zwama, Rotterdam.

the ship still managed to complete at least two passenger runs to the Gulag. *Dzhurma* returned to Gulag duties immediately after World War II and is known to have operated on these routes in the late 1940s. It was during this time, 1948–49, that a witness states that the ship was used to carry U.S. servicemen to imprisonment in the Kolyma Gulag.[14]

Dzhurma was probably employed on general cargo duties after the population of the Gulag camps declined in the 1950s. It was removed from *Lloyd's Register of Shipping* and the *Russian Maritime Register of Shipping* in 1968 at the same time a new *Dzhurma* was built in Poland for the Soviet Union.[15] Its final disposition remains unknown, but it was probably scrapped in the Soviet Union in 1968.

DALSTROI (ДАЛЬСТРОЙ, DALSTROY, YAGODA)

The second ship of the Gulag fleet—and the namesake for the Kolyma organization itself—would likely have paralleled *Dzhurma* in infamy except for the fact that it served only half as long in its odious duties.

Dalstroi was originally named *Almelo* and, like *Dzhurma*, was built in Flushing by Koninklijke Maatschappij "deSchelde" and operated by VNS and KNSM.[16] At 6,948 gross tons and 448 feet in length, it was slightly larger than *Dzhurma*. It too was sold during the Great Depression to Dal'stroi, the transaction being personally arranged by Eduard Berzin in 1935. The

The Dutch freighter *Almelo* was the first ship acquired for the Dal'stroi fleet and was given the name *Dalstroi*. It was destroyed in 1946 in a violent explosion, blamed on Latvian prisoners. *Source*: Collection of Roel Zwama, Rotterdam.

ship arrived in Nagaevo Harbor on September 16, 1935, under the command of a Captain Glejzer.[17]

With the transfer to the Soviet Union, *Almelo* was registered as UPLA, home ported in Nagaevo, and renamed *Yagoda*, after the then head of the NKVD.[18] Given the ongoing Communist Party purges, it was a risky proposition to name any ship after a living member of Soviet leadership. Sure enough, in 1936, just after having the ship named after him, Genrikh Grigoryevich Yagoda was arrested for crimes against the state, executed, and declared a "nonperson"; his image was literally scratched out of the archives. Clearly, it would not do to operate a ship named for a disgraced nonperson, and *Yagoda* became *Dalstroi*.

There is ample evidence that *Dalstroi* was used in Gulag service. One can find published passengers' accounts for 1939 and unpublished passengers' accounts from 1938, 1940, and 1942.[19] In addition, there are other reports of operations in 1936, 1937, 1939, 1940, and from 1937 to 1940.[20] Perhaps the most famous passenger aboard *Dalstroi* was Sergei P. Korolev, who was taken to Kolyma aboard the ship in 1938.[21]

Dalstroi played an important role in World War II as a cargo ship transferring American Lend-Lease cargo to the Soviet Union. During the war *Dalstroi* even rescued survivors of a Japanese cargo ship sunk by a U.S. submarine.[22] The ship was extensively modified and overhauled by the United States during World War II, courtesy of the American taxpayers; by the end of 1945, over $1.4 million had been spent to overhaul and upgrade the ship, which is a very significant amount, roughly equal to the cost of a new Liberty merchant ship. *Dalstroi* was again repaired in Vancouver, British Columbia, following wartime damage in August 1945. It returned to cargo operations following these repairs until it exploded with great loss of life on July 24, 1946.[23]

FELIX DZERZHINSKY (ФЕЛИКС ДЗЕРЖИНСКИЙ, NIKOLAI EZHOV, FELIKS DJERJINSKY)

The circumstances that led to the creation and use of *Felix Dzerzhinsky* in Gulag service had everything to do with the development of a revolutionary technology in the first decades of the 1900s—radio—and the unsuccessful attempts of the submarine (undersea) cable industry to defeat this competitive threat to its monopoly on rapid long-distance communications. The ship would not have been built were it not for radio, it would not have been put up for sale except for radio, and it was purchased by the Soviets in part because of radio.

Submarine telegraph and telephone cables were a big business at the turn of the century. But the industry was threatened by wireless communication. One way it responded was by improving the performance of undersea cables by using "loaded" cable technology, which boosted transmission rates ten-fold.[24]

But the new cables were much heavier, and the undersea lines built with the technology challenged the capacity of the fleet of cable-laying ships then in use, in particular across the long distances of the Pacific. This was especially true for the gap between Bamfield in British Columbia and Fanning Island in the Pacific, at 3,466 nautical miles the longest continuous segment of submarine cable in the world. In 1902, even before the development of loaded cable, a new large cable ship christened *Colonia* had been constructed specifically to carry the massive bulk of cable needed to fill the Bamfield-Fanning gap. But with the development of loaded cable, even this capacity was insufficient. It was clear to the Telegraph Construction and Maintenance Company (Telcon), the company responsible for laying the cable along this route, that a still bigger ship was needed.

The answer was the *Dominia*. Built for Telcon in 1926 by Swan, Hunter & Wigham Richardson Ltd. in Newcastle, the *Dominia* was by far the largest specialized cable-laying ship yet constructed. It measured 489 feet in length and had a capacity of 9,273 gross tons, about twice the size of most large cable-laying ships. Four massive holds contained about four thousand miles of loaded submarine cable, the largest cable capacity of any ship constructed to that time.[25]

Once launched, the ship was very busy, completing the Bamfield-Fanning portion of the Pacific cable in the late 1920s and many other submarine cables in the Caribbean and Europe.[26] *Dominia* also played a major role in the repair of the transatlantic cables disrupted by seismic activity in November 1929. Those aboard, afloat for the next several months on this emergency mission, did not suffer, as an official history of Telcon recalls: "All this did not prevent those aboard *Dominia* enjoying Christmas. Everyone was in fancy dress and to read through the menu of the Christmas dinner, with the choice of wines and liqueurs, is to bring back dim but nostalgic memories."[27]

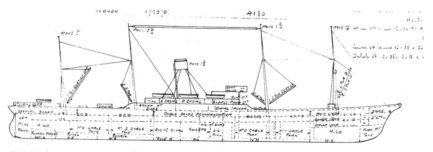

Original arrangements sketch for *Dominia*, which later became Dal'stroi's flagship. *Source*: Tyne-Wear Archive Services.

Despite the new capabilities embodied by *Dominia,* the submarine cable industry continued to be overtaken by wireless transmission technologies. In 1935, Telcon merged with its former archrival Siemens Brothers and pursued a plan to rationalize the fleet as part of a desperate cost-saving strategy. With the Bamfield-Fanning cable completed, the unique demands for a ship of *Dominia*'s size no longer applied, and as it was the most expensive cable-laying ship to operate, the owners decided to put it up for sale.[28]

Once again, the Soviet Union appeared as the only buyer during this period of economic depression. Arrangements were made in 1936 for the purchase of *Dominia* by the Soviet Union, with the exact date of transfer on January 6, 1937. One of the most appealing aspects of the ship for the Soviets was its modern radio equipment, which led to its assignment as the flagship of the NKVD fleet. *Dominia* was given the name *Nikolai Ezhov* after the then head of the KGB, Nikolai Ivanovich Ezhov. The new addition to the fleet, under the command of Capt. Pavel Illarionovich Feodor, steamed to Amsterdam for a several-month refit and then via Odessa, Port Said, and Singapore to Nagaevo, arriving in late July. It was greeted at the dock by Berzin himself.[29]

A few years before, the naming of a ship after Ezhov's predecessor, Yagoda, led to some awkwardness when the latter was executed shortly afterward. The Gulag ship-naming curse continued—almost immediately after having a ship named after him, Nikolai Ezhov was declared a "nonperson" and executed. The Soviets must have learned the folly of naming Gulag ships after existing heads of the NKVD given the rate of turnover in that position in the late 1930s. By renaming the new ship *Felix Dzerzhinsky*—after the founder of the NKVD, by then dead over a decade—they avoided this unseemly problem. (Lavrenti Pavlovich Beria, Ezhov's successor, wisely

In its time, *Dominia* was the largest cable-laying ship ever built. In 1937 it was sold to the Soviet Union and renamed *Felix Dzerzhinsky. Source*: Tyne-Wear Archive Services.

decided against naming any Gulag ships after himself, which might in part explain why he survived until 1953 before being executed.)

Several sources document the use of *Felix Dzerzhinsky* in Gulag service. One source indicates the ship made eight trips between Magadan and Vladivostok in the second half of 1937, making the trip in an average of four days, about half what the other steamers required.[30] There exists an unpublished biographical account of its use in 1940.[31] A former Dal'stroi sailor identified it as a member of the core Gulag fleet from 1937 to 1940.[32] One prisoner identifies it as part of a four-ship Gulag convoy in 1938 and also recounts a story told him by another prisoner of the *Felix Dzerzhinsky*'s role in rescuing prisoners from the wrecked *Indigirka* in 1939.[33] *Felix Dzerzhinsky* was also reported as escorting *Dzhurma* to port following a riot and fire aboard the latter in 1939.[34] It is reported the ship was in Nagaevo Harbor in December 1947, but it is not known if prisoners were carried on this trip.[35]

During the war, *Felix Dzerzhinsky* made about a dozen trips to the United States. Like its sister ships in the Gulag fleet, *Felix Dzerzhinsky* was extensively overhauled and modernized while in the United States. *Felix Dzerzhinsky* also participated in special cargo operations during World War II, one of which involved the transport of gold from Magadan to Nikolaevsk-on-Amur in 1944.[36] In addition, in the last days of the war and immediately afterward *Felix Dzerzhinsky* was used to transport former Soviet POWs recently released from captivity in German camps to new captivity in Dal'stroi's camps.[37]

Information on the postwar use of the ship is scarce; Conquest states it was converted into a fish factory ship, but he does not cite a source for that information.[38] In the middle and late 1950s the ship continued to appear in standard ship registries, such as *Lloyd's Register of Shipping* and Talbot-Booth's *Merchant Ships*, though still under the old name of *Nikolai Ezhov*. (It was quite common for the Soviet Union not to bother informing Western organizations about changes to its Gulag fleet.) The *Russian Maritime Register of Shipping* confirms that the ship, was taken off the register in 1978 or 1979; presumably it was scrapped.

SOVIETSKAYA LATVIA (СОВЕТСКАЯ ЛАТВИЯ, SOVETSKAYA LATVIA, SOVLATVIA)

Sovietskaya Latvia was constructed in 1926 as *Childar* by Kockums in Malmö, Sweden. It was a medium-sized steamer of 4,138 gross tons, measuring 378 feet in length. The ship was operated for several years in standard merchant service by the shipping firm Wiel & Amundsens based in Halden, Norway. In contrast to other ships used in the Gulag operation, which were powered by traditional triple-expansion steam engines, *Childar* was propelled by modern diesel engines.

Childar in the 1930s. It was later purchased by a Latvian shipping company and then confiscated by the Soviet Union in 1941. *Source*: Karl Osterman.

The Gulag career of *Sovietskaya Latvia* was very nearly preempted by a gale off the northwest coast of the United States. In May 1934, *Childar* was involved in a memorable incident off the coast of Washington state that made a hero of a U.S. Coast Guard skipper but also left several of *Childar*'s crew dead. The incident occurred while *Childar*, with twenty-nine crew members and one passenger aboard, left Longview, Washington, on the way to South Africa with a heavy load of lumber. Leaving port in the teeth of a southerly gale, *Childar* ran aground the North Spit Bar off the mouth of the Columbia River, an area notorious as a graveyard for ships. Stuck fast with its bow aground and the stern settling, the ship was struck broadside by a series of waves that sent the deck cargo into the seas and ripped off or destroyed all of the lifeboats. Three crew members were washed overboard and lost in the raging sea. Fearing for their lives, the crew sent off an SOS, which was received by a number of ships in the area. Then the mast was ripped overboard by the waves, and the radio went dead.

The Coast Guard cutter *Redwing*, under the command of Lt. A.W. Davis, left port within the hour intent on rescuing the crew and, if possible, the ship as well. It reached *Childar* as darkness approached and managed to secure a towing line to the ship. Exploiting the force of the waves, which lifted *Childar* slightly each time they passed, the *Redwing* was able to refloat the ship and tow it into deeper water. However, *Childar* was not out of danger. The damage to the ship was extensive, and it was in danger of breaking up and sinking. Three seriously injured and eighteen others were taken off and transferred to the cutter, leaving a skeleton crew of six aboard as *Redwing* slowly towed *Childar* north toward Puget Sound, reaching safe water only after an all-night vigil.[39] Though written off as a total loss, *Childar* was eventually acquired by the Henneseid shipping company and rebuilt in the Burrard Dry Dock in North Vancouver, Canada. The ship was renamed as *Aakre,* once again under Norwegian registry.[40]

Aakre was sold in 1939 to the Latvian shipping company Apvienota Kugniecibas Akc. Sab. (United Shipping Company of Latvia) and renamed *Hercogs Jçkabs* (*Hercogs Jekabs*) after Duke Jacob, a former ruler of Kurland (now Latvia), who developed a thriving shipbuilding operation in the late 1600s. But this symbol of past Latvian greatness was not to last very long, as was the case with Latvian independence itself. In June 1940, the Soviet Union occupied and annexed Latvia. On October 6, 1940, the Supreme Soviet of the Latvian SSR issued a decree that in effect turned over the maritime resources of Latvia—including its ships—to Soviet authorities. At this time, *Hercogs Jçkabs* was in Caljano, Peru, having spent the previous few months operating up and down the East Coast of the United States and then the western coast of South America. Capt. H. Mieielsons decided to obey orders from the new Soviet-led Latvian government to hand over the ship to Soviet authorities. His was the only Latvian ship to comply with the order to sail to a Soviet port.[41]

It almost did not happen. Latvian officials from the pre-Soviet government still in Washington attempted to frustrate the ship's return to Latvia and convinced port officials in Caljano on August 17, 1940, to arrest the ship, in effect putting the ship under the authority of the court and thereby preventing its departure. But Soviet influence must have prevailed, for on December 16, 1940, the decision was reversed, and the ship began a long

Childar almost never made it into Gulag operation. It was nearly lost after running aground on the North Spit Bar off Washington state. *Source:* Andrews; © Superior Publishing Company.

voyage across the Pacific to Vladivostok, where the Latvian crew was removed and taken by rail back to Riga. On February 18, 1941, *Hercogs Jçkabs* was formally taken over by the Soviet Union, renamed *Sovietskaya Latvia,* and transferred to the NKVD fleet.[42] *Sovietskaya Latvia* was registered internationally as UUEQ and operated in the Pacific with Soviet registration M-11546.

Firsthand stories of use in Gulag service are limited in the case of *Sovietskaya Latvia.* There exists a published account of a passenger voyage in 1949, as well as unpublished accounts of voyages in 1941, 1946, and 1949.[43] There are other reports of the ship in Gulag service from 1937 to 1940, which of course seems unlikely, given the fact the ship was not in Soviet hands until 1941.[44] *Sovietskaya Latvia* is known to have been operating in Nagaevo Harbor in December 1947, but no reports have surfaced that it carried prisoners on this trip.[45]

During World War II, *Sovietskaya Latvia* was used on Lend-Lease duties, making about a dozen trips to and from the United States and Canada. Just as the ship was almost lost in 1934 as a result of nature, it was also nearly destroyed in March 1943, this time as a result of human effort. While the ship was docked in Vancouver, a disgruntled crewman by the name of Vojtuyk schemed to blow it up and flee to the West; the plot was evidently spoiled by Soviet intelligence officers operating in the United States.[46]

Sovietskaya Latvia was also extensively repaired and upgraded during World War II courtesy of the United States and Canada—which is noteworthy, since the ship was reemployed on Gulag transport duties immediately after the war. The initial repairs took place in Burrard Dry Dock, the very same location where *Childar* was made seaworthy following its near loss on the Columbia bar in 1934.[47]

The ship was deleted from *Lloyd's Register of Shipping* in the 1959–60 edition. According to Swedish sources, *Sovietskaya Latvia* sailed to Kobe, Japan, in 1962, evidently for scrapping. It was not deleted from the *Russian Maritime Register of Shipping* until 1967.

KULU (КУЛУ)

Kulu was the third Dal'stroi ship purchased in the Netherlands. It was built in 1917 by Nederlandsche Scheepsbouw-Maatschappij in Amsterdam as *Batoe* and operated by the Stoomvaart Maatschappij Nederland (SMN), also known as the Nederland Line.[48] This line provided services from the Netherlands to the Dutch colonies in the East Indies. SMN over time was absorbed by KNSM.[49]

Batoe, which measured 6,492 gross tons and was 420 feet in length, operated for many years on the Dutch East Indies routes. But the Great Depression caused a major reduction of worldwide trade, which led to a crisis in the shipping industry. Moreover, the English pound, the currency in which

Batoe was the final Dutch ship purchased for the initial Dal'stroi fleet. Renamed *Kulu*, it later was transferred to the military, and afterwards, to regular cargo operations. *Source*: Collection of Roel Zwama, Rotterdam.

shipping rates were quoted, was devalued 25 percent, which led to a decline in revenues. Operating costs, however, denominated in other currencies, did not decline. By the end of 1930, of the sixteen ships operated by SMN, about half were laid up. The only solution was to scrap the older ships and sell some of the newer ones.[50] For this reason, *Batoe* was transferred to Soviet owner-ship on July 27, 1935, and registered internationally as UPMH, based in Nagaevo. Assigned Soviet registration was M-11731, the ship was renamed *Kulu*, after the large river in the Soviet Far East.

There are no published firsthand accounts of Gulag voyages on *Kulu*. There exists at least one unpublished passenger account from 1937.[51] Other accounts record use of *Kulu* on the route in 1936 and 1937. Solzhenitsyn describes a specific incident involving the ship in 1938.[52]

The year 1938 was the last in which *Kulu* served in the NKVD Gulag fleet, for in the middle of that year *Kulu* was requisitioned by the Soviet Navy for a special assignment, though until now that mission has not been de-scribed.[53] On July 29, 1938, Japanese forces attempted to seize Soviet ter-ritory near Lake Khasan, southwest of Vladivostok. Soviet forces were mobilized in response; *Kulu* was requisitioned to transport munitions into the region and wounded soldiers out.[54] The conflict (known to Japanese historians as the battle for Changkufeng) was short-lived, with hostilities winding down only two weeks after they began. With peace restored to the region (for a while), *Kulu* was transferred to the regular merchant fleet of the Far East Shipping Company and apparently did not serve again as a trans-port ship in the Dal'stroi fleet. This explains why *Kulu* is not listed as one of the ships in the core NKVD fleet in a 1945 interview with a former sailor on the Magadan run.[55]

The record of *Kulu* after World War II is unclear, but the ship was evidently still in use in the late 1950s. It is listed in U.S. naval intelligence reports as part of the Soviet merchant fleet in 1945; it also appears in the 1952–53 *Lloyd's Register of Shipping* and in Talbot-Booth's 1959 edition of *Merchant Ships*.[56] It was removed from *Lloyd's Register of Shipping* in 1960. However, the final story is more interesting and perhaps more fitting. It turns out that while *Kulu* no longer sailed the seas, its hull was still afloat. In early 1978 the ship was converted to a non-self-propelled floating workshop, moored in Vladivostok's Golden Horn Harbor, and deleted from the *Russian Maritime Register of Shipping*. *Kulu* ended up serving as the offices for a search and rescue organization in the Russian Far East and also providing space for workshops in support of the Far Eastern fishing fleet. In December 1995, following a fire on board, it was sold for scrap to merchants in China.[57] But the sea would not so easily give up a ship that had played such an infamous role in history. On November 8, 1995, after seventy-eight years of life, under tow from Vladivostok to the scrap yard, the hulk of the old *Kulu* sank in a typhoon in the Sea of Japan.

INDIGIRKA (ИНДИГИРКА, INDIGHIRKA)

Indigirka is one of the more interesting ships of the Gulag fleet, in part because most of the previous authors on Kolyma history have perpetuated a case of mistaken identity. There were in fact two ships by this name stationed in the Soviet Far East in the 1930s, and previous Western authors have generally described the wrong one as having been involved in the 1939 accident off Hokkaido.

The first ship of this name (which we shall call *Indigirka-1886* to avoid confusion) was constructed in 1886 by Scott's in Greenock, Scotland, as the *Tsinan*, the last of a class of four ships purchased by China Navigation Company, a forerunner of the Swire Group. *Tsinan* was used for many years to transport immigrants and other passengers between China and Australia until trade with Australia was diminished following restrictions on Chinese immigration and tariffs on the importation of sugar and rice. China Navigation Company abandoned the Australian market (until after World War II) and transferred *Tsinan* in 1907 to the Shanghai-Japan route.[58]

In 1909, *Tsinan* was sold to Ping An Steamship Company of Shanghai and renamed *Tsinanfu*. The following year *Tsinanfu* was sold to J. Christensen of Bergen, Norway. In 1914, *Tsinan* was sold to Russian interests and became part of the Russian Volunteer Fleet Association, an organization founded in 1878 by wealthy Russians to fund the acquisition of auxiliary steamships for their country's navy. It was at this point that the vessel's name became *Indigirka*.[59]

But this arrangement was not to last long. The British government's wartime shipping controller requisitioned *Indigirka* in 1917 and assigned it to

Tsinan. Most sources mistakenly claim this ship, also operated by the USSR as *Indigirka,* was the one lost in 1939. *Source:* Swire Group.

the management of Turner, Morrison & Company, and later in 1918 to Jardine Matheson. At this point its name became once again *Tsinan.* Upon termination of World War I, the ship was returned to Russia under its new Soviet government, was again named *Indigirka,* and was provided with registration RAFL. One has this image of weary crew members looking askance at news that once again the ship's name must be repainted.

On March 20, 1923, *Indigirka-1886* was mobilized as an auxiliary cruiser and was included in the navy of the Far Eastern Republic, the nominally independent republic in Siberia established by the Soviet Union. It returned to merchant use on July 6, 1923, performing basic trade duties for its Soviet owners until being assigned as a depot ship for salvage service in 1933.[60] At this point *Indigirka-1886* seems to disappear from the records, suggesting that it was no longer operated as a seagoing vessel.

In 1938 the Soviet Union acquired a vessel named *Commercial Quaker* and renamed this new ship *Indigirka.* (While it was not unheard of for the Soviet Union to operate two merchant ships of the same name simultaneously, a far more typical pattern was to reassign a name to a new ship once the prior namesake had been removed from the registry.) This second *Indigirka* was completed as hull number 114 in 1920 by Manitowoc Shipbuilding in Wisconsin as part of the Emergency Fleet Corporation's shipbuilding program during World War I. The name of the ship was to have been *Lake Galva,* but a last-minute decision was made to rename the ship *Ripon* in honor of the college town near Manitowoc. One of the "Lakers" class of standard ships built to EFC design number 1044, *Ripon* measured 253.42 feet in length, 43.75 feet in width, and 25.75 feet in height—

Steamship *Ripon* is launched on a cold December day in 1919. It was later sold to the Soviet Union and renamed *Indigirka*. *Source*: Wisconsin Maritime Museum.

dimensions based on the size of locks used on the St. Lawrence Seaway. It had gross tonnage of 2,689 and net tonnage of 1,667.[61]

Ripon was acquired from the U.S. government in 1926 by Malsah Steamship Company and renamed *Malsah*. Two years later it was acquired by the Commercial Pioneer Steamship Company and renamed *Commercial Quaker*.[62]

It was when *Kulu* was reassigned from the Dal'stroi fleet to the Soviet Navy in 1938 that Dal'stroi went looking for a replacement and acquired *Commercial Quaker*. This second *Indigirka* then traveled from New York via the Panama Canal, reaching Vladivostok on July 20, 1938. It made its first visit to Magadan in early August and returned to Vladivostok. One of the prisoners aboard this journey was Thomas Sgovio, an American communist sentenced to the Gulag during the Great Terror.[63] Presumably *Indigirka* made many other journeys to Magadan until it last arrived in Nagaevo Harbor in early December 1939.[64] From there it took its fateful journey to the rocks off Sarufutsu.

Most Western historians have cited *Indigirka-1886* as the ship involved in the Sarufutsu incident, and indeed it is a model of this ship that appears the Vladivostok maritime museum's exhibit on this incident. It is generally assumed that the new *Indigirka* (ex-*Ripon*) entered the fleet as a replacement for the older ship lost off Japan. But it is clear from photographic evidence that the ship that ran aground off Hokkaido in 1939 was the *Indigirka* completed in 1920 as the *Ripon* and acquired in 1938.[65] (In fact, the original news story about the incident in the *New York Times* got it right, all the way back in December 14, 1939.) A source of ambiguity might be that the second *Indigirka* is listed in 1942 *U.S. Naval Intelligence Reports* (ONI-208R) as active in the Soviet fleet, although subsequent issues do not include this ship. *Indigirka* is also listed in *Lloyd's Register of Shipping* up through the mid-1950s. Given the confusion of the war years and the difficulty of tracking Soviet merchant ships, it is seems clear that this listing in *Lloyd's* is incorrect.

ABOVE DECKS: THE OFFICERS AND CREWS OF THE NKVD FLEET

While much is known of the ships in the Dal'stroi fleet, somewhat less is documented about the captains, officers, and crews who manned these ships during the Gulag voyages. But it is possible to piece together enough information to shed light on the people who served aboard the NKVD fleet. Ironically, the three sources paint the same set of officers and crewmen in very different colors: as criminals, victims, and heroes.

One source of information is from former prisoners who made the journey to Kolyma aboard the NKVD fleet. Certainly these prisoners paint a cruel picture, specifically charging some of the officers and crews with forcing female prisoners into prostitution and with tolerating or even encouraging the robbery, beating, and murder of political prisoners aboard ship by common criminals. Other atrocities attributed to the ships' personnel include the use of firehoses in subzero conditions to suppress insurrections (with the result that masses of still-living prisoners were frozen together), and the use of live-steam hoses to fight fires (which led to prisoners being boiled to death). The image of the Dal'stroi officers and crew given by these sources is barbaric.

A second source of information is from Russian maritime historians in the Far East. Researcher Alla Paperno of Vladivostok and Magadan-based author Aleksandr G. Kozlov have documented the careers of several captains who served aboard these ships. These authors report that for the most part the officers and crew aboard the Gulag ships were volunteers from the Far Eastern fleet. But they also report that subtle or overt pressure was placed on crewmen to accept postings on the Dal'stroi ships. Officials offered a carrot as well as a stick—there are some indications that pay rates were higher for crews on the Gulag ships than for those of regular merchant ships. Certainly there were incidental benefits to the Gulag duty. For one thing, the shipping season was only six or eight months long, and crews spent the rest of the time with their families in Vladivostok. Several former crewmembers speak of a special comradeship on Gulag duty.

Paperno and Kozlov also describe the hazards for service on the Gulag ships, particularly for the officers. For example, the Great Terror in Kolyma in late 1937 did not end with the arrest of execution of Dal'stroi head Eduard Berzin. It filtered down through the Dal'stroi organization; several of the Gulag ship captains were affected. Vil'cheka Nikolay Iosifovich was captain of *Dalstroi* until July 1937, when he was arrested and executed. His replacement as captain of *Dalstroi*, Alexander Dmitrievich Rjabokon', was likewise arrested, on November 6, 1937, and shot for alleged espionage. Capt. Pavel Illarionovich Feodor of *Felix Dzerzhinsky* was somewhat more fortunate. Feodor, denounced by one of his own officers, who perhaps aspired to replace Feodor as captain of the ship, was arrested shortly after Berzin in December 1937 but escaped execution and was released in 1944 and rehabilitated in 1956. Capt. N.L. Lapshin of *Indigirka* was arrested after the ship ran aground in 1939 and was subsequently put to death, though this was related to his professional incompetence. Not all of the fatalities were inflicted by the Soviet secret police: Capt. Vsevolod Martinovich Bankovich was killed when *Dalstroi* exploded in 1946.

Interestingly, the most illuminating material on the careers of the Gulag ship captains and officers comes from a third source, a forty-thousand-word book, published in Russia, that never once mentions the word "Gulag" or makes any reference to transport of prisoners. This book consists of a compilation of interviews by Capt. Petr Osichanskii, of the Far Eastern Association of Sea Captains, with Capt. Pavel Pavlovich Kuyantsev, a former officer in the Far East fleet.[66] The interviews evoke the adventures of a band of adventurous sea captains in the 1930s and 1940s, a group of maritime heroes who faced and overcame the real dangers of the sea. While the material never links these individuals with the Gulag, the ships involved will sound familiar: *Dzhurma, Dalstroi, Felix Dzerzhinsky, Sovietskaya Latvia,* and *Indigirka* all figure prominently. There are references as well to *Svirstroi, Smolensk, Kashirstroi, Nevastroi, Minsk, Nogin, Erevan, Kamenets-Podolsk,* and *Vitebsk.* While many of the stories are about the adventures aboard ships on Gulag voyages, as demonstrated by a careful consideration of dates and locations, one would never guess the fact from the material itself.

Despite all of the dangers, of causes both natural and human, some officers survived their years aboard the Gulag fleet. Kuyantsev, who served at various times on *Svirstroi, Kashirstroi, and Dalstroi,* and who commanded *Felix Dzerzhinsky,* retired from the maritime service after an illustrious career to become a painter of watercolors, well known in Vladivostok circles until his death in the late 1990s.

Chapter 10

The Western Connection

[Dzhurma] has been a very satisfactory performer. . . . The specifications submitted by the Soviets call for a general overhaul and some hull repair resulting from ice damage. . . . We recommend favorable action.
—U.S. War Shipping Administration

The involvement of the West in the Kolyma transport operation dates back to the first mass shipment of prisoners in 1932.[1] These convicts were carried to the bleak cliffs of Nagaevo in U.S.-built freighters sold by the U.S. government to a Soviet agent only two years earlier. In all, about four-fifths of the ships used in Gulag transport service—and all of the NKVD-operated ships—were built in the United States or Western Europe, and virtually all were overhauled at some point in the United States and Canada during World War II. In all likelihood the West was an unwitting accomplice, as it was not until well after that war that that the atrocities of Kolyma were widely reported and discussed, despite mounting evidence beginning in the early 1940s.

THE CURIOUS CASE OF JOHANN G. OHSOL

The Kolyma Gulag fleet was largely built in the West and sold to Soviet officials in the 1930s. This was a time of great economic turmoil in the United States and Europe, and shipowners in those depressed regions were only too happy to sell idle hulls to Soviet customers, especially when the latter were willing to pay in cash. In most cases, the freighters eventually used to support the Gulag were sold to Soviet marine ministries as part of a massive buildup of the Soviet merchant fleet.

The largest single group of Gulag ships was supplied via a curious series of transactions in late 1929 and early 1930 involving Johann G. Ohsol, operating out of New York City.[2] These ships were owned by the U.S. government as late as 1930, but just two years later they were hauling the first waves of slave laborers to the Kolyma mines.

Johann Gottfried Ohsol was an interesting figure. Born in Latvia, he was a elected in February 1907 to the Second Duma in Russia, one of sixty-five Social Democrats elected. The Second Duma was dissolved by the tsar in June 1907, and all sixty-five Social Democrats were sentenced to exile for conspiracy and revolutionary behavior. Ohsol escaped to Finland and emigrated to the United States, arriving in 1907 on White Star's *Adriatic*. Upon arrival in the United States, Ohsol, then twenty-eight years old, described himself to authorities as a "lecturer" but shortly after commenced work with the Eugene Dietzgen Company on East 43rd Street in New York.[3] In 1909 he began study for a Ph.D. in economics in Harvard, a course of studies that would last a decade.[4]

Ohsol was forced to defend himself publicly in 1913 against charges that he was either a "revolutionist" or spy operating on behalf of radical forces in Russia.[5] In 1919 he was accused publicly by Senator James E. Watson as being a "Soviet advocate of the most virulent type who never fails to express the greatest admiration for Lenin and Trotsky."[6] In 1921 he held the position of director of the Commercial Department of the Former Russian Soviet Government Bureau and later was a founder of Amtorg, the Soviet trading company and front for intelligence activities in North America.[7] In mid-1933 he was raked over the coals during a congressional hearing for alleged support of Soviet efforts to undermine the United States.[8]

In late 1929, just after the devastating crash on Wall Street, and with the Western economies crumbling, Ohsol managed to find $1.2 million in cash and purchase twenty-five surplus merchant ships from the U.S. Shipping Board, the organization established during World War I to manage the large numbers of cargo ships built to carry American troops and supplies to France. These ships had originally been constructed by the Emergency Fleet Corporation in World War I and after the conflict, being deemed surplus, had been laid up at various locations on the East Coast. The Soviets paid the U.S. authorities a total of $560,000 for these ships, receiving a significant discount—in most cases about 30 percent—off the original asking prices.[9]

Within months these twenty-five ships turned up in the hands of Soviet authorities, this at a time when the U.S. government did not even recognize the legitimacy of the Soviet regime. That recognition did not occur for another three years, just about the time the ex-U.S. ships delivered a second year's allotment of slave laborers to Kolyma. At least seven of these twenty-five ships ended up in the Gulag fleet during the early 1930s: *Aledo, Bellingham, Chebaulip, Masuda, Dallas, Galesburg,* and *Puget Sound*. Two of them, *Bellingham* (as *Nevastroi*) and *Dallas* (as *Dneprostroi*), also probably made numerous trips to Magadan during the peak shipment years in the late 1930s.

It seems clear that Ohsol was acting directly as an agent of the Soviet Union when he purchased the twenty-five ships from the U.S. government, and indeed this relationship was openly admitted in later years. It is unclear, however, in the archival records when the United States knew the ships were to be operated by the Soviet Union. Records of the Shipping Board indicate only that "a firm offer has been received for the purchase" of the ships and provide no additional information on Ohsol.[10] Records of the Maritime Commission indicate only that a Johann G. Ohsol took possession of the ships in late January and early February 1930 in Boston, New York, Baltimore, and Norfolk.[11] But contemporary newspaper reports indicate that Ohsol had received permission from the State Department to transfer the ships to another country, without naming the Soviet Union but specifically identifying Siberia and the Baltic as likely destinations.[12] The only stipulation was that the ships not be used in trade with the United States for a period of years, this provision being designed to aid U.S. ship operators at a time of oversupply.

Ironically, had Ohsol returned to the Soviet Union—a Social Democrat, Latvian patriot, and contemporary of Lenin—in all likelihood he would have been swept up in the Great Terror of 1937 and very possibly could have been dispatched to Kolyma on one of the very ships he purchased on behalf of the Soviet government. Had he escaped the Terror, he might have been taken prisoner in the first mass deportation of Latvians—numbering approximately fourteen thousand—in the months following Soviet occupation of Latvia in June 1940. Had he survived the war, he might have been one of the twenty thousand to forty thousand Latvians arrested and sent to the Gulag in March 1949.

Ohsol's views of the Soviet Union and Stalin evidently changed after the brutal absorption of Latvia into the Soviet Union following World War II. In the late 1950s Ohsol worked on, but never completed, a history of the Latvian uprising of 1905–1907 as part of a broader historical study of the Communist Party of the Soviet Union. He continued to advocate Latvian causes until his death in 1968 in a nursing home in Pennsylvania. Coincidentally, that was the same year the last of his ships was removed from the *Lloyd's Register of Shipping*. One wonders if Ohsol was aware of his contribution to the creation of the fleet that made possible the initial Kolyma operation.

SELLING SHIPS TO THE NKVD

U.S. government officials could probably not have predicted how the ships acquired by Ohsol would be used. But in at least three cases in the Netherlands, ships were sold directly and personally to Eduard P. Berzin, the commander of the Dal'stroi Gulag. He personally visited the Netherlands to negotiate the purchase of *Dzhurma, Dalstroi,* and *Kulu,* the first three ships of the NKVD Gulag fleet, and most likely he was also involved directly in the purchase of *Felix Dzerzhinsky* from its British operators.[13] There is no evidence that the operators, Dutch government, or British government knew of Berzin's role within the NKVD, but this may be a topic worth further inquiry. One other transaction may be of interest in this regard. In early 1937 Dal'stroi acquired *Indigirka* from Commercial Pioneer Steamship Company, a U.S.-based shipping company. Again, records that have surfaced to date do not indicate that the sellers knew of the potential use of the ship, but this may be worth further investigation.

The Arsenal of Democracy Provides Gulag Ships to the Soviet Union

During World War II, the United States transferred massive amounts of war materiel to the Soviet Union. Roughly eleven billion dollars in supplies were sent from the United States to the Soviet Union between mid-1941 and late 1945.[14]

The best known of the transport routes was from East Coast ports to Murmansk, a route that put convoys within striking range of German submarines and aircraft, with horrendous losses as a consequence. What is less well known is that about half of the tonnage shipped to the Soviet Union made its way via the Pacific Ocean in Soviet merchant ships. The Pacific route had the advantage of relative safety, since Japan and the Soviet Union were not at war until mid-1945. Of course, this route had the singular disadvantage that "any bullet sent by that route had to travel half way around the world before it could be fired at a German."[15]

It would have been suicide for ships of the United States to attempt this route after the attack on Pearl Harbor, since the track passed very close to Japan. Therefore only Soviet ships could be used. But it became clear early on that the Soviet fleet was not up to the task, so the United States transferred a number of ships to the Soviet Union. This transfer started with about a hundred older merchant ships but ultimately included thirty-eight brand-new Liberty ships and five more advanced Victory ships, all built in the early 1940s. The initial plan was to have the Soviet Union return these ships following the war, and indeed a few of the older ships were returned—but not one of the modern Liberty or Victory ships.

Several of the ships were lost during the war, and another two dozen were returned to the United States at its conclusion, leaving ninety-six ships in Soviet hands. Another eight ships were returned in March 1948, and four others had sunk by that time, leaving eighty-four in the Soviet fleet. [16] These ships provided considerable service for the Soviet Union, carrying a variety of cargo to many destinations and accounting for a full 25 percent of Soviet merchant fleet tonnage as late as 1954, nine years after the war ended.[17]

It seems clear that the cargo included forced laborers and that the destinations included Magadan. There are a number of reports that the Soviets used some of these ships after the war to transfer prisoners to the Kolyma camps, including perhaps U.S. military personnel. The data are strongest for *Nogin* and the Liberty ship *Erevan,* for which the various claims are supported by firsthand reports. Secondary sources suggest the Liberty ships *Kamenets-Podolsk, Erevan,* and *Odessa,* along with the prewar passenger ship *Balkhash,* were also used to support Kolyma transport operations. There are even reports that some of the new Liberty ships were almost immediately put to use on Gulag transport duties during the war, including a trip by *Odessa* with three thousand female prisoners in 1943.[18]

By 1967, only forty-eight of the original Lend-Lease ships were still in service, including all of those mentioned in the context of Gulag service above, with the exception of *Nogin,* by then fifty-four years old and presumably scrapped. The others remained active in the Far East fleet for at least several years.[19]

There is a twist to the Lend-Lease story that involves a Gulag ship. According to the memoirs of Maj. George R. Jordan, *Kashirstroi,* one of the original fleet of Kolyma ships from 1932, sailed on October 3, 1943, from Portland to Vladivostok with Lend-Lease cargo that included, quite contrary to formal export controls, some forty-five pounds of uranium nitrate. According to Jordan, this shipment was specifically authorized by Henry Hopkins, who was overseeing the Lend-Lease program for President Roosevelt. He implies that the elements in the administration were keen to support Soviet atomic weapons development and used Lend-Lease shipments as a way to transfer critical materials to the Soviet Union.[20] Others suggest the amount transferred had been approved in advance by the leadership of the U.S. nuclear weapons program, and had been calculated precisely so as to avoid providing the Soviets with sufficient material for practical use.

Maintaining and Upgrading the NKVD Gulag Fleet

It is known that each of the six ships of the NKVD Dal'stroi fleet operated on the Gulag routes prior to the Soviet Union's involvement in World War II. At least two of them (*Dzhurma* and *Dalstroi*) are known to have operated on Gulag routes at times during the war. All three of the NKVD ships that survived the into the late 1940s (*Dzhurma, Felix Dzerzhinsky,* and *Sovietskaya Latvia*) are known to have operated on Gulag routes in the years following the war.

What is not well known is that the NKVD ships made numerous visits to ports in the United States and Canada in the years 1942 to 1945—

immediately after, between, or concurrently with their years of Gulag operation. Moreover, all of these NKVD ships, and many others used in Gulag service, were extensively repaired and upgraded during these visits, courtesy of the U.S. and Canadian taxpayers. In at least some cases it seems the ships went almost directly from a North American repair facility to Vladivostok in order to pick up a load of forced laborers for the Gulag.

The arrival of Soviet merchant ships into U.S. and Canadian harbors during the early days of the war was a topic of considerable interest. Some of the first repairs were conducted in early 1942, when four ships, including *Sovietskaya Latvia*, arrived at Burrard Dry Dock in North Vancouver, Canada. As reported in an unpublished history of that shipyard, "Discipline on the Russian ships was very strict and there was always a political agent on board who was senior to the captain. When members of the crew went ashore, they always went in pairs. Even the captain was not allowed to go alone."[21]

Robert Hennig, a former worker at the Lake Washington Shipyard outside Seattle, recalls:

> We also repaired several larger Russian ships and freighters. I know there were lots of Russian ships repaired in shipyards in Seattle. A lot of these Russian ships had lots of women in their crews. Some even had women captains. We were not allowed to take pictures. The Russian crewmembers couldn't speak English but they did know two words: "new one." They would point to a part of machinery about to be repaired and say "new one!"[22]

Dzhurma

The *Dzhurma*'s first known visit to the United States was to San Francisco, probably in late January 1942.[23] The ship spent four months, from February 2 to June 6, 1942, in San Francisco undergoing major repairs and upgrades. *Dzhurma* then moved to Seattle for other modifications, begun on June 9 and completed in eleven days, following which the ship was loaded with Lend-Lease cargo destined for the Red Army. On July 2, 1942, it sailed for the Soviet Union. The ship returned to San Francisco in late September that year, undergoing an additional week's repairs starting on September 30.

Dzhurma made its next nine visits to Portland to pick up Lend-Lease cargo, arriving on November 14, 1942; February 4, 1943; April 20, 1943; June 17, 1943; August 23, 1943; October 26, 1943; January 12, 1944; May 13, 1944; and September 15, 1944. On at least the first four of these visits, *Dzhurma* spent a total of forty-one days undergoing additional repairs and modifications. By that point, total costs for the overhaul work on *Dzhurma* exceeded $305,000, a sizable sum in those days.

The interval between *Dzhurma's* visits to the United States averaged forty-five to sixty days throughout late 1942, 1943, and early 1944. However, the intervals increased to ninety to a hundred days in mid-1944, the prime sailing

A Soviet merchant ship undergoing repair in the Todd Seattle shipyards during World War II. This ship appears to be either *Nevastroi*, *Kashirstroi* or *Shaturstroi*. *Source*: Todd Pacific Corp.

season to the Kolyma port at Magadan, which is often blocked by ice during the winter and spring. Evidence exists of *Dzhurma*'s use to transfer forced laborers to the Gulag on July 25, 1944, which might explain the ship's extended absence from the United States around that time.[24]

On December 1, 1944, *Dzhurma* again arrived in San Francisco to pick up cargo. A visit to Portland in March 16, 1945—in the waning months of the war in Europe—led to a more extended visit lasting over three months, during which *Dzhurma* again was given extensive overhauls and repairs costing at least two hundred thousand dollars. Some of the work was designed to repair ice damage from previous voyages. In any case, the budget of two hundred thousand was approved in late March 1945.

Interestingly, death plagued this ship even in American waters. In Portland in April 1945 a Soviet merchant sailor, confined to his quarters after becoming drunk, committed suicide. The suicide was discussed within the Soviet intelligence apparatus in the United States. It was also picked up by American intelligence.[25]

Soviet merchant ship officers meet with a representative of a U.S. shipyard (left) during World War II. The conversation occurs under the fatherly gaze of Joseph Stalin. *Source*: Todd Pacific Corp.

Debates over additional work, costing fifty thousand dollars, were still being held in late September 1945, after the end of the war. This additional work, above and beyond the two hundred thousand dollars approved in March, involved repairs to 240 feet of bilge keel, major repairs to the en-

Dzhurma in San Francisco Harbor in February 1942. Over the next 138 days the ship underwent extensive overhaul and modification in San Francisco and Seattle. *Source*: U.S. Coast Guard.

gine, structural repairs to the hull and decking, and various fixes to pipes and tanks.

Vancouver was the destination for another visit on October 10, 1945, almost a month after World War II had ended. The ship was overhauled in Burrard Dry Dock in North Vancouver as late as 1946.[26] In all, *Dzhurma* visited the United States or Canada at least fifteen times and received at least $558,000 in repairs, upgrades, and modifications. To put it in perspective, this represents about one-third the price to the U.S. government of acquiring a brand-new Liberty ship during World War II.

The upgraded and overhauled *Dzhurma* was assigned to additional Gulag transport duties after World War II. As related earlier, there are firsthand reports data of its use on such routes in 1949 and 1950.

Dalstroi

Dalstroi was the recipient of even more extensive upgrades from Canada and the United States. The ship arrived in Vancouver in March 1942 and spent two months, starting March 16, undergoing war-related modifications costing just over sixty-nine thousand dollars. On May 18, 1942, *Dalstroi* arrived in Seattle and for the next four months underwent a very significant overhaul and upgrade costing over $1.2 million—a massive sum for a ship of this size in 1942. On additional visits during 1942 and 1943, *Dalstroi* received still more upgrades. By the end of 1943, over $1.37 million had been spent to overhaul and upgrade the ship. An additional fifty-four thousand was spent in early 1944 for work in Portland.

Dalstroi made another ten trips to the United States from 1942 to 1945. In most cases, the interval between visits was fifty-eight to seventy-six days. However, as with *Dzhurma*, in mid-1942 and mid-1944—the prime sailing

Dalstroi in San Francisco Harbor during October 1942. Over a period of 188 days, the ship was upgraded and repaired at a cost of over $1.2 million—almost the cost of a new Liberty ship. *Source*: U.S. Coast Guard.

season to Magadan—the ship was absent for well over a hundred days, suggesting its use on other duties during that time. In fact, there exists an unpublished firsthand account of *Dalstroi*'s use on Gulag duties during 1942, and other reports of its use in 1944.[27]

Coincidentally, during the war *Dalstroi* and some of the other Gulag ships departed from their normal missions of misery to support a humanitarian effort—the special Gripsholm mission to provide Red Cross supplies to Allied POWs and internees being held by Japan in China and Southeast Asia.[28] The Soviets acted as intermediary in this case between the United States and Japan. In December 1943 in Portland some 2,500 tons of supplies were loaded aboard five Soviet merchant ships—including *Dalstroi* and *Felix Dzerzhinsky*—and taken to Nakhodka.[29] (Sometime later the supplies were collected by the Japanese merchant ship *Awa Maru* and delivered to several sites in the region. On the return voyage, the *Awa Maru,* though marked with large white crosses and traveling under an American guarantee of safe passage, was sunk by the U.S. submarine *Queenfish.* Over two thousand men, women, and children were lost.)[30]

Dalstroi was the recipient of yet further overhaul and repair work in 1945. After a visit in early January, the local Soviet engineer overseeing maintenance operations on Soviet ships requested dry-docking and major repairs. About $332,000 was spent in May 1945 to cover main engine and hull repairs, as well as similar work. This sum, well above the initial estimate of $235,000 authorized in March, was a topic of extended discussion within the War Shipping Administration and the Foreign Economic Administration. By war's end, the U.S. government had funded over $1.7 million in repairs to *Dalstroi,* or roughly what a new, larger, and more modern Liberty ship would have cost.

Felix Dzerzhinsky

Felix Dzerzhinsky made at least thirteen visits to the United States in World War II, first arriving in San Francisco in March, 1942, for overhaul work totaling the modest sum of $1,758. Over the course of the next year, another five visits to Seattle, Portland, and San Francisco occurred, and additional work was performed during each visit. By June 1943, expenditures on repairs accumulated to over $206,000. In March 1944, authorization was received to build a platform for hauling locomotives on the deck of the ship; this work was probably performed in Portland.

Felix Dzerzhinsky was employed on a special mission in December 1945, picking up 796 former Russian POWs from Portland on December 31 and returning them to the Soviet Union. The ship was modified in the Portland shipyard for additional passenger capacity prior to that voyage—various U.S. memos refer to the installation of large numbers of cots. It is widely reported that former Russian POWs were often sent to the Gulag after their repatria-

Felix Dzerzhinsky, flagship of the Dal'stroi fleet, in San Francisco in March 1942. The ship visited the U.S. over a dozen times in WWII. *Source*: U.S. Coast Guard.

tion. Given this, it is certainly possible that *Felix Dzerzhinsky* delivered the group immediately from the United States to the Kolyma camp system. It has already been reported that *Felix Dzerzhinsky* was used to move former Russian POWs from German camps to the Kolyma camps later in 1945.[31] One wonders if the United States was aware of the ultimate destination of the former POWs, at the time under American jurisdiction and on U.S. soil, as they walked the gangway onto the Soviet ship.

Sovietskaya Latvia

Sovietskaya Latvia, another ship in the core Gulag slave fleet, also benefited from the generosity of the United States and Canada during World War II. In March 1942 the ship spent 129 days in Vancouver undergoing major repairs. Four visits later, in April 1943, *Sovietskaya Latvia* spent another forty days undergoing repairs, this time in Portland and San Francisco. By this point, total expenses had accumulated to over $460,000.

Additional work was performed during 1944 and 1945. In June 1944, ninety-five thousand dollars was approved for repair work. In early 1945, another four hundred thousand was requested, in part to support conversion of the ship to carry locomotives. This amount came as a surprise to the

Foreign Economic Administration but was ultimately approved. Even this proved not enough, as another $250,000 ultimately was approved to cover overruns even as late as September 27, 1945—after the war had ended. In total, over $1.3 million was spent to repair and upgrade *Sovietskaya Latvia*.

A FINAL IRONY

During World War II, the United States and Canada played host to each of Stalin's slave ships, on average about a dozen times. At least two of the ships were performing services for the Gulag between visits to the United States and after receiving U.S.-funded upgrades and repairs. A third ship was modified by American shipyards to carry hundreds of released Soviet POWs away from the United States, most likely on a direct trip to the Gulag. Other ships were provided free of charge to Soviet authorities, which placed them in Gulag service after the war, and possibly during the war.

Overall, twenty-four ships that appear to have served in the Gulag fleet were repaired in the United States and Canada during the war at a total cost between eight and nine million dollars. Some of these ships may have made only one or two voyages and had only limited repairs made. But all four of the remaining ships in the core NKVD fleet were repaired, and interestingly, these four ships, despite being some of the most modern in the group of twenty-four, accounted for half of the total expenditure. In short, ships on which thousands died and hundreds of thousands of others were taken to their death were provided, or made more efficient and effective, by the generosity of the U.S. and Canadian taxpayer. Perhaps the most interesting aspect of this issue is that more than half a century after it all happened, the story is only now being unveiled.

But in a final and subtle twist, the United States also benefited from the visits of Gulag transport ships during World War II. In the mid-1940s, the

Minsk in San Francisco during World War II. *Source*: U.S. Coast Guard.

Dneprostroi in San Francisco in 1942, ten years after making the maiden voyage of the Gulag fleet. *Source*: U.S. Coast Guard.

forerunner of the National Security Agency initiated a major program, code-named "Venona," to break the Soviet ciphers used in communications between agents and Soviet intelligence and KGB headquarters in Moscow. U.S. code breakers were making little progress until an analyst, Samuel Chew, noticed patterns in the encrypted messages that matched the activities of Soviet merchant ships sailing for the Soviet Union with Lend-Lease supplies. The Soviet military intelligence organization in San Francisco was sending routine notifications of these sailings back to Moscow—declassified Venona transcripts contain many of these messages. Since the United States also knew of these sailings, it was able to exploit these patterns to begin the process of breaking the code.[32] Over the following decades, the Venona project provided U.S. analysts with tremendous insight into Soviet espionage operations in the United States.

The ship *KIM* played a minor but nonetheless interesting role in an espionage incident involving Venona. On September 19, 1945, a secret Soviet message was transmitted from Moscow to London requesting an expedited reply to a previous message regarding "the conclusion about KIM." The message was intercepted and subsequently decoded by U.S. intelligence officials, who pondered what the reference to "KIM" might mean. Evidently, they checked the movements of the ship *KIM* and concluded that as it had never sailed to London, the message might very well contain a rare accidental reference by name to the famous British agent of the Soviet Union, Kim Philby.[33]

Chapter 11

What Did the West Know, and When Did It Know It?

There are about 200,000 people in the city. . . . Just what they all do
for a living I could not make out, as Vladivostok is not a commercial
port to any extent.
—Adm. Harry E. Yarnell during a visit to Vladivostok in August 1937

Those miserable wretches, as well as Japanese flack and fighter planes,
are etched on my memory today as if I saw them yesterday.
—2nd Lt. Gilbert S. Arnold, U.S. Army, Magadan, 1944

What did the West know?[1] How aware were the United States and Europe
of the activities underway in the Kolyma region? When European ships were
sold to the Dal'stroi organization, and when these same ships were overhauled in the United States during World War II, did the Western powers
understand to what use these ships were applied? When shipyard workers
noticed the horrible smells from the holds of *Dzhurma, Dalstroi,* and *Felix
Dzerzhinsky,* were they able to relate the odors to the nature of the cargo
carried aboard ship?

The most likely scenario based on evidence surfaced to date is that the
West was a vital but unwitting accomplice in the Kolyma transport operation. But how did this happen? Were the United States and Europe bliss-
fully ignorant, were they duped, or did they deceive themselves, perhaps
disregarding emerging stories about Kolyma in favor of more pressing considerations, such as the defeat of global fascism? It is hard to answer the
question directly six decades after the events took place. At best, there is
indirect evidence to support either the complicity or ignorance of the West
prior to the end of World War II, though it is now clear that unambiguous
and ample evidence existed in late 1945 to make clear the situation in Kolyma
and the role of the transport ships.

However, it is also clear now that prison camps and shackled inmates in Magadan were witnessed by U.S. military personnel as early as September 1943, though they may not have understood what they were seeing or linked it to a Gulag. In August 1943 British prime minister Winston Churchill forwarded to American president Franklin Roosevelt a highly confidential report that mentioned the movement of Polish prisoners to Kolyma. To put this into context, the report appeared well before many of the repairs were made to the Gulag fleet and before the transfer of at least one of the Liberty ships subsequently used for transport of Gulag prisoners. It was also before the now-infamous visit of the American vice president to Magadan on a fact-finding trip, after which he reported back to America on the happy condition of the Kolyma "volunteers."

PUBLISHED INFORMATION ON THE KOLYMA CAMPS

One place to start is with contemporary literature on the Kolyma system. When were the existence of the Kolyma camps and the role of the Gulag ships revealed in published works? The first wave of published records of the Kolyma camps and the Gulag transport fleet appeared in 1945. They had been drafted by former Polish prisoners captured in large numbers by the Soviets in 1939 and released in 1943, their numbers much diminished by overwork and starvation. These former captives provided vivid accounts of their experiences in the Kolyma camps, which were collected and published by Polish authors Sylvester Mora (a pseudonym for Kasimierz Zamorksi) and Piotr Zwierniak in a 1945 book *Sprawiedliwooœœ Sowiecka* (Soviet Justice), released initially in Polish and French.[2] The following year a similar book written by an anonymous author and featuring an introduction by T.S. Eliot was published in London in English. This book, *Dark Side of the Moon*, reported similar stories of Polish prisoners in the Kolyma system and contained vivid and horrific tales of the transport ships.[3]

The second wave of information on the Kolyma operation came from the emerging body of Gulag studies at the end of World War II. Details of the Kolyma transport operations were revealed for the first time in a Russian-language newsletter, Социалистический Вестник (*Sotsialisticheskyi Vestnik*, or Socialist Bulletin), published in New York at the end of 1945.[4] The newsletter contains an interview with a former sailor in the Gulag fleet and provides considerable detail on the fleet operations, though it does not describe in detail experiences of the passengers aboard ship. Two years after this article was published, Gulag scholars David Dallin and Boris Nicolaevsky published their path-breaking work *Forced Labor in Soviet Russia*, which contained extensive and vivid material on the Kolyma system in a chapter appropriately entitled "The Land of White Death."[5] Dallin and Nicolaevsky provided information on the transport fleet, including the first published account of the *Dzhurma-Chelyuskin* incident, but they did not present detailed accounts of experiences on board the Gulag ships, focusing instead on the ample horrors of the Gulag camps themselves. Similar information on the transport fleet was presented by Silvester Mora in his 1949 pamphlet *Kolyma: Gold and Forced Labor in the USSR.*[6]

The third wave of information on Kolyma was produced in the form of autobiographical works from former prisoners released in the late 1940s. These books contained very vivid and personal details about the horrors of life aboard the transport ships, identifying a number of ships by name. Vladimir Petrov's book *Soviet Gold: My Life as a Slave Laborer in the Siberian Mines* was published in 1949.[7] This was followed two years later by Elinor Lipper's amazing *Eleven Years in Soviet Prison Camps.*[8] Similar autobiographical works by former prisoners emerged over the next twenty years.

The final wave of information appeared in 1978, when British historian Robert Conquest published *Kolyma: The Arctic Death Camps,* focusing on the history of the Kolyma camp system and its brutality. Drawing extensively from a large number of published and unpublished autobiographical works, Conquest presented a very detailed account of life aboard the Gulag transport ships and attempted for the first time to compile a comprehensive list of the transport fleet.[9]

OTHER CONTEMPORARY LITERATURE

There was considerable interest in the West regarding economic development of the Soviet Arctic in the middle of last century. As the Dal'stroi organization played a large role in this development, it is logical to investigate contemporary writings to determine whether a careful reader might have gleaned sufficient information to reveal the Soviet activities in Kolyma. Such a review indicates that these Western observers and researchers were unaware of the Kolyma operations during the 1930s and that published information on this topic did not occur until the late 1940s and early 1950s, concurrent with the revelations described above.

One of the first books to describe forced labor in connection with Siberia—but not the Kolyma region—is a 1937 book by British journalist H.P. Smolka, *40,000 against the Arctic,* a glamorous portrayal of heroic socialist struggle by a forward-looking Soviet Union to develop the far north.[10] Visiting the Dudinka camp on the lower Yenesei, Smolka had come away impressed with the difficult but humane conditions of the prisoners and the enlightened and supportive attitude of the camp staff, even joking that he had difficulty knowing when he was in a labor camp, since the prisoners seemed so contented and unrestricted. However, Smolka limited his visit to the regions administered by Glavsevmorput (his sponsor for the trip) and did not venture into the darker territory of Dal'stroi. His book does not mention Magadan, Ambarchik, the Kolyma region, or the Dal'stroi empire, and none of these towns or regions appears on his maps of the area.

In 1938, John Littlepage, an American mining engineer employed in the Soviet Union in 1930s, wrote a book of his experiences entitled *In Search of Soviet Gold,* in which he refers to widespread use of forced labor:

> The authorities have never given out figures of the total number of men and women put to forced labor; I have heard the number estimated at anywhere from one to five million. Thousands of the small farmers rounded up during and after 1929 have since regained their freedom, but so far as I could see the number of forced laborers remained fairly constant up to the time I left Russia in 1937. The recent purges, which affected hundreds of thousands of persons, undoubtedly added to the labor army.[11]

But Littlepage's work was focused on western Siberia, and his journeys did not take him to the remote Kolyma region. He mentions nothing of Dal'stroi or the Kolyma operations. Also, his description of the conditions in the forced labor camps greatly understated the brutality later made evident in the Kolyma system:

> During the first years after 1929, when the whole country was in an uproar from so many social upheavals occurring simultaneously, forced laborers were treated worse then they were later. The police simply couldn't cope with the problem of handling so many people at once, and it took years to build up an efficient organization. Thousands of them didn't have decent quarters to live in or sufficient food. But this wasn't deliberate, as I see it; the police simply were given more to do than they could handle properly. Later the forced labor camps became better organized, and those I have observed in recent years were orderly and reasonably comfortable. They had schools and cinema theatres, and the inmates didn't live a very different life from ordinary Soviet citizens.[12]

Also in 1938, Harvard researcher Timothy A. Taracouzio published an exhaustive review of Soviet Arctic activities in *Soviets in the Arctic*.[13] It contains considerable detail about the logistical and economic development of the far north, a region that included but extended far beyond the Dal'stroi-administered regions in the Soviet Far East. Despite its scope and detail, Taracouzio's work does not even mention Dal'stroi or provide any information whatsoever on forced labor operations in that region. His book contains a number of detailed maps on this part of the Soviet Union; none locate Magadan or Ambarchik.

One can only conclude that the existence of large-scale forced labor operations in the Kolyma region were generally unknown within the years leading up to World War II, at least within the community studying Soviet development in the far north. By contrast, a study of Soviet arctic development written in 1952 by Terrance Armstrong of the Scott Polar Research Institute explicitly identifies the Dal'stroi organization and the role of "convict labor" in its Kolyma mining operations.[14] The maps in Armstrong's book clearly and correctly locate Ambarchik and Magadan. Similarly, Constantine

Krypton's 1956 book on the Northern Sea Route confirms the role of forced labor in the region: "Forced labor is an important source of manpower for the Kolyma gold mining area. . . . Human values and political considerations aside, forced labor is no final solution to the labor problem. . . . [The] rapid physical deterioration of forced laborers also calls into question the economic expediency of the system."[15]

POSSIBLE GLIMPSES INTO THE KOLYMA GULAG

On at least four occasions the possibility arose that the West, and in particular the United States, might have stumbled onto the Kolyma Gulag operations in advance of the public revelations in the mid-1940s. This emerged in part because of the elevated level of military cooperation between the United States and Soviet Union in the early 1940s.

Visit by the USS *Augusta* to Vladivostok

In 1937 the U.S. Navy cruiser *Augusta* and its escorts paid a call at Vladivostok during a trip to the Far East.[16] This was the first visit by a U.S. warship to Vladivostok in fifteen years. *Augusta* was the flagship of Adm. Harry E. Yarnell, the commander in chief of the U.S. Asiatic Fleet; he and his fellow officers, as well as the sailors and marines of the force, roamed the city and met with local officials.

This visit, from July 28 to August 1, occurred in the middle of a period in which large numbers of convict laborers were shipped to the Kolyma Gulag. One would expect the Soviets to restrict the Americans' access to prisoners and the transport operations, so it is unlikely that the crew of the *Augusta* had any firsthand exposure to the Gulag infrastructure during these four days. It is possible the shipment operations were suspended for a while, which would be consistent with survivor Nadezhda Surovtseva's report of a huge backlog of prisoners in Vladivostok at this time awaiting shipment, a situation that led to an outbreak of typhus.[17] It would be ironic if that outbreak, which affected not only the prisoner transit camps but the free citizens of Vladivostok, was caused indirectly by the visit of USS *Augusta*.

A letter about this visit from an officer or crewman of the *Augusta* (the author remains unknown) describes extensive "lavish entertainment" organized by the Soviets but makes no mention of any observations that would suggest the city was a major transshipment point for Gulag slave laborers.[18] A letter from Admiral Yarnell to the Chief of Naval Operations written during the Vladivostok stay and forwarded to President Roosevelt makes no reference to any Gulag operations but does raise questions about what activities occupy the two hundred thousand inhabitants: "Just what they all do for a living I could not make out, as Vladivostok is not a commercial port to any extent."[19]

The USS *Augusta* and escorts in Vladivostok harbor in July 1937. The ships in the background may include two used in Gulag operations. *Source*: The photo collection of the late Col. Charles. E. McPartlin, Jr., USMC (ret).

A photograph of the harbor taken by Charles McPartlin, Jr., one of the marines aboard the USS *Augusta,* shows the cruiser lying alongside its escort of destroyers amid the usual array of ships in any large harbor. Anchored in the background, near the point where prisoners were loaded aboard Gulag transports, are two large cargo ships that match very closely the profiles of *Nevastroi* and *Dneprostroi,* two of the ships known to be used in Gulag transport operations from Vladivostok in the late 1930s.[20]

The Wreck of *Indigirka*

The wreck in December 1939 of the steamship *Indigirka* with almost nine hundred Gulag prisoners aboard was reported widely around the world. For once the hidden Soviet operations in the Sea of Okhotsk were on the point of being laid open for the world to see—here was a Gulag ship spilling its prisoners onto the rocks of the Japanese coast. However, the Soviet Union managed to acknowledge the disaster but yet mislead the international community as to the real mission of the ship and nature of her cargo. A *New York Times* report of December 14, 1939, is typical of how the story was reported in the West: "The *Indigirka*, a 2,690-ton ship, was taking 1,139 Soviet fishermen, their wives and children from Nagaevo, Kamchatka to Vladivostok at the close of the fishing season."[21]

Similar articles appeared in the *Times* of London and the *Sydney Morning Herald*. Interestingly, the true point of origin (Nagaevo) is identified by name by the *New York Times*—perhaps the first time this city is mentioned by name in the West—but misplaced in Kamchatka rather than Kolyma. The contemporary coverage makes no reference to Kolyma, Magadan, or the Gulag.

World War II Intelligence Reports

Prior to World War II it appears the United States had little knowledge that a major Gulag facility was operating in the Kolyma region. For example, an intelligence report written in May 1942 describing the feasibility of transporting military aid to the Soviet Union via the Kolyma River presents in detail the logistical issues involved but makes no reference whatsoever to the existence of a Gulag operation, nor does it mention the existence of Magadan, by then a substantial town:

> Another North Siberian route partly developed by the Russians is as follows: The Kolyma river south to Byrybylym (approximately 350 miles south of the mouth of the Kolyma)—unimproved road south to Ust-Utinaya improved road to Nagayevo, an excellent port on the Sea of Okhotsk, ice-free for six months. Thence coastwise to Nikolaevsk. The route has the same limitations as the others. However it is shorter, but on the other hand more susceptible to attack by the Japanese. The latest data on this route are of 1938.[22]

A similar report prepared a few months later acknowledges the existence of a port in Nagaevo and a general aura of secrecy surrounding the area, but Magadan again remains unmentioned:

> Nagayevo, the terminus of the two-lane highway from ust-Utinaya, is situated on Tauiskaya Bay in the Sea of Okhotsk. It is an important naval and military air base. Limited marine repair facilities are available. The population is believed to be 15,000. Ice conditions hamper shipping from late December to late March, but a channel may be kept open by the use of icebreakers. Dock and wharf facilities have been greatly improved and storage facilities for gasoline and oil have been built. Although great secrecy has been kept by the Soviet government in respect to the development of Nagayevo, captains of merchant ships which have sailed to this port have rendered detailed reports on its present stage of development.[23]

The United States and Soviet Union were allies during the Second World War, and Lend-Lease operations in the Pacific provided at least some opportunity to lift the veil on the Kolyma operations. After all, Ambarchik, the port at the nexus of the Kolyma River and Arctic Ocean, was a regular destination for Lend-Lease shipments along the Arctic route, with an average of six or seven ships calling each season.[24] At least a handful of ships on the main Pacific route traveled directly from U.S. West Coast ports to Magadan.[25] Finally, the town of Seimchan, the vital link between the Magadan port and the Kolyma River, was a major refueling station on the Alaska-Siberian (ALSIB) route, over which hundreds of U.S.-built aircraft were ferried to the Soviet Union.[26]

As a practical matter, Lend-Lease did not lead to a major U.S. presence in the Soviet Far East. Despite repeated suggestions, Soviet authorities discouraged the United States from sending liaison personnel to the region and insisted that only Soviet personnel pilot the aircraft along the ALSIB air route, despite their desperate need for qualified airmen in the combat with Nazi Germany. Moreover, the cargo ships bringing supplies to the Far East ports were manned by Soviet crewmen in order to avoid Japanese intervention—the Soviet Union and Japan being not yet at war.

But there is one clear occasion during the war during which explicit reference was made to the shipment of prisoners to Kolyma. In August 1943, Prime Minister Churchill forwarded to President Roosevelt a confidential report (so sensitive it was to be returned to Churchill after it was read) on the massacre of Polish prisoners in the Katyn Forest. That report, received by Roosevelt on August 13, 1943, mentions "rumors which have been current during the last two and a half years that some of the inmates of Kozielsk, Starobielsk and Ostashkov had been transported towards Kolyma."[27] This could very well be the first time Kolyma was mentioned in the West in the context of a destination for prisoners.

Moreover, it was clear that by 1944 U.S. officials knew of the existence of an organization by the name of "Dal'stroi," even if they did not understand the mission of that organization. A naval intelligence report from July 1944 correctly identifies the Dal'stroi fleet (at that time) as encompassing *Dzhurma, Dalstroi, Felix Dzerzhinsky,* and *Sovietskaya Latvia.*[28]

American Witnesses to the Gulag

However, it is now clear there were American witnesses to the Kolyma Gulag during the war. Several dozen U.S. military personnel witnessed firsthand the presence of Gulag camps around Magadan, perhaps as early as September 1943, and were in a position to inform their superiors about this as early as December 1943, and certainly by February 1944.

In a little-known aspect of World War II, almost three hundred U.S. pilots and crewmen on bombing missions to Japan were interned in the Soviet Union after diverting battle-damaged or fuel-starved aircraft to Soviet territory. In fact, on the very first American attempt to bomb Japan—the famous Doolittle Raid in April 1942—one of the aircraft landed in the Soviet Union, and its crew was interned. All of the pilots and crewmen were eventually released to U.S. authorities, following "escapes" organized with the connivance of the NKVD. It was not possible simply to turn over the flight crews, because the Soviet Union was officially neutral in the war against Japan until August 1945.

A sizable number of these pilots were moved to the internment camp in Tashkent via Magadan, and many kept vivid memories of the horrors of the forced labor camps, where they witnessed shackled prisoners being marched to and from work assignments. The first group to transit through Magadan was a crew of ten from a B-24 that crash-landed in Kamchatka on August 12, 1943. This group, under the command of Lt. James R. Pottenger, arrived in the city on September 6, 1943, and spent the next four days in this capital of the Kolyma Gulag. As Otis Hays, Jr., the author of *Home from Siberia,* reports:

> Although they were not allowed to leave the second floor of the building where they were confined in Magadan, the airmen for the first time since leaving Petropavlosk were able to observe outside activities through the windows. They could see cargo ships discharging Lend-Lease vehicles so new that the American Army white-star symbols had not been eliminated. In the opposite direction they could see a stockade whose watchtowers contained guards, searchlights and machine guns. Daily they viewed groups of shackled prisoners who were marched from the stockade in the mornings and then back in the evenings.[29]

The Pottenger crew was released to U.S. authorities in Tehran in February 1944, but before that, in December 1943, it was visited by a U.S. military doctor from the Moscow mission, Maj. John F. Waldron. It is unclear if these airmen reported their observation of the stockade and ranks of shackled prisoners, either during Major Waldron's visit or upon their release. (The last member of the crew passed away in 2002.)[30] A member of another crew, who did not personally pass through Magadan but spent extensive time with the Pottenger crew, writes, "In my opinion, the Pottenger crew never realized they were in Magadan, let alone [knew] the history of the Gulag Slave Camp. At this early stage of the war in 1943 there was little or nothing known about Russia or Siberia."[31] It does not appear the Pottenger crew came away from Magadan eager to relay stories of their observations there.

But later crews did (see Table 11.1). [32] In September 1944 a group of seventeen U.S. airmen were moved to Magadan, where they witnessed scenes of forced labor. The following month, another group also witnessed the prison camps at first hand. Yet another group passed through Magadan in November 1944 and saw evidence of forced labor that shocked at least one American as much as had his experience of air-to-air combat. These last three groups were all released in February 1945, well before the last round of repairs to the Dal'stroi ships in U.S. shipyards.[33] It remains undocumented whether these groups relayed their observations to U.S. officials. The available interrogation transcripts do not specifically mention any observations.

VISIT BY THE U.S. VICE PRESIDENT TO MAGADAN

Until mid-1944, official American exposure to the Kolyma region was at best indirect and circumspect. But that was all to change when in June of that year Vice President Henry A. Wallace led an entourage of Americans

Table 11.1
Interned American Military Personnel Transiting Through Magadan

Unit	Crew (Listed by Commander's Name)	Date First Interned In Soviet Union	Dates In Magadan	First Contact with US Officials	Final Escape From USSR
Army 404th	Pottenger	12 Aug 43	6-10 Sep 43	23 Dec 43	18 Feb 44
Navy VB-136	Lindell	13 Aug 44	12-14 Sep 44	5 Oct 44	30 Jan 45
Navy VB-136	Cowles	20 Aug 44			
Navy VB-136	Dingle	28 Aug 44			
Army 77th	Head	10 Sep 44	17-22 Oct 44	30 Nov 44	
Navy VB-136	Wayne	17 Sep 44			
Army 404th	Ott (part)	25 Sep 44			
Navy VB-135	McDonald (part)	11 Sep 44			
Navy VB-135	McDonald (part)	11 Sep 44	7-11 Nov 44		
Army 404th	Ott (part)	25 Sep 44			
Army 77th	McQuillan	1 Nov 44			

Source: Compiled from accounts of individual crews as described by Otis Hays in *Home From Siberia: The Secret Odysseys of Interned American Airmen in World War II* (College Station: Texas A&M University Press, 1990).

on a three-day visit to Kolyma as part of a month-long visit to Soviet Asia and China. The vice president flew from Alaska in a special aircraft along the ALSIB route, landed at Seimchan and then continued on to Magadan, the capital of the Dal'stroi region.

Historians have since learned that very special preparations were made for his visit. The convicts were moved out of sight, and NKVD officials took their places, donning new clothing. Watchtowers and barbed-wire barricades were removed. Wallace was entertained in high style at banquets, at the theater, and at a ballet orchestrated by Gridasova Alexandra Romanovna, wife of the Dal'stroi commander, Ivan Nikishov. It is clear the Dal'stroi authorities went to considerable trouble to deceive Wallace, and that they were highly successful.[34]

A book by Wallace appeared in 1944 shortly after his return to the United States (and his replacement by Harry S Truman on the Democratic ticket for the 1944 election). Wallace's book makes strange reading today. It describes Dal'stroi as a "combination of TVA and Hudson Bay Company." According to Wallace, the "Kolyma Gulag miners are big, husky young men who came out to the Far East from European Russia. They were keen about winning the war."[35] He comments on the ideal working conditions and the favorable pay rates in Kolyma compared to Moscow. Wallace does mention forced labor once in his book, in a reference to the penal practices of the tsars of prerevolutionary Russia. In latter years, Wallace regretted his book and acknowledged that he had put too positive a spin on his observations.

The town of Magadan and Nagaevo Harbor. This photo was taken from the aircraft carrying Vice President Henry A. Wallace in 1944. *Source*: U.S. Army.

Vice President Henry A. Wallace (right) with Ivan Fedorovich Nikishov, the Dal'stroi
commander. The ship in the background appears to be one of the Liberty ships provided free to the Soviet Union by the United States. *Source*: U.S. Army.

How could Wallace have come away from Kolyma so blinded to the forced
labor empire surrounding him? Conventional wisdom suggests the Soviet
deception was so impressive that any unsuspecting observer would have been
similarly misled. There is clearly truth in this. The real question is the extent to which Wallace was unsuspecting. The evidence indicates that some
U.S. intelligence sources were aware of strange activities taking place outside Nagaevo a full two years before his visit. Churchill forwarded to
Roosevelt a report mentioning movement of prisoners to Kolyma a full year
before Wallace traveled there. But the fact remains that no evidence has surfaced that any of this information actually made its way to Wallace—who,
after all, was rarely privy to the secrets of the Roosevelt administration.

Conspiracy theorists point to Wallace's pro-Soviet stances during and after
World War II and to his circle of associates who shared these leanings. Ac-
companying Wallace to Magadan was Owen Lattimore, a policy advisor on
Asia during the war who was accused after the war of having communist
sympathies. In 1943, while still in good standing, he wrote a book on the
issues of Asia for wartime and postwar America.[36] In another of the ironies
of the period, the foreword to that book was written by none other than
Adm. Harry E. Yarnell, whose flag had flown aboard USS *Augusta* during
its 1937 visit to Vladivostok.

In summary, it seems probable that the Soviet Union managed to keep
the operations of the Kolyma Gulag hidden from the West for a decade or

more. This was not challenging, given the remoteness of the region and the difficulty of access. Moreover, it seems possible that the operations of Otto Shmidt's Glavsevmorput provided an easy way for the Soviets to explain any unusual activity in the far north during the critical formative years. Indeed, the scientific and industrial activities of Glavsevmorput were widely reported in the West during the 1930s, often in heroic terms. Whether intentionally or not, Glavsevmorput effectively distracted analysts seeking to unravel activities in eastern Siberia.

Chapter 12

Kolyma Today

The surrounding Magadan Region, an area larger than Texas and California combined, has lost a third of the 390,000 inhabitants it had a decade ago. . . . According to the Red Cross, the average life expectancy in Chukotka, which borders on the Magadan Region, may be as low as 34 years.

       —U.S. News & World Report, January 1999

A statue of Eduard Petrovich Berzin, the founder of the Dal'stroi Gulag system, sits outside the Magadan city hall.[1] Berzin is today viewed by some observers as a victim of Soviet repression; indeed, as he was executed during the Great Terror, such status is technically justified. However, one wonders if such a depiction oversimplifies the complex story of the Kolyma Gulag system he created, in which a million or more suffered and in which a hundred thousand or more probably perished.

  Another statue outside Magadan has been dedicated to the millions who suffered in the Great Terror. The statue reminds one observer of the giant stone heads on Easter Island.

*   *   *

A museum to record Gulag history has been created on the premises of one of the former prisons in Magadan. The other part of the same building is occupied by a scrap-metal dealership.

*   *   *

The city of Bellingham, Washington, has reached out to a sister city across the Pacific, specifically the port of Nakhodka, which is a few hours outside Vladivostok. During the peak years of Gulag prisoner transport, Nakhodka was a very busy place, as it was the starting point for many of the voyages to the Kolyma camps. One of the ships that made the journey was *Nevastroi*. For some, the name of *Nevastroi* is forever associated with Nakhodka, sister city to Bellingham.

It is fitting, then, to remember that when *Nevastroi* was launched in the United States in 1918, it was given the name *Bellingham*, after this same city.

* * *

In 1997, major mining companies—including the Australian giant Broken Hill Proprietary, Ltd.—began to acquire properties in Kolyma with a view toward renewing the gold mining operations. BHP's interest was in the Vodorazdelnaya property, which contains a quartz-vein deposit that might hold over thirteen tons of gold.[2] In 2000, under the new leadership of American CEO Paul Anderson, the Australian company abandoned Vodorazdelnaya. Anderson indicated he could not support investments in areas of the world that "none of my senior managers can find on a map."[3]

* * *

A computer game was released in the late 1990s and became the subject of feverish Internet dialogue. The game, "King's Quest 2," took place in the mythical kingdom of Kolyma.

* * *

A Canadian company was formed in the early 1990s with the name Kolyma Goldfields. It was listed on the Vancouver stock exchange and had as its business mission the exploitation of mineral resources left over from Gulag mining operations. In late 1999 the company announced its intention to acquire the Internet auction business BidCrawler and to change its name from Kolyma Goldfields to BidCrawler Online.com, Inc.[4] About six months later, the Internet bubble burst.

* * *

Eco-tourism has exploded in the Kolyma region, and trips to abandoned Gulag sites are common. One tourist, Vladimir Dinets, reports that "following old roads, you sometimes get to dilapidated remains of wooden barracks and wire fences, now used by foxes and shrikes. Skulls from mass graves are sometimes offered to foreigners as souvenirs."[5]

* * *

Fisherman and writer Fen Montaigne traveled across seven thousand miles of Russian landscape to indulge his passion for angling. He stumbled across the shallow graves of Gulag victims while fishing the Kolyma River. The customers of Internet retailer Amazon.com found his book, *Reeling in Russia*, popular, assigning it an average four stars out of a possible five on Amazon's rating scale.

* * *

In 1977, a perfectly preserved baby mammoth was found by a bulldozer driver buried in the Kolyma permafrost. The baby was named Dima and became famous around the world. A second mammoth was found in the ice of eastern Siberia and became the subject of a major scientific attempt to reanimate the species through genetic engineering.

Solzhenitsyn reports that during the 1930s, starving Kolyma Gulag prisoners came across specimens of ancient and previously unknown animals perfectly preserved in the permafrost—and promptly ate them.

* * *

One senses that not much of importance has happened in the Kolyma River Valley over the last twenty years, or even since the end of the Gulag operations in the mid-1950s. Perhaps the silence is a godsend, to allow us to hear better the echoes from the two decades in which the peace of this quiet and empty land was shattered by the brutality inflicted by man upon man.

In comparison with the 1930s, 1940s, and 1950s, relatively few ships call today at Magadan, a city that was founded only in the 20th Century and grew only as a direct result of Stalin's decision to build a Gulag system in the Kolyma River Valley. The ships of Stalin's slave fleet are mostly long gone, having been lost during World War II, destroyed in accidents after the war, or cracked apart by Japanese and Chinese scrap dealers in the 1960s and 1970s.

We are left only with the records of those ships—their wakes. Fortunately, the wakes are clear enough to allow us to reconstitute the era and, perhaps for a short time only, to bring ourselves into more direct contact with the experiences of the Kolyma Gulag.

Appendix A:
Other Western-Built Ships
of the Gulag Fleet

Although before the war some of the vessels . . . were suitable, their charter prohibited their use in passenger service; and passengers continued to be carried on vessels without proper accommodations.
—Constantine Krypton, *The Northern Sea Route and the Economy of the Soviet North*

While six ships served in the core NKVD fleet supporting Dal'stroi, many other ships transported prisoners to the Kolyma Gulag.[1] Some were used over many years, while others may have made only one journey. Many were acquired secondhand from the large number of "British Standard ships" built during World War I and used after the war in commercial cargo operations. Some were provided to the Soviet Union free of charge during the World War II Lend-Lease program. A few were requisitioned from a defeated Germany at the end of World War I. Each has its story.

WAR VETERANS

Three of the ships that served in the core NKVD fleet were veterans of war drafted into occasional Gulag service.

Dekabrist (Декабрист, Decabrist)

Dekabrist is one of the few ships known to be in Gulag service before 1945 that is not included in lists of Gulag transports compiled by historians Robert Conquest or David Dallin. It is also the only Gulag transport ship also known to have been involved in military operations in four different wars—an example of an ordinary merchant ship living through extraordinary times.

Dekabrist was launched by Vickers, Son & Company in Barrow-in-Furness in 1902 as *Vickerstown* and then renamed in 1903 as *Franche-Comte*. A twin-screw merchant ship, large for its time, it displaced 7,363 gross tons and measured 476 feet in length.[2] The ship was purchased by a Monsieur Le Boule from Le Harve, but by all accounts it remained laid up in Barrow for about a year, until April 27, 1904, when *Franche-Comte* went to sea for the first time with nominal sailing orders for a French port. But the ship never arrived in France—during the journey the destination was changed to Libau (now Liepaja, Latvia). *Franche-Comte* was drafted as an auxiliary transport in the Russian Second Pacific Squadron, with a new name, *Anadyr*.[3]

The explanation for such an intriguing event becomes clear when presented in the context of the times. In February 1904, Russia suffered a major defeat at the hands of the Japanese at Port Arthur in Manchuria, and by midyear the Russian Pacific squadron had been nearly annihilated. Without a Pacific Fleet to speak of, the tsar decided to send major units from his Baltic and Black Sea Fleets on a long journey around the world to do battle with the Japanese and avenge the earlier humiliations. This was an eighteen-thousand-mile expedition, and the Russians had to complete it largely on their own. Since this Second Pacific Squadron needed to be largely self-sufficient, a small armada of transport ships was assembled, and one of these was *Franche-Comte*, renamed and redesignated an auxiliary cruiser. The ship was equipped with eight 57 mm French guns, strengthened with some minimal armor, and manned by a crew of sixteen officers and 245 men.[4]

The Second Pacific Squadron left the Baltic in late October 1904 and arrived in the Far East in late May 1905. Nearing a likely confrontation with Japanese forces, the fleet commander, Admiral Rozhdestvensky, dispatched most of the auxiliary ships to safe locations, retaining eight to accompany the combatants as they steamed forward to battle. This logistical group included two hospital ships, two tugs, a repair ship, and three transports—one of which was *Anadyr*. As the fleet approached Japan, *Anadyr* took the lead position in the column of transports, following the two divisions of battleships. The Japanese fleet was ready and waiting; it had been practicing for this moment ever since the Second Pacific Squadron had sailed from the Baltic half a year earlier. Despite the Russians' heroic efforts, it was never going to be an even battle.

The two fleets met off the coast of Korea in the Straits of Tsushima. In a matter of moments virtually the entire Russian fleet was sunk or captured by the Japanese in one of the most decisive and one-sided naval battles in history. *Anadyr* was fortunate enough to be one of the very few Russian ships to escape. Just before shooting began, *Anadyr* fled the scene of battle and escaped to Madagascar, and then back to Russia.[5] Its wartime service concluded, at least for the time being, the auxiliary cruiser reverted to an ordinary freighter and plied the oceans in the service of commerce.

Anadyr had a major overhaul in 1915 and at some point participated in World War I. It was handed over to the Soviet government in March 1918 but only a month later was laid up in port. As before, no one seemed to know what to do with the ship. On October 9, 1918, *Anadyr* was activated and returned to sea. Just over a year later, on October 25, 1919, it was assigned to the Baltic Fleet in the young Soviet Navy but returned to commercial service with the freight operator Transbalt, on June 4, 1920.[6] The following year it was again drafted into military service as a naval auxiliary. After 1922, it returned to civilian registration with the name *Dekabrist,* operating with registration UOML.[7] It spent at least some of that time operating in the Pacific, from Vladivostok.[8]

One mission is known. In 1940 *Dekabrist* transported large numbers of Poles taken captive in the early days of World War II to imprisonment in Kolyma.[9] This seems to have been the only time the ship served the Gulag administration.

Dekabrist was employed on the infamous "Kola run" during World War II, transporting Lend-Lease cargo from U.S. and Canadian ports to Murmansk on the Kola Peninsula, or around the peninsula to Archangel'sk on the White Sea.[10] On one particularly heroic voyage, ending on December 20, 1941, *Dekabrist* was the first ship to bring into Murmansk vital engineering cargo, operating on this journey without escort and in radio silence, all of the while facing the constant threat of air and submarine attack.

But the fate of this seagoing transport of the arctic was sealed by decisions involving a land military campaign in Africa. In late 1942, the Allies decided to open a new front against the German forces in North Africa, and in order to assemble the amphibious invasion force, escort ships on Lend-Lease escort duty were diverted to Africa. The Allies simply did not have enough ships both to escort merchant ships to the Soviet Union and support Operation Torch's landing force—and invasion troops took priority over Lend-Lease cargo.

But the Western Allies were also conscious of the need for conspicuous support for Stalin's forces, which at the time were engaged in heavy combat against German invaders. The halting of Lend-Lease convoys at that time might have undermined Stalin's confidence in that Allied support. The Teheran Conference—the first meeting of Winston Churchill, Franklin Roosevelt, and Joseph Stalin—was just around the corner, and it is likely the British and Americans did not want to appear to be undercutting their Russian allies at such a delicate time. So the decision was made to send a group of merchant ships back on the Kola run without escort, sailing individually in the hope that they could sneak through to Murmansk. *Dekabrist* was added at the last minute to the twelve ships already selected for this near-suicidal mission, code-named Operation FB.[11]

For *Dekabrist*, which had narrowly escaped destruction at the battle of Tsushima, this voyage was a disaster. *Dekabrist* was torpedoed by German

Ju-88 aircraft on November 4, 1942. Another four ships in Operation FB were sunk, and three others turned back long before reaching their destination. Of the thirteen ships sent to the Soviet Union, only five managed to complete the journey.[12] It was a loss nearly as decisive as the one at Tsushima thirty-seven years before.

Nineteen men survived the sinking of *Dekabrist* but found themselves stranded at the top of the world, drifting in small boats amid a cold and desolate sea. The men eventually found their way to Hope Island (Hopen), a small outcropping of land south of Spitzbergen. Here they were stranded for two years, during which time sixteen of the men died, one by one, from hunger, cold, or illness. The three survivors were finally rescued when Germans arrived on Hope Island to establish a weather outpost—though in this case "rescue" meant a transfer to a German concentration camp. These three survivors were ultimately freed by advancing Soviet armies.[13] The hut constructed by the *Dekabrist* survivors on Hope Island, home to this dwindling band of sailors over a two-year period, remains intact to this day.

Following the loss of *Dekabrist* in 1942, the Soviet Union acquired another ship from the United States under Lend-Lease and gave it the same name. The second ship is the subject of an amazing story, which while not directly related to Kolyma operations, nonetheless involves the shipment of large numbers of convicts. This second *Dekabrist* was supposedly carrying ten thousand former Soviet soldiers—ex–prisoners of war rescued from German confinement—to a Gulag camp in Chukotka in 1950.[14] (The estimated number of passengers is likely inflated, as is typical in these stories.) The convicts mutinied, seized control of the ship, and decided to set a course for America.

One can imagine the impact the arrival of such a ship off U.S. shores would have had during the Cold War. To preclude this unacceptable prospect, Stalin supposedly ordered his air forces to intercept *Dekabrist* at sea and sink it. (The story is told by one of the pilots assigned this mission and is verified by two other witnesses to the orders.) Severe weather precluded the intercept mission from launching, but by the time the weather cleared the mutiny had failed. Upon return to Soviet shores, according to at least one account, all ten thousand convicts were shot. These allegations have yet to be validated, but for many of the passengers who traveled aboard the Gulag fleet and endured the horrors of the voyages to Kolyma, such a story would be all too believable.

Kiev (Киев)

Kiev was a 5,822-ton, 449-foot cargo ship built in 1918 by Flensburger Schiffsbau Gesellschaft in Flensburg, as the *Waldenburg*. In its short (twenty-four-year) life span, *Kiev* was witness to some of the major geopolitical events of the twentieth century. It was completed just after the conclusion of World

War I and as such became embroiled in the postwar negotiations between the Council of Four (the United States, Britain, France, and Italy) and the new government of the defeated Germany. To offset losses in the merchant fleet caused by submarine warfare, the postwar reparations imposed upon Germany included the forfeiture of all ships over a thousand tons. All large ships were confiscated and handed over, mostly to Britain (74 percent) and to a lesser extent to the United States, France, and Italy. Flensburger Schiffsbau Gesellschaft had just completed nine large freighters, all of which were promptly handed over to the Allies.

One of these was *Waldenburg*, and thus began the first phase of the ship's career. It was delivered to British authorities in June 1919 and renamed *Maritime*. It was bought in 1922 by the W. Thomas Shipping Company of London and renamed *Cambrian Queen*. In 1928 it was sold to North German Lloyd of Bremen, with the name *Remscheid*. It operated with registration UOWZ.

The second phase of this ship's career occurred in 1932 with its sale to the Soviet Union and thereafter—if reports from authors Dallin and Nicolaevsky are accurate—with its use in Gulag service as *Kiev*. The Gulag career of *Kiev* was evidently brief. Dallin and Nicolaevsky report that it was used in Gulag service only from 1940 to 1941, though no published, first-hand accounts of passengers on *Kiev* have surfaced.[15]

The third phase of *Kiev's* short career involved its role in the second major global conflict of the twentieth century, World War II. *Kiev* was assigned to Lend-Lease duty in 1942, sailing with convoy PQ-12 from Reykjavik on March 1 of that year, arriving twelve days later at a port on the Kola Peninsula. However, *Kiev* was not so fortunate on the return voyage as part of convoy QP-10; *Kiev* was sunk by the *U-435* on April 13, 1942.[16] Six members of the crew perished as *Kiev* capsized within seven minutes of the attack. The remaining crew members were saved by a British corvette.[17]

Following the loss of *Kiev*, another ship—a former British Standard ship built in 1919—was assigned this name. There are no reports of this ship's having been used in Gulag service.

Minsk (Минск)

Minsk was probably a near sister ship to *Kiev*, 449 feet long with cargo capacity of 5,949 tons, slightly larger than *Kiev*. It was constructed in 1918 as the *Forst* by Flensburger Schiffsbau Gesellschaft, originally for the Deutsche-Australische Dampfschiffs-Gesellschaft. Like *Waldenburg* above, in 1919 *Forst* was surrendered following Germany's defeat in World War I and taken over by the British government's Shipping Controller, for which it was managed by G. Dodd & Company. In 1921, *Forst* was purchased by Hogarth Shipping Company Ltd., better known as the Baron Line, and renamed *Baron Ogilvy*. In 1924 it returned to German ownership with a sale to

Roland-Linie A.G., at which point the name changed to *Murla*. It was acquired by the Soviet Union in 1932 and renamed *Minsk*. The new acquisition was based in Odessa and registered internationally as UOWY and in the
Soviet Union as M-11650.[18]

Minsk is listed among the Gulag fleet for the years 1940 and 1941 by
historians Dallin and Nicolaevsky.[19] It was one of the more capable ships on
this route: equipped with three decks and seven holds, it was able to carry a
wide variety of cargo (including passengers) on individual voyages.[20] There
is independent confirmation of a passage to the Kolyma camps in 1940 and
a second confirmation of a voyage to Kolyma in 1951.[21] *Minsk* was in
Nagaevo Harbor in December 1947 when two crew members were killed
in an explosion, but it has not been revealed whether prisoners were aboard
at the time.[22] As with other Gulag ships, *Minsk* served on convoy duties
during World War II, making many trips between Vladivostok and the United
States.[23] The ship survived the war, but its final disposition is unknown. It
was removed from *Lloyd's Register of Shipping* in 1959–60 but was still included in the *Russian Maritime Register of Shipping* in 1965, as based in
Nakhodka.

FROM TACOMA TO KOLYMA

Many of the Soviet Gulag ships were built in the United States to a British
design for purposes of defeating a German adversary, only to end up in Soviet
hands. How did this come about?

Unrestricted submarine warfare became a reality during World War I, and
the losses within the merchant fleet were horrific. From the need to replace
these losses emerged a massive shipbuilding program in which the British
Shipping Controller orchestrated the ordering of 821 new merchant ships
from shipyards in Britain, the United States, Canada, Japan, Hong Kong,
and Shanghai. To save money and time, the ships were built to standard
designs and have since been known as "British Standard ships."

Shortly after the United States entered the war in 1917, the federal gov-
ernment issued an order requisitioning all steel ships under construction in
American shipyards, which included many of these British Standard ships.
In addition, the Emergency Fleet Corporation, under the supervision of the
U.S. Shipping Board, launched its own major program of ship construction,
its vessels to be built in many of the same yards that were busy fulfilling
British orders. The United States produced in World War I more standard
ships than any other country. Most, however, were not completed until 1918
or 1919, leaving some 1,500 ships on the books of the U.S. Shipping Board
in the years immediately after the war.

The Seattle Construction and Drydock Company of Seattle, Washington,
received an order from Great Britain for the construction of six standard ships
of 7,500 deadweight tons as part of the British "War" series of cargo ships.

They were intended for the Imperial Munitions Board but were placed on the order books of Cunard in order to protect the nominal neutrality of the United States. These ships were taken over by the U.S. government, about the same time that the shipbuilder itself was taken over by the Todd Drydock and Construction Company of New York.[24] The Seattle facility did not survive long. Looking to expand, the new owners developed a new "greenfield" facility outside Tacoma and gradually shifted work away from the original Seattle site, which was closed down just two years after the acquisition.[25]

Four of the ships in the British order eventually became *Shaturstroi, Nevastroi, Kashirstroi,* and *Syasstroi,* all of which served in the Gulag fleet. These were fairly standard two-deck steel merchant ships with triple-expansion steam engines; they measured about 4,800 gross tons and 380 feet in length. The design of these ships was very successful and became the model for the "Cascade" series of ships constructed for the U.S. Emergency Fleet Corporation in World War I.

Todd itself survived the downturn in shipbuilding after World War I and went on to become one of the major commercial and naval shipbuilders in the United States, operating shipyards in New York, Tacoma, Seattle, Los Angeles, Oakland, and Houston. The decline in naval shipbuilding was to hit the company hard in the last part of the twentieth century; while the company continues today as Todd Pacific Shipyards in Seattle, it is but a shadow of its former self.

Kashirstroi (Каширстрой)

The Seattle Construction and Drydock Company was preparing to construct *War Artist* in 1918 on behalf on the British Shipping Controller when the order was taken over by the U.S. Shipping Board. Construction was shifted to the new Tacoma facility; the ship, hull number C1, was launched as *Tacoma* but was completed with the name *Chebaulip.*[26] It measured 4,838 gross tons and 380 feet in length.[27]

Chebaulip's initial service was in the nitrate trade for Wessel Duval & Company.[28] For a brief time, from July 1918 until May 1919, *Chebaulip* served in the U.S. Navy's Overseas Transportation Service, making several runs to Europe, Africa, and South America in support of American forces overseas.[29] Then, like its sister ships, it was returned to the U.S. Shipping Board for general cargo duties. These it performed—making a trip to Petrograd in September 1922—until March 14, 1923, when it was laid up in Norfolk. It remained there until sold to an agent of the Soviet Union in February 1930.[30] Later in 1930 it arrived in the Soviet Union and was assigned the name *Kashirstroi,* Soviet registration M-1152, and international registration UOBG. It was based in Odessa until 1936, when the homeport was changed to Vladivostok.[31]

Kashirstroi is documented as one of the first ships to bring prisoners to the new camps in Magadan, in mid-1932.[32] This one trip is the only published reference to *Kashirstroi* in Gulag use, though this certainly does not preclude employment at other times, especially in the 1932 to 1934 period. The ship's final status remains unrevealed, but its last reported service was in 1955. It was removed from *Lloyd's Register of Shipping* in the 1959–60 edition.

Nevastroi (Невастрой)

Nevastroi was launched by Todd shipyards in Tacoma as the *War Herald* in 1918 on behalf of the British Shipping Controller, but it was completed as the *Bellingham* on behalf of the U.S. Shipping Board. It measured 4,838 gross tons and 380 feet in length.[33] It served for one year in the U.S. Navy's Overseas Transportation Service, ferrying cargo between North America, South America, and Europe, but was then was returned to the Shipping Board, under the control of which it remained throughout the 1920s.[34] From 1919 to 1923 it made numerous trips carrying metals, grains, and other general cargoes between East Coast ports and Europe, after which it was deemed surplus. On July 22, 1923, *Bellingham* was taken under tow to Norfolk from Baltimore and two days later arrived at Camp Eustis, Virginia, where it apparently remained until it was towed again to Newport News, Virginia, on February 12, 1930, to be prepared for sale.[35]

Bellingham was acquired by the Soviet Union in 1930, renamed *Nevastroi*, and registered as UOBF; it was based in Vladivostok, probably as part of the NarkomVodTrans Pacific fleet. (The name is probably that of one of Stalin's industrial projects on the Neva River, which flows from northwestern Russia through St. Petersburg into the Gulf of Finland.) *Nevastroi* served not only in the Gulag fleet but also in the Soviet operations against Japan at the very end of World War II. It was damaged and possibly lost on August 16, 1945, during the Soviet attacks against Seishin, when it struck a mine laid by an American submarine or aircraft.[36] In any case, it was deleted from *Lloyd's Register of Shipping* in the 1959–60 edition.

There is only one reported incident of *Nevastroi*'s use in the Gulag fleet, which is by Aleksandr Solzhenitsyn in 1938, but it is likely the ship was used repeatedly in the period 1937 to 1940.[37]

Shaturstroi (Шатурстрой)

Shaturstroi was launched in Tacoma as *War Guide* on behalf of the British Shipping Controller but was completed as *Puget Sound* in 1918 after the ship was requisitioned by the U.S. Shipping Board. *Puget Sound* measured 4,838 gross tons and 379 feet in length. The Shipping Board continued to own the ship throughout the 1920s; its homeport was Seattle.[38] The ship was laid up on May 7, 1924, after discharging cargo in New York, where it remained until sold in February 1930.[39]

Puget Sound was acquired by the Soviet Union in 1930 and was renamed *Shaturstroi*, operating with registration UOVH; its new name was in honor of the major electrical generating plant in the town of Shatur, southwest of Moscow. (Other surplus U.S. ships named after such projects were *Volkhovstroi, Dneprostroi, Svirstroi, Syasstroi,* and, as noted above, *Nevastroi*.)[40]

Its first mission in July 1930 may have been to bring several aircraft and related factory material to establish an aircraft plant in Rostok.[41] Eventually based in Vladivostok as part of the NarkomVodTrans Pacific fleet, *Shaturstroi* survived World War II in the Pacific and was reported in service as late as 1968.[42] While its final disposition is unknown, it was deleted from *Lloyd's Register of Shipping* in the 1969–70 edition.

The one confirmed report of *Shaturstroi* in Gulag service comes from Ivan Krevsoun, as cited in Victor Kravchenko's book *I Choose Justice*.[43] Krevsoun describes an incident in which a passenger aboard *Shaturstroi* jumped overboard when the ship passed near Japanese fishing boats. He was subsequently rescued by these fishing boats, the only reported case of a prisoner escaping from a Gulag ship while at sea.

Syasstroi (Сясьстрои)

Syasstroi was built in Tacoma by Todd Shipyards, although many writers have mistakenly reported the ship as having been launched in Seattle. Construction actually began in the Seattle Construction and Drydock Company, but work was moved to the new Todd facility in Tacoma shortly after the two companies merged. Measuring 4,844 gross tons and 380 feet in length, the ship was completed in Tacoma as *Masuda* on behalf of the Barber Company and was requisitioned by the U.S. Shipping Board for wartime purposes. The Shipping Board owned the ship throughout the 1920s and sold it in 1930.[44] Upon arriving in the Soviet Union the ship was assigned registration code UOVG and the name *Syasstroi*, after a major pulp and paper facility in northwestern Russia.

There is very little information available on *Syasstroi*'s service in the Soviet Union and no firsthand reports of its use in moving forced labor to Kolyma. In fact, there would be no evidence at all of its use in carrying prisoners had the ship not run aground on June 10, 1936, off the southern coast of Karaginski Island in the Bering Sea, near Cape Krasheninnikova. According to at least one source, the ship was carrying 1,090 "workers" on this voyage, and a major rescue operation was launched involving the freighters *Itelman* and *Suchan* and the tug *Kit*.[45] The ship's destination is unknown, but its position upon grounding was consistent with a voyage from Vladivostok through the Bering Strait to a destination such as Ambarchik.

It is uncertain if *Syasstroi* survived this incident. According to Lloyd's Casualty Reports the ship was lost in the Bering Sea in October 1936—possibly written off at this late date due to damage received in this same incident. Another source suggests the ship was lost on April 1, 1939, having foundered on a reef in the Okhotsk Sea.[46]

THE GULAG SHIPS OF STATEN ISLAND

A series of ships was constructed for the British Shipping Controller by Standard Shipbuilding in its new shipyard on Shooter's Island, a fifty-one-acre site just north of Staten Island and about three miles southeast of Elizabeth, New Jersey. Standard Shipbuilding constructed these nine 7,300-deadweight-ton dry-cargo ships almost in sight of the Statue of Liberty; four of them eventually found their way into Soviet hands. These were conventional two-deck steel ships measuring 377 feet in length and propelled by triple-expansion steam engines. Three of these ships—*Dneprostroi, Svirstroi,* and *Volkhovstroi*—saw Gulag service. The final ship, *Aleut,* was evidently not used in Gulag operations but was converted to a whale factory ship.[47]

Standard Shipbuilding itself did not survive the decline in the industry's fortunes after the war and went out of business shortly after completing these ships, abandoning the island in 1922. Shooter's Island, which had earned its name during colonial days as a favorite site for duck hunting, is today a bird sanctuary, surrounded by several dozen wrecks—all that is left from its former life as a major shipbuilding center.

Dneprostroi (Днепрострой)

Dneprostroi was built as the *Dallas* in 1918; it measured 4,757 gross tons and 377 feet in length. It was owned by the U.S. Shipping Board and operated out of New York throughout the 1920s.[48] Like so many of its contemporaries, it was then deemed surplus and on May 5, 1924, was laid up in Norfolk, Virginia. It did not move again until February 2, 1930, when it was towed to Baltimore, to be prepared for sale five days later to the Soviet Union. The new owners renamed the ship *Dneprostroi* and based it in Vladivostok, with international registration UOBH and Soviet registration M-11506.[49] The ship was named after the massive hydroelectric works constructed on the Dnieper River in the central Ukraine between 1927 and 1932, one of the most ambitious of Stalin's industrial development projects.

Dneprostroi served in Gulag transport at least twice, once in 1932 and then again 1938.[50] During World War II, *Dneprostroi* participated in two Atlantic convoys, PQ-12 in March 1942 and QP-10 in April 1942. It later saw service in the Pacific theater, including many visits to the United States.[51] It was still in service in the mid-1950s. According to the *Russian Maritime Register of Shipping, Dneprostroi* was eventually converted to a floating workshop in Kamkatchka and was broken up in the Vladivostok shipyard in 1965.

Svirstroi (Свирьстрой)

Svirstroi, a sister ship of *Dneprostroi,* was constructed as *Aledo* in 1919 and thereafter was operated mostly by the U.S. Shipping Board, out of New York.[52] It made numerous trips to such destinations as Glasgow and Rotterdam, as well as Jacksonville (Florida) and other U.S. East Coast ports until it was laid up in Fort Eustis, Virginia, on July 16, 1924. It remained there until towed to Baltimore in February 1930 and prepared for sale.[53] *Aledo* was sold to the Soviet Union in 1930, renamed *Svirstroi,* and was at least initially based in Odessa, with registration UOBE.[54] (The ship was named after hydroelectric works constructed on the Svir River, which flows between Lake Onega and Lake Lagoda in northwestern Russia.)

The only confirmed use of *Svirstroi* in Gulag service was in 1932.[55] However, another source reports that *Svirstroi* made a journey to Nagaevo Bay the year before, though the nature of the cargo on that voyage is unspecified.[56] As the founding of the Gulag in Nagaevo did not occur until 1932, it is possible this source is mistaken about the date and that the reference is in fact to the voyage made in 1932, or that it is to a voyage unrelated to the Gulag.

The final fate of *Svirstroi* remains uncertain. *Svirstroi* and three other ships of the Soviet Far East fleet (*Sergei Lazo, Krechet,* and *Simferopol*) were being overhauled in Hong Kong when on December 8, 1941, the Japanese launched attacks on British forces there. The Soviet ships were subjected to artillery and air attack as the Japanese forces pushed back the British and Canadian defenders from the mainland onto Hong Kong Island. The Soviets, neutrals in the war against Japan, protested, and the Japanese agreed to allow the Soviet crews to leave the ships.

But there are conflicting reports about the actual fate of *Svirstroi* during this period. One generally authoritative source suggests the ship was destroyed by Japanese aircraft in Hong Kong on December 12, and that its wreckage remained aground off Tsun Wan, before being scrapped in 1950.[57] Indeed, it is reported by at least one observer that two wrecked merchant ships were in this vicinity in 1945 and that shortly after the war local residents claimed the abandoned hulls were Russian ships caught during the Japanese attack.[58]

It is commonly held in Russian maritime circles that *Svirstroi* was bombarded and sunk by Japanese artillery in Hong Kong Harbor on December 18, 1941.[59] Students of the 1941 siege of Hong Kong would be right to question this account, however, for by December 18 the Japanese were already in control of Kowloon Bay, where *Svirstroi* (and *Sergei Lazo*) were anchored. Why would Japanese artillery sink a valuable ship in territory already under Japanese control? An explanation may be found in the papers of Gen. C.M. Maltby, commander of the defending forces:

> In the early hours [of December 18] a 60-pounder gun which had been brought up into North Point under cover of darkness (Lt. J.S. Vintner commanding) attempted to sink three freighters in Kowloon Bay suspected of being used for observation posts or being prepared as "jumping off places" for an attack. Only shrapnel was available but by obtaining hits on the waterline one 4,000 ton ship was holed and settled down.[60]

It thus appears possible that *Svirstroi*, a 4,700-ton ship—and one originally built to support British war aims in World War I—was the victim of British artillery strikes.

However, a third scenario exists in which *Svirstroi* survived the attacks in Hong Kong and was then impressed into service in the Japanese merchant fleet. There are reports within some Russian sources that two of the four Soviet ships in Hong Kong survived the attacks and were confiscated by the Japanese, though *Svirstroi* is not one of those specifically mentioned. Yet of these four ships only *Svirstroi* appears in the recognition manual for Japanese merchant ships issued by the U.S. Office of Naval Intelligence (ONI) in 1944.[61] According to that document, *Svirstroi* was captured by the Japanese in Hong Kong in 1941 and placed in the merchant shipping fleet.

If *Svirstroi* was impressed into Japanese service, and if, as it seems clear, did not survive the war, then what was its fate? There are no records of a ship with that name having been sunk after 1941. But *Svirstroi* shared the same design with two other ships in the Japanese merchant fleet, *Ryuzan Maru* and *Kenzan Maru*, and it is at least possible that *Svirstroi* was confused with one of these ships. Indeed, two merchant ships named *Ryuzan Maru* are reported sunk during the war, and four by the name *Kenzan Maru* were also reported lost in that same conflict. The submarine USS *Finback* reported sinking a cargo ship identified as *Ryuzan Maru* on July 31, 1943. (This submarine ten months later would rescue future U.S. president George H.W. Bush.) It seems apparent from the available records that this victim was the sister ship to *Svirstroi*. Another cargo ship identified as *Ryuzan Maru* is listed as having succumbed to a mine laid by U.S. aircraft off Hangkow, China, on January 27, 1945.[62] But this vessel was only half the size of the *Svirstroi*. Therefore it is unlikely the missing *Svirstroi* has been confused with *Ryuzan Maru*.

Circumstances are less clear for *Kenzan Maru*. A merchant steamer of that name is listed in the official U.S. Navy chronology as having been sunk by the submarine USS *Albacore* on November 25, 1943. This vessel appears to be the sister ship to *Svirstroi*. Another ship named *Kenzan Maru* sank following a collision off northern Japan in January 1943, but this freighter was much smaller than *Svirstroi*. An American B-24 air raid at Makassar on May 5, 1945, is credited with sinking yet another cargo ship named *Kenzan Maru*, and there is some ambiguity of the actual identity of this ship, as it is otherwise unaccounted for. However, that same report suggests that a gunboat named *Kenzan Maru* was sunk by B-24 aircraft at Makassar on May 7, 1945, and if this report in actuality refers to the same ship above, as is typically assumed, then the mystery disappears.[63] On the other hand, if the gunboat sunk on May 7 was a different ship than the cargo vessel sunk two days earlier, then there is at least a possibility that the remains of *Svirstroi* can be found off the coast of Sulawesi, Indonesia.

While the fate of *Svirstroi* remains uncertain, that of the crew is documented. In December 1942 the survivors of *Svirstroi* and three other Soviet ships attacked in Hong Kong finally made their way back to the Soviet Union.[64] Their ships had been among the first of many losses of Soviet maritime units during the war. The crews on these voyages—the "fiery flights"—were later recognized with a memorial of bronze plaques in Vladivostok. In May 2000, in a sign of the times, the heavy plates, with the names of the lost crew inscribed in recognition of their sacrifice, were vandalized and stolen, presumably for the scrap value of the metal.

Volkhovstroi (Волховстрой)

Volkhovstroi was built as the *Galesburg* in 1918 for the U.S. Shipping Board. It was operated by the Wyman S. Company on transatlantic routes until June 1920, when that company entered liquidation and the ship was placed in the hands of the receiver, a Mr. G.W. Sterling. It was returned to the government under court order in 1921 and was laid up at Caldwell's Landing on the Hudson River at Jones Point, New York, not far from the site where American rebels had laid cables across the river to disrupt the movement of British ships in the Revolutionary War.[65]

Galesburg remained at Caldwell's Landing until moved under tow to Boston in January 1930 in preparation for sale to the Soviet Union. The Soviets assigned their new ship registration UOVF and relocated it to Vladivostok.[66] It was renamed *Volkhovstroi* (after a hydroelectric plan on the Volkhov River constructed in 1926). Slightly larger than its sisters, at 4,943 gross tons, *Volkhovstroi* served with *Svirstroi* and *Shaturstroi* in the initial Magadan fleet in 1932 and may have made other voyages in the early 1930s.[67] During World War II it carried Lend-Lease cargo between the United States and Soviet Union.[68] Its final disposition is unknown; it was deleted from *Lloyd's Register of Shipping* in the 1959–60 edition.

LEND-LEASE GIFTS FROM AMERICA

A number of ships were supplied to the Soviet Union in support of Lend-Lease operations during World War II. Several of these ended in Gulag service, at least on an occasional basis.

Balkhash (Балхаш, Balhash, Balkash)

Balkhash was a combined passenger/cargo ship of 6,806 gross tons and 423-foot length operating with international registration UOYT. *Balkhash* was constructed as the *Manoa* by Newport News Shipbuilding in 1913 for the Matson Navigation Company and was used to support the burgeoning tourist and cargo trade to Hawaii in the years around World War I. Unusually for the period, *Manoa* was constructed with engines aft instead of amidships, a design considered quite ugly by passenger ship purists.[69]

Following the attack on Pearl Harbor, the *Manoa* was called into military service and was sold to the U.S. Maritime Commission. In turn she was transferred to the Soviet Union in 1943 as part of the Lend-Lease program and renamed *Balkhash*, replacing a ship with the same name that had been sunk by German air attacks in 1941 during the evacuation of Tallinn.[70] The ship was assigned Soviet registration M-11744.

There are two indications of the use of *Balkhash* in the Gulag system. The first relates to the transfer of Estonian prisoners after World War II.[71] The second involves an unpublished personal account of a voyage to the Gulag aboard this ship (though the year is not stated).[72] Incidentally, there is at least one account of the original *Balkhash*'s having been used to move prisoners to the camps in the Archangel'sk area, but no such accounts that relate to Kolyma.[73]

In 1956 *Balkhash* was modernized in China and equipment was added to restore the ship to its original mixed cargo and passenger configuration. On June 22, 1964, *Balkhash* was transferred to the Far Eastern Shipping Company, and on December 13, 1966, it was decommissioned and turned into a floating base for repair of navigation equipment for the Vladivostok merchant fleet.[74] The ship was deleted from the *Russian Maritime Register of Shipping* in 1967 and supposedly broken up in the Soviet Union sometime after that date. According to one source this took place in the late 1970s, though another lists the vessel as a repair hulk in Vladivostok as late as 1985.[75] There are reports that it was still afloat in Vladivostok in the mid-1990s, and it may today still reside amid the detritus of Vladivostok Harbor.[76]

Nogin (Ногин)

Nogin is an interesting ship, in that it may represent an unusual and horrific irony—a ship provided free to the Soviet Union by its ally the United

States and subsequently used, if recent reports are accurate, to take American military personnel to the Kolyma Gulag.

Nogin was constructed in 1919 in Seattle, Washington, by the Skinner & Eddy Corporation. Skinner & Eddy was a phenomenon at the time, the equivalent of the Seattle-based "dot-com" start-ups some eighty-five years later. The shipyard had been formed in 1916 and rapidly became the largest in the city, employing many thousands of workers; it had launched its first ship at the end of 1917. But the success was short-lived; the shipyard ceased operations in 1920 after the U.S. government canceled major orders and the shipyard suffered a major workers' strike. The cancellation of orders eventually led to a seventeen-million-dollar lawsuit against the government, a suit that was ultimately decided against the company's interests by the U.S. Supreme Court in 1924. (It is a precedent still cited today.)[77] The site of the shipyard, twenty-five and a half acres, was sold in 1923 to Pacific Steamship Company but later became a "Hooverville," a shantytown, during the Great Depression.

But before Skinner & Eddy folded, it managed to produce seventy-five ships for the Emergency Fleet Corporation. (Incidentally, the construction yard was adjacent to the Seattle Construction and Drydock Company's facility that produced *Nevastroi* and *Shaturstroi*.) Skinner & Eddy constructed several types of ships, including fourteen of the "Editor" model (EFC design 1105).[78] One of these "Editor" ships was *Eldridge* (often mistakenly recorded as *Elridge*), a classic three-island freighter measuring seven thousand gross tons and 409 feet in length. For several years *Eldridge* was operated by the Admiral Oriental Line, including one notable journey in May 1926 to Osaka, Japan, in which the ship's carpenter attacked and killed the captain, J.H. MacNichol.[79]

In 1928 *Eldridge* was taken over by the Tacoma-Oriental Line, one of the Dollar Line companies, and was renamed *Tacoma*. In 1937, after several crippling strikes, the bankrupt Tacoma-Oriental Line was sold off to pay Dollar Line debts, and *Tacoma* was acquired by Matson Navigation Company, the owners of the *Manoa* (later *Balkhash*). With the sale, *Tacoma* was renamed *Ewa*. In 1942, *Ewa* was by sold Matson to the U.S. Maritime Commission. In 1943, the ship was transferred to the Soviet Union and renamed *Nogin,* replacing a ship of the same name built in the United Kingdom in 1915, sold to the Soviet Union some years later, and destroyed in 1942.[80] Both ships were probably named after V.P. Nogin, one of the early Bolsheviks, who had died in 1924.

Nogin, operating with registration UOWQ, was employed in Lend-Lease convoys during the war, not without incident. On June 15, 1943, *Nogin* was seized by Japanese naval forces and taken to Otomaru, where it was held for six weeks before being released to continue on its way to Vladivostok.[81] *Nogin* also participated in at least one military operation, the 1945 invasion of Seishin; it was damaged by an American-laid mine but survived. It also appears to have accidentally rammed *Dalstroi*, another Gulag ship involved in this operation.[82]

There are four reports of *Nogin*'s use in Gulag operations. The first involves the transfer in 1949 of freed prisoners from the Soviet atomic-weapons facility Arzamas-16 into exile in Magadan.[83] There are also indications that *Nogin* took Estonian prisoners to imprisonment in the Kolyma Gulag in the years after World War II.[84] There is in addition a firsthand report of passage on *Nogin* in 1948.[85] Finally, according to a witness, *Nogin* is one of four ships that may have transferred former U.S. servicemen from World War II to the Kolyma Gulag camps in 1948 and 1949.[86]

In 1946 *Nogin* was transferred to the Ministry of the Merchant Marine.[87] According to the *Russian Maritime Register of Shipping*, the old freighter was towed to the Italian port of La Spezia in late 1967 for demolition. It was removed from *Lloyd's Register of Shipping* in the 1968–69 edition, but according to the CIA *Nogin* was presumed scrapped by 1967.[88]

Lvov (*Львов*)

Lvov was another old merchant ship transferred to the Soviet Union, late in the war, in 1945. *Lvov* was constructed as *West Norranus* by Southwestern Shipbuilding in San Pedro, California, in 1920, as part of the Emergency Fleet Corporation's acquisition program in World War I. As a standard "USSB West" ship, *West Norranus* measured 5,435 gross registered tons, 3,392 net registered tons, and 410 feet in length. Having arrived well after the war ended, *West Norranus* was incorporated into the U.S. Shipping Board's fleet of surplus ships.[89] (A rarity for those times, the shipbuilder actually survived the ship. Southwestern Shipbuilding became a division of Bethlehem Steel in 1922, was spun off in 1983, and still operates today as South West Marine.)

In 1926 *West Norranus* was acquired by the Dimon Line and was renamed *Pacific Pine*. As was the case with many shipping companies in those bleak years, the Dimon Line fell on hard times in the 1930s, and *Pacific Pine*, which had cost approximately one million dollars to build, was sold at auction in July 1932 for only fifteen thousand dollars.[90] Later in 1937 the ship was renamed *Maine* and served in the California Eastern Lines.[91] *Maine* was transferred to the Soviet Union in February 1945 as part of the Lend-Lease program and renamed *Lvov*, operating with registration URBG.[92] The only indication of *Lvov*'s having been used as a Gulag transport ship comes from statements of former Estonian prisoners in the Kolyma Gulag for the period immediately after the war.[93]

Lvov was reassigned to the Baltic Steamship Company in early 1950 and was renamed *Istra* shortly thereafter. According to some sources, the ship was scrapped toward the end of the 1950s. But a formerly classified CIA report of 1967 suggests that *Istra* was converted as a barracks ship sometime before 1962.[94]

There is opportunity for confusion regarding *Lvov*, as two ships by this name operated in the Soviet fleet during World War II. The other *Lvov* was a small passenger ship of 2,034 tons and 345-foot length, constructed in 1933 by United Naviones de Levantes as the *Ciudad de Tarragona* and seized by the Soviet Union during the Spanish Civil War. The Soviets drafted the ship into military service as a floating headquarters and hospital ship, assigning it the name *Lvov*.[95] The ship was demobilized in 1944 and reverted to its original name, most likely as the newly obtained and larger *Maine* was to be assigned the name *Lvov*.

Odessa (Одесce)

The United States constructed about 2,700 Liberty ships during the war, often completing ships in a few weeks. Hull number 1553 of that group was the *Mary Cassatt*, a ship of the EC-2-S-CI type built by Permanente Metals Corporation of Richmond, California, over a six-week period culminating in delivery on May 13, 1943.[96] It measured 7,176 gross tons and 423 feet in length and sailed under international registration UUML. In Soviet service it would carry registration M-11950 and later be assigned a new Russian registration code, 430071.

Mary Cassatt was almost immediately handed over to the Soviet Union, renamed *Odessa*, and employed on Lend-Lease operations in the Pacific. Its first voyage was relatively uneventful, but not so the second voyage. On October 3, 1943, while traveling from Akutan (Alaska) to Petropavlosk, *Odessa* was hit by a torpedo that created a massive hole in hold number five. Despite the damage, the ship stayed afloat and sought refuge in Akomten Bay in Kamchatka for repairs.[97] There is uncertainty to this day as to the identity of the submarine that struck *Odessa*, though the best evidence points to the American *S-44*, which was operating in the area and was itself sunk only four days later by a Japanese destroyer.

On its third mission, in December 1943, *Odessa* was assigned a special cargo of three thousand young women sentenced to the Gulag for fraternizing with German troops during the Nazi occupation of Soviet territory. *Odessa* was assigned to transport these women from Vladivostok to a barren location farther up the coast. Here these prisoners constructed the new port of Vanino, which later became a major transshipment point for prisoners from the Trans-Siberian Railway to Magadan.[98] This is the only confirmed use of *Odessa* in transporting Gulag prisoners.

From March 23, 1946, on, *Odessa* was operated by the merchant marine ministry in conventional cargo roles. *Odessa* retired from active service in 1977 and since then has been used as a repair shop for the crab and fishing fleets in the Russian Far East under the ownership of Dalmoreprodukt. It is still afloat today in Vladivostok, the only Gulag transport ship known to survive.[99] It is also one of only three surviving Liberty ships, of the 2,700 built, and the only survivor amongst the Liberty ships constructed in the yards of famed shipbuilder Henry J. Kaiser.

Vitebsk (Витебск)

John Minto was a Liberty ship assigned hull number 2021 and displacing 7,176 gross tons. It was built in just four weeks in May–June 1943 by the Oregon Shipbuilding Corporation in Portland. It was immediately transferred to the Soviets, renamed *Vitebsk*, and assigned international registration UUMN and Soviet registration M-11949.[100] The only indication of use of *Vitebsk* in the Gulag system relates to the transfer of Estonian prisoners after World War II.[101]

On March 23, 1946, *Vitebsk* was transferred to the Ministry of the Merchant Marine, which on June 22, 1964, handed it over to the Far East Shipping Company. *Vitebsk* was decommissioned on December 29, 1971.[102] The records of the *Russian Maritime Register of Shipping* indicate that *Vitebsk* for a short time regained its original U.S.-assigned name of *John Minto*— just long enough for one last voyage from Kure to Taiwan for scrapping. It arrived in Kaoshiung in 1972 and was promptly broken up.

Erevan (Ереван, Jerevan, Erivan)

Joseph Watt was a Liberty ship with hull number 2,042, also constructed by the Oregon Shipbuilding Corporation in Portland. Measuring 7,175 gross tons, it was delivered in July 1943 after a four-week construction period and transferred to the Soviets, who renamed the ship *Erevan* and assigned it registration UOCF.[103] There are two indications of use of *Erevan* in the Gulag system. There is a firsthand account from a freed prisoner of passage from Magadan in 1948.[104] There is also a secondhand report on the use of *Erevan* to transfer of Estonian prisoners to Magadan in the years after World War II.[105] *Erevan* was transferred to the merchant marine ministry on March 23, 1946, and the Far East Shipping Company on June 22, 1964. It was decommissioned on May 5, 1975, and presumably was scrapped shortly thereafter.[106]

Kamenets-Podolsk (Каменец-Подольск)

The *Robert S. Abbott* was another Liberty ship constructed (in a different shipyard than *Mary Cassatt*) by Permanente Metals in Richmond, California. It was delivered in April 1944 after just four weeks under construction.[107] It was transferred directly to the Soviet Union and renamed *Kamenets-Podolsk*, with international registration UNZW and Soviet registration M-11742. (An earlier ship named *Kamenets-Podolsk*, built in the United Kingdom in 1915, had been destroyed in 1941.)[108]

The only indication of the use of *Kamenets-Podolsk* in the Gulag system relates to the transfer of Estonian prisoners after World War II.[109]

On September 22, 1948, the ship was transferred to the Far East Shipping Company. *Kamenets-Podolsk* was rebuilt in 1950 and reclassified as a combined cargo and passenger ship. On February 12, 1970, it was transferred to the Ministry of Fishing and used as a mother ship for the Vladivostok fishing fleet.[110] *Kamenets-Podolsk* was converted to a non-self-propelled workshop in 1977 and was promptly deleted from the *Russian Maritime Register of Shipping*. According to those records, it was sold in July 1988 for demolition in Nakhodka, but it is conceivable that the ship remains afloat there today.

FURNESS'S TIMBER CARRIERS

In the mid-1930s, the Soviet Union exported large amounts of timber to Western Europe from Arctic ports, principally from the booming timber city of Igarka, located in the Far North along the Arctic coast. It must have infuriated the Soviet authorities that the trade in Soviet timber was dominated by British shipping lines. In an attempt to correct this imbalance, the Soviet Union commissioned a series of seven specialized timber carriers from Furness shipyard in Haverton, Hill-on-Tees, in Britain. These ships, designed specifically for Arctic operations, included *Arktika, Belomorcanal, Belorussia, Revolutsioneer, Dickson, Igarka,* and *Komsomolsk*. At least the last two of these were used in Gulag service, according to some authors.

Igarka (Игарка)

Igarka was built in 1936 as a specialized timber carrier, registered as UPON internationally and M-11645 in the Soviet Union, and was based in Archangel. The ship was relatively small, at 327 feet in length and 2,900 gross tons.[111] It was named after the Arctic port, a major center of timber exporting during the Stalin years.

Gulag scholars David Dallin and Boris Nicolaevsky reported in 1947 that the *Igarka* was used in Dal'stroi service starting in 1940.[112] However, there are no published firsthand accounts of voyages on the *Igarka* to the Kolyma camps. U.S. wartime records indicate that the ship was used in Pacific Lend-Lease operations during World War II.[113] The *Igarka* was renamed *Ilelny* in 1952.[114] According to the *Russian Maritime Register of Shipping*, it was broken up in Inchon by the Ssang Yong Industry Company in 1974.

Komsomolsk (Комсомольск)

Komsomolsk was a sister ship of *Igarka,* also built in 1936 by Furness; it was registered as UPOT and based in Archangel'sk. It was named after Komsomolsk, a Soviet planned city in the Far East, itself named after the Komsomol, the All-Union Leninist Communist League (Kommunisticheskiy Soyuz Molodezhi)—or, as it is more commonly known, the Young Communists League. As with *Igarka,* historians Dallin and Nicolaevsky reported that the ship was used in Dal'stroi operations in 1940. Independent confirmation of this is lacking, but again like *Igarka, Komsomolsk* was used in World War II on Lend-Lease operations in the Pacific.[115] According to Russian maritime records, *Komsomolsk* was broken up in the first part of 1962.

The *Komsomolsk* should not be confused with *Komsomol,* a merchant ship built in the Soviet Union in the 1930s and sister ship to the *KIM,* another ship used in Dal'stroi operations (see Appendix B). *Komsomol* was constructed in 1932 by Severney Shipbuilding Yard in Leningrad.[116] In October 1936, *Komsomol* brought the first shipment of Soviet armor to the Republican forces in Spain fighting against Nationalist forces in the Spanish Civil War. *Komsomol* was to be attacked and sunk by the Nationalist cruiser *Canarias* on December 12, 1936, off the coast of Oran, while carrying crated aircraft to Spain.[117]

Sylvester Mora, in his listing of Gulag ships operating in the early 1940s, presents a list identical to that of Dallin and Nicolaevsky, except that *Komsomolets* is included rather than *Komsomolsk.*[118] There was a ship named *Komsomolets,* a tanker seized in Germany in 1939 while under construction (as the *Dorsanum*) for Britain, and then sold by the Germans to the Soviet Union in 1940.[119] *Komsomolets* was requisitioned by the Soviet Navy in 1941 and sunk by a U-boat in August 1942.[120] As a newly built tanker in the service of the Soviet Navy, *Komsomolets* was an unlikely ship for Gulag service. Also, as Mora's listing of Gulag ships in 1949 otherwise exactly matches that of Dallin and Nicolaevsky in 1947, his identification of *Komsomolets* could be in error.

Appendix B:
Soviet-Built Gulag Ships

As a transition between cargo and passenger-and-freight ships, the Baltic
factory constructed five series (two units in each) of steamship such as
Anadyr. . . . With significant cargo capacity they traded off on passenger
transport with only limited comfort. Places for 3rd-class passengers were
thus equipped on two decks.

—История Отечественного Судостроения
(History of Domestic Shipbuilding)

As part of its five-year plans, the Soviet Union embarked on a major program of shipbuilding.[1] Activity accelerated in the late 1920s and early 1930s,
principally in the Leningrad area. Some of these new ships were specifically
designed for operations in Arctic waters, and it is not surprising that some
appear to have been used in Gulag service. However, most proved quite
unsuitable for the task and were eventually replaced in favor of specially designed transport ships of greater speed and size.

BALTIC'S PASSENGER/CARGO SHIPS

Several Gulag transports were members of a class of nine passenger/cargo
vessels constructed in the Baltic Shipbuilding and Engineering Works in
Leningrad, a company that survives today as Baltiysky Zavod. These ships,
some 315 feet long and about 3,600 gross tons—about half the size of
Dzhurma—were the mainstay of merchant ship activity along the Northern
Sea Route in the 1930s, supplying the northern terminus of the Kolyma
camp system, at Ambarchik. Except for two such voyages involving a total
of three ships, it is hard to find unambiguous data that the passengers on

these voyages were Gulag prisoners, though it seems a logical conclusion, given the destination and timing of the voyages, and it is for this reason that these ships are included in this review.

Sakhalin (Сахалин)

Sakhalin, which was constructed in Leningrad in 1930, has the dubious distinction of being the first ship to carry prisoners to Nagaevo Bay, and the ship on which the newly appointed leader of Dal'stroi, Eduard P. Berzin, arrived at Nagaevo. This voyage culminated on February 4, 1932, when *Sakhalin,* possibly with icebreaker support, reached Nagaevo with approximately 150 forced laborers, mostly engineering and technical personnel rounded up in the purges.[2]

The *Sakhalin* is one of the few ships mentioned by name in official Soviet documents related to the creation of Dal'stroi, possibly in relation to another trip with Gulag passengers. Specifically, on October 26, 1932, instructions were issued to Narkomvod to make available to Dal'stroi a motor vessel "such as *Sakhalin*" for a trip to Nagaevo in November 1932, and to provide use for such a ship during the winter of 1932–33.

Several writers, including historian Robert Conquest, have described *Sakhalin* as an icebreaker, but this is a mistake. No such icebreaker has ever been identified in the Soviet fleet, and a number of original source documents clearly describe it as a conventional steamship, not an icebreaker, albeit one hardened for service in Arctic waters.[3]

The ship was renamed *Krasnoyarsk* in 1939 and survived World War II.[4] Its final disposition is unknown.

Anadyr (Анадырь, Anadir)

Anadyr was constructed in Leningrad in 1930 and operated with international registration UOFX and Soviet registration M-11591. It was named after the river in eastern Siberia. In 1932, it was part of the fleet of six merchant ships that formed the first large-scale convoy to Ambarchik, near where the Kolyma empties into the Arctic Ocean. Along with *Suchan* (below), *Anadyr* carried about a thousand Gulag prisoners on this trip.[5]

In 1935, *Anadyr* again traveled from Vladivostok to Kolyma, but this time instead of returning it traveled further west to Igarka and then all the way to Murmansk. This complete passage of the Northern Sea Route was a major achievement, coming only three years after the first one-season transit.[6]

Anadyr made additional trips to Ambarchik in 1938 and in 1939 or 1940.[7] Little is recorded of this ship after these pioneering voyages to the northern reaches of the Kolyma region. According to the *Russian Maritime Register of Shipping,* *Anadyr* was renamed *Vertikal* in 1966 and served as a training ship, based in Vladivostok. It was broken up in 1970 in the Soviet Union.

Suchan (Сучан, Soutchan)

Suchan was built in 1930 in Leningrad, a sister ship to *Anadyr;* it was named after another river in the Soviet Far East. It accompanied *Anadyr* on the first voyage from Vladivostok to Ambarchik in 1932, passing through the La Perouse Strait between Sakhalin and Hokkaido and carrying its share of a thousand prisoners.[8] *Suchan* met its end on a similar voyage in June 1938, when it foundered in the La Perouse Strait along the classic route from Vladivostok to the Soviet Far East.[9] Evidence has not yet surfaced that it was carrying prisoners on this trip, but that is certainly a possibility, especially since this was one of the peak years of shipments from Vladivostok to Magadan. If so, it is entirely possible that hundreds of Gulag prisoners perished on this voyage. The name *Suchan* was reassigned during World War II to a new Liberty ship provided by the United States as part of the World War II Lend-Lease program.

Khabarovsk (Хабаровск)

Khabarovsk was another sister ship to *Anadyr,* built in 1932 and operating with international registration UOIA and Soviet registration M-11586. It was named after the Siberian city. It made a trip from Vladivostok to Ambarchik in 1933, the year following the voyage of *Suchan* and *Anadyr.* While it is unknown if it carried Gulag prisoners on this journey, this would be a logical conclusion. The profile for this voyage fits almost perfectly the account of the *Dzhurma's* 1933–34 voyage, as originally reported by Russian émigrés David Dallin and Boris Nicolaevsky and repeated often since then.[10] The final disposition of *Khabarovsk* is unknown, but the vessel appears to have survived World War II.

Sverdlovsk (Свердловск)

Sverdlovsk was yet another sister ship to *Anadyr,* built in Leningrad in 1931 and operating with registration UOHV. It accompanied *Khabarovsk* on the 1933 mission to Ambarchik and very possibly carried prisoners on this voyage.[11] Little is known of the history of *Sverdlovsk;* it probably did not survive World War II.[12]

Smolensk (Смоленск)

Smolensk was yet another ship in this series, built in Leningrad in 1931 and operating with registration UOHS. It accompanied *Suchan* on the 1934 mission to Ambarchik and most likely carried at least some Gulag prisoners on that trip. *Smolensk* was impressed into the Soviet Navy during World War II and converted to an auxiliary minesweeper and transport. It is probable that *Smolensk* was an early casualty of the war, as a new ship by that name was registered in 1944.[13] *Smolensk* played a more heroic role in 1934 when it rescued many of the members of the crew of *Chelyuskin* in 1934 after that ship sank beneath the Arctic ice.

BALTIC'S ARCTIC CARGO SHIPS

The Soviet Union ordered a series of twelve cargo ships specially strengthened for Arctic operations. These were constructed by Baltic Shipbuilding and Engineering Works. These twelve cargo ships were fairly small: only 2,336 gross tons and 285 feet in length, or about a third of the size of *Dzhurma*. There is no published firsthand evidence that these ships were used to transport Gulag prisoners, but several historians have reported this, based on unrevealed sources.

Uritskii (Урицкий)

Uritskii was constructed in 1929 by Baltic Shipbuilding and Engineering Works in Leningrad.[14] Registered as UOAX, *Uritskii* made frequent trips to the Kolyma Arctic ports in the early 1930s, including participation in the first large-scale convoy in 1932, in company with *Anadyr* and *Suchan*.[15] It made another such trip in 1935 and may have made others.[16] There is no direct evidence that these trips involved the transport of Gulag prisoners, but one cannot know with certainty. The link of *Uritskii* to Kolyma comes from historians Dallin and Nicolaevsky, who write that the ship was used on Gulag transport duties in 1940 and 1941.[17] During World War II, *Uritskii* was used on convoy duties in the Atlantic, including the infamous Operation FB voyages to the Soviet Union.[18] The final disposition of the ship is unknown. *Uritskii* was removed from *Lloyd's Register of Shipping* in the 1959–60 edition, and there are no records of it in the archives of the *Russian Maritime Register of Shipping*.

Rabochii (Рабочий, Robachi, Rabotchy)

Rabochii was a sister ship to *Uritskii*, built in 1928 by Baltic Shipbuilding and Engineering Works.[19] It is noted for two events during its relatively short life of less than a decade. In 1935, *Rabochii* was the first steamship to sail the difficult Northern Sea Route directly from Archangel'sk to Ambarchik and then back again in one season.[20] Historians David Dallin and Robert Conquest each contend that it carried Gulag prisoners on this trip, and that is certainly a possibility.[21] In another such voyage in 1937, *Rabochii* met with less good fortune. The 1937 shipping season along the Northern Sea Route was a disaster; eighteen merchant ships and eight of the nine Soviet ice-breakers became stuck in ice and were forced to spend the winter at sea. Only one Soviet icebreaker remained free to unlock the twenty-six icebound ships. Help for *Rabochii* did not arrive in time: in January 1938, the ice pack crushed the ship and it sank, though without loss of life.[22]

SEVERNEY SHIPS

The Leningrad area was the center of Soviet shipbuilding in the 1920s and 1930s, home to several shipyards, including the Baltic Shipbuilding and Engineering group mentioned above. The nearby Severney "A. Zhdanov" Shipbuilding Yard, named after Leningrad party boss Andrei Alexandrovich Zhdanov, was another major builder of Soviet merchant vessels, at least one of which was used in Gulag operations. The shipyard survives today, renamed in 1989 the Severnaya Verf (Northern Shipyard).

KIM (КИМ)

KIM was a large freighter constructed in 1932 by Severney Shipbuilding Yard "A Zhdanov" in Leningrad, one of a series of four. It was registered as UPON internationally and M-11698 in the Soviet Union; it was based in Odessa. *KIM* (the acronym for Communist Youth International—Коммунистический Интернационал Молодёжи) measured almost four hundred feet in length and displaced 5,114 gross tons. Little has been documented of *KIM*'s early history except that in October 1936 it sailed from the Soviet Union to Spain with a cargo of crated aircraft for use by Republican forces in the Spanish Civil War, returning with a portion of the Republican gold reserves for safekeeping in the Soviet Union.[23] During World War II, *KIM* operated in the Pacific as part of the merchant fleet.

The only explicit reference to Gulag service by *KIM* is by writer Varlam Shalamov, who describes an incident December 1947 in which a rebellion was put down by hosing the holds with freezing water.[24] The *KIM* was broken up in the Soviet Union in 1971, according to the *Russian Maritime Register of Shipping*.

Notes

PREFACE

1. *Stalin's Arctic Disaster* [video] (Toronto: CineNova, 1997).

2. For example, some years before, and to much international approval, the Soviet Union had rescued the survivors of the airship *Italia* after it crashed in the Arctic. The rescue was part of a multinational initiative that included the United States.

CHAPTER 1: HERE STONES CRY

1. The account of the loss of *Indigirka* is taken from several sources. These include a contemporary newspaper article: "700 Believed Dead on Russian Vessel," *New York Times*, 14 December 1939, 14. Firsthand testimony from a survivor is quoted in Vladimir Petrov, *Soviet Gold: My Life as a Slave Laborer in the Siberian Mines* (New York: Farrar, Straus, 1949), 403–407. Additional material, including another survivor's testimony, is available from the papers of a December 1998 conference organized by the Far Eastern Marine Academy and Primorskje Branch of the Russian writers Union in Vladivostok: V.P. Bolotov, ed., "Документы о Гибели Парохода Индигирка в Районе п.Саруфуцу (о.Хоккайдо) в 1939 году [Documents about the destruction of the steamship *Indigirka* in the area of Sarufutsu (off Hokkaido) in 1939]" (1998), www.vld.ru/ppx/Indigir/Docs.htm (December 2002). The topic is covered in I. Muromov, *Сто Великих Кораблекрушений* [A hundred great shipwrecks] (Moscow: Veche, 1999), 356–59. Another source is a semifictional book by Lev Kniazev, *У Врат Блаженства* [At the gates of bliss], www.vld.ru/ppx/Knyazev/Blazh.htm (December 2002). Another account, but one without any reference to a Gulag connection, is in Petr Osichanskii, *П.П. Куянцев: Я Бы Снова Выбрал Море* . . . [P.P. Kuyantsev: I would again choose the sea . . .] (Vladivostok: Far Eastern Association of Sea Captains, 1998), 57–59. This is a compilation of interviews with P.P. Kuyantsev, a merchant captain in the Soviet Union in the 1930s. One of the most complete versions has been prepared by Teruyuki Hara of the University of Hokkaido: インディギルカ号の悲劇-1930年代のロシア極東

[The *Indigirka* tragedy: The Russian Far East in the 1930s] (Tokyo: Chikuma Shobo, 1993).

2. Petrov, 404.

3. The "white stains" reference is from the captain's testimony before the subsequent investigative panel.

4. William J. Spahr, *Zhukov: The Rise & Fall of a Great Captain* (Novato, Calif.: Presidio Press, 1993), 29.

5. Hara, 12.

6. Ibid., 18.

7. "Here Stones Cry," by Oleg Matseev.

8. Immigration and Naturalization Service, "Immigration to the United States" (2001), www.ins.usdoj.gov/graphics/aboutins/statistics/300.htm (December 2002). This was admittedly a slow period for U.S. immigration.

CHAPTER 2: THE LABOR CAMPS AT THE END OF THE WORLD

1. Vladimir Dinets, "Hitchhiking to Oimyakon and Beyond" (1999), www.hotcity.com/~vladimir/kolyma.htm (December 2002).

2. David Y. Dallin and Boris I. Nicolaevsky, *Forced Labor in Soviet Russia* (New Haven, Conn.: Yale University Press, 1947), 108.

3. Michael Jakobson, *Origins of the GULAG* (Lexington: University Press of Kentucky, 1993), 130.

4. Dallin and Nicolaevsky, 113.

5. Timothy A. Taracouzio, *Soviets in the Arctic* (New York: Macmillan, 1938), 121. Taracouzio actually refers to Narkomvod as the agency, but this was not formed until it was separated from its parent agency, NarkomPut'.

6. David Nordlander, *Capital of the Gulag: Magadan in the Early Stalin Era, 1929–1941* (Chapel Hill: University of North Carolina, 1997), 34, 46.

7. Dallin and Nicolaevsky, 114.

8. M.I. Khlusov, *The Economics of the Gulag and Its Part in the Development of the Soviet Union in the 1930s: A Documentary History* (Lewiston, N.Y.: Edwin Mellen Press, 1999), 22. The specific reference is from "Decision of the Central Committee of the Communist Party: About Kolyma," November 11, 1931.

9. "Постановление № 516 Совета Труда И Обороны 13 Ноября 1931 Г. [Council of Labor and Defence, decision 516, November 13, 1931]," www.gulag.ru/page/doc/doc3.htm (December 2002).

10. There is some confusion regarding the words represented by the acronym "Dal'stroi," at least upon its formation in 1931. No formal definition appears in the official Soviet decrees of the time Dal'stroi was formed. Most authors write that when formed "Dal'stroi" stood for "Far Eastern Construction Administration" or "Far Eastern Construction Trust." However, others, including David Nordlander and John McCannon, write that "Dal'stroi" when formed actually stood for "Far Northern Construction Trust." See Nordlander, 86, and John McCannon, *Red Arctic: Polar Exploration and the Myth of the North in the Soviet Union, 1932–1939* (New York: Oxford University Press, 1998), 7. In the late 1930s the acronym was formally linked in official documents to the phrase "Main Administration for Construction in the Far North" (Главное управление строительЬство Дальнего Севера).

11. Dallin and Nicolaevsky mistakenly identify the individual as Reingold Berzin, an error that continues to be repeated in later years. See, for example, Dallin and Nicolaevsky, 116, and Jakobson, 130.

12. R.H. Bruce Lockhart, *British Agent* (New York: G.P. Putnam's Sons, 1933), 314.

13. Gordon Brooke-Shepard, *Iron Maze: The Western Secret Services and the Bolsheviks* (London: Macmillan, 1998), 91–115. Berzin is therefore almost certainly the only Dal'stroi commander to have been featured as a character in a theatrical production, the *Reilly, Ace of Spies* television serial.

14. Nordlander, 82.

15. Jakobson, 119–20.

16. Nordlander, 79, 87.

17. Ibid., 96.

18. Roy Medvedev, *Let History Judge: The Origins and Consequences of Stalinism* (New York: Columbia University Press, 1989), 508.

19. Varlam Shalamov, *Kolyma Tales* (London: Penguin Books, 1994), 368–69.

20. Thomas Sgovio, *Dear America* (New York: Partners' Press, 1979), 139.

21. Roy Medvedev, 509.

22. Robert Conquest, *Kolyma: The Arctic Death Camps* (New York: Viking Press, 1978), 219–20.

23. Silvester Mora, *Kolyma: Gold and Forced Labor in the USSR* (Washington, D.C.: Foundation for Foreign Affairs, 1949), 1.

24. Nordlander, 255.

25. Ibid., 261. Other sources suggest that he was executed. See, for example, Sgovio, 154.

26. Mora, 2. The identity of ships in 1940 is provided by Marion Sloma, "Lasciate Ogni Speranza," www.najmici.org/kolyma/ksiazka11.htm (December 2002).

27. See, for example, Sylvester Mora and Piotr Zwierniak, *Sprawiedliwоœæ Sowiecka* [Soviet justice] (Wlochy, 1945). See also *Dark Side of the Moon* (London: Faber and Faber, 1946).

28. Central Intelligence Agency, *Recent Developments in The Soviet Arctic*, CIA/SC/RR 82 (October 13, 1954), www.foia.ucia.gov (Washington, D.C.: Office of Research and Reports, December 2002). A formerly top secret report declassified in 1999.

29. Data on Kolyma gold production is from A.I. Shirokov, "Первое Десятилетие 'Дальстроя' [First decade of Dal'stroi]," www.gulag.ru/page/histori/1ten.htm (December 2002). Data on world production of gold is from the Chamber of Mines of South Africa, "Estimated Western World Gold Production (1887–1991)" (2002), www.bullion.org.za/Level3/Economics&Stats/Goldmindata.htm#estimated (December 2002).

30. I.D. Batsaev, "Колымская Гряда Архипелага Гулага, Заключенные [The Kolyma range of the Gulag archipelago]," *Исторические Аспекты Северо-Востока России: Экономика, Образование, Колымский Гулаг* [Historical aspects of Russia's northeast: Economics, formation of the Kolyma Gulag]" (1996): 50. The Batsaev data are cited in Stephen G. Wheatcroft, "Victims of Stalinism and the Soviet Secret Police: The Comparability and Reliability of the Archival Data—Not the Last Word," *Europe/Asia Studies* 51:2 (1999): 315. The Batsaev data also match data presented by Shirokov.

CHAPTER 3: DEVELOPMENT OF THE GULAG FLEET

1. John Harbron, *Communist Ships and Shipping* (London: Adlard Coles, 1962), 140.

2. The rate of fleet expansion is based on records of ships in the Soviet merchant fleet at various points in time. Data on ships from 1940 and 1945 were obtained from *Soviet Merchant Ships 1945–1968* (Homewell, Havant, Hampshire: Kenneth Mason, 1969). Data for 1939 were obtained from Roger W. Jordan, *The World's Merchant Fleets 1939: The Particulars and Wartime Fates of 6,000 Ships* (London: Chatham, 1999). Data for 1935 were based on *Lloyd's Register of Shipping: 1935–36* (London: Lloyd's Register of Shipping, 1936). Supplemental data on many ships were obtained from Jürg Meister, *Soviet Warships of the Second World War* (London: Macdonald and Jane's, 1977).

3. Habron, 140.

4. *Soviet Merchant Ships 1945–1968*, 227.

5. John McCannon, *Red Arctic: Polar Exploration and the Myth of the North in the Soviet Union, 1932–1939* (New York: Oxford University Press, 1998), 6.

6. Derek Watson, *Molotov and Soviet Government: Sovnarkom, 1930–41* (New York: St. Martin's Press, 1996), 142.

7. D.M. Long, *The Soviet Merchant Fleet: Its Growth, Strategy, Strength and Weaknesses 1920–1999* (London: Lloyd's of London Press, 1986), 11.

8. Watson, 152.

9. McCannon, 37.

10. Ibid. However, the merchant fleet owned by Glavsevmorput was never very large. Ships directly owned by Glavsevmorput included several built specially for Arctic service: *Chelyuskin,* acquired from Copenhagen in 1933 and lost in 1934; *Dejnev,* built in Lenningrad in 1937; two tankers acquired from Japan, *Nenets* and *Yukagir;* and the Levaneskiy, built in 1940 but not delivered for Arctic service until 1946. Other ships transferred to Glavsevmorput shortly after its creation include *Makarov, Davydov, Dobrynia Nikitich,* and *Truvor.*

11. Linda Trautman, "The Fall of the Commissariat of Ice 1935–1938," October 18, 2000, 6, note 13. Paper presented to the Soviet Industrialisation Project Series, University of Birmingham. Quoted with permission.

12. Watson, 139–40.

13. McCannon, 172.

14. Meister, 277.

CHAPTER 4: PRISONER TRANSPORT OPERATIONS

1. Epigraph: William Barr, "First Convoy to the Kolyma: The Soviet Northeast Polar Expedition, 1932–33," *Polar Record* 19:123 (1979): 563.

2. David Y. Dallin and Boris I. Nicolaevsky, *Forced Labor in Soviet Russia* (New Haven, Conn.: Yale University Press, 1947), 117.

3. Aleksandr G. Kozlov, "От Истории Колымских Лагерей: 1932–37 [From the history of the Kolyma camps: 1932–37]," *Краеведческие Записки* [Notes of the Museum of Regional History] (1991): 61–91.

4. Robert Conquest, *Kolyma: The Arctic Death Camps* (New York: Viking Press,

1978), 218. Conquest estimates that one-third of the initial batch of prisoners perished.

5. David Nordlander, *Capital of the Gulag: Magadan in the Early Stalin Era, 1929–1941* (Chapel Hill: University of North Carolina, 1997), 101.

6. Victor Kravchenko, *I Choose Justice* (New York: Charles Scribner's Sons, 1950), 290–91. Kravchenko relays the experience of passenger Ivan Krevsoun.

7. This conclusion is based on the monthly data for arrivals to the Kolyma camp during 1932. In most months during the shipping season that year, prisoner arrivals are in multiples of a thousand or 1,500. In other months they are in multiples of 150, the same number as on the initial voyage of the *Sakhalin*. Also, according to Ivan Krevsoun, he was one of 1,500 convicts aboard *Svirstroi* in 1932. See Kravchenko, 290.

8. Conquest, *Kolyma: The Arctic Death Camps*, 222.

9. Kozlov, 70–78.

10. Barr, 563. There is potential for confusion regarding ships named *Anadyr*. The ship described here was a new ship, built two years before in the Baltic ship works in Leningrad. Another Gulag ship, *Dekabrist*, was named *Anadyr*, but was renamed in the early 1920s well before the new *Anadyr* was built. The first records of *Dekabrist* having been used in the Gulag fleet do not occur until around 1940.

11. Conquest, *Kolyma: The Arctic Death Camps*, 222. Conquest also places the date as 1933, but this is likely a mistake, as this historic voyage was well documented.

12. I.D. Batsaev, "Колымская Гряда Архипелага Гулаг, Заключенные [Kolyma range of the Gulag archipelago]," *Исторические Аспекты Северо-Востока России: Экономика, Образование, Колымский Гулаг* [Historical aspects of Russia's Northeast: Economics, formation of the Kolyma Gulag]" (1996): 50. The Batsaev data are cited in Stephen G. Wheatcroft, "Victims of Stalinism and the Soviet Secret Police: The Comparability and Reliability of the Archival Data—Not the Last Word," *Europe/Asia Studies* 51:2 (1999): 315.

13. Kozlov, 78.

14. Aad Schol, *Koninklijke Nederlandsche Stoomboot-Maatschappij* [The Royal Netherlands Steamship Company] (Alkmaar: De Alk bv., 1998), 53–55.

15. There is opportunity for confusion arising out of the ship *Felix Dzerzhinsky*. A *Felix Dzerzhinsky* was built in Leningrad but was renamed *Ural* in 1937 at the same time as the new *Felix Dzerzhinsky* was added to the Gulag fleet. This new ship, a converted British cable layer, was much larger and perhaps considered a more fitting testimonial to the founder of the NKVD, operator of these ships. The ship renamed *Ural* continued in merchant use until converted to an auxiliary minelayer in 1940.

16. As discussed in a later chapter, this outbreak corresponded with the presence of U.S. warships in Vladivostok Harbor, which may have forced a suspension of prisoner shipments.

17. Nadezhda Surovtseva, "Vladivostok Transit," in *Till My Tale Is Told*, ed. Simeon Vilensky (Bloomington: Indiana University Press, 1999), 184. Surovtseva mistakenly reports *Kulu* as *Kula*. (There are no records of a Soviet merchant ship by the name *Kula* operating in that era.)

18. "Кровью Омытое Советское Золото [Blood-washed Soviet gold],"

Социалистический Вестник [Socialist bulletin] 21–22 (December 10, 1945), 579–80. An interview with an anonymous sailor in the Soviet Union.

19. Department of the Navy, Office of Naval Intelligence, "Soviet Merships in Pacific—Index of," July 1, 1944, Navy Department Intelligence Report FT-49-441, folder MR450 (7): Location of Russian Ships 1943–1945, Map Room File, Franklin D. Roosevelt Library.

20. Conquest, *Kolyma: The Arctic Death Camps,* 221. However, Conquest also makes the point that the primary data on which homeport information is based (*Lloyd's Register of Shipping*) is often inaccurate.

21. Alla Paperno, *Тайны и История: Ленд-Лез Тихий Океан* [Secrets and history: Lend-Lease Pacific Ocean] (Moscow: Terra-Book Club, 1998), 223.

22. Tables 4.1 and 4.2 identify sources of firsthand evidence on the operation of Gulag transport ships over the period from 1932 to 1952. The time period is divided into sections: Initial years, Core Fleet years, Pre-War Surge years, World War II, Post-War Surge years and Final years. Where a firsthand account exists of a specific ship being used in a specific year, initials corresponding to the source of that account have been entered into the appropriate cell. The initials correspond to firsthand sources as indicated below. Where information other than a firsthand account indicates a ship was used in a given year, the corresponding cell has been shaded.

AG: A.V. Gorbatov, *Years Off My Life* (New York: W.W. Norton, 1964), 124–126.

AS: Aleksandr I. Solzhenitsyn, *The Gulag Archipelago: 1918–1956* (Boulder, Colo.: Westview Press, 1998), vol. 1, 581–82.

BD: Memorial (Kursk), "Джафарова Берта Самойловна [Dzhafarova Berta Samoblovna]," www.memorial.krsk.ru/martirol/dj_dl.htm (December 2002).

BL: Sakharov Center, "Лесниака Бориса Николаевича [Lesnyak Boris Nicolaevich]," <http://www.sakharov-center.ru/adcs/bio/99.htm> (July 2001).

CK: Sylvester Mora and Piotr Zwierniak, *Sprawiedliwoœæ Sowiecka* [Soviet justice] (Wlochy, 1945), 213. This book contains testimony of a Polish prisoner identified only as "C.K."

DA: Memorial (Tomsk), "Есть люди нелегкой судьбы... [There are people of hard destiny . . .]," <http://www.memorial.tomsk.ru:8100/memo/lud/ade.htm> (August 2001). This is a biography of Daniel Egorovich Alina.

EG: Evgenia Semyonovna Ginzburg, *Journey into the Whirlwind* (New York: Harcourt, Brace and World, 1967)

EL: Elinor Lipper, *Eleven Years in Soviet Prison Camps* (Chicago: Henry Regnery Company, 1951), 92–4.

IK: Victor Kravchenko, *I Choose Justice* (New York: Charles Scribner's Sons, 1950), 288–91. Kravchenko relays the story of Ivan Krevsoun, a passenger aboard *Svirstroi* who also witnessed *Volkhovstroi* and *Shaturstroi.*

IP: Zhores A. Medvedev, "Stalin and the Atomic Gulag," *Spokesman Books* (2001): 105, www.spokesmanbooks.com/spokesman/spksmn_69.htm (December 2002). This article cites an unpublished letter from I.P. Samokhvalov.

GL: Elena Glinka, "The Big Kolyma Streetcar," *Russian Life* 31:3 (March 1998): 40.

GN: Nadezhda Grankina, "Notes by Your Contemporary," *Till My Tale Is Told*, ed. Simeon Vilensky (Bloomington: Indiana University Press, 1999), 138–39.

KA: Sylvester Mora and Piotr Zwierniak, *Sprawiedliwoœæ Sowiecka* [Soviet justice] (Wlochy, 1945). The book reports on the personal testimony of a passenger identified only as "K.A."

KO: Е.Е. Starobinskij, "Менеджмент и психология в бизнесе: Королев С.П. [Management and psychology in business: Korolev, S.P.]" (2001), <http://www.ukrinter.com/ssart_board_view.asp?ID=17&MID=4> (January 2002).

LG: "Восстание троцкистов на Колыме [Troskyite insurrection in Kolyma]," www.gulag.ru/page/zk/v_Trozk/v_trozk.htm (December 2002). Manuscript detailing the transport of L.I. Girshik to the Kolyma Gulag.

LR: Larissa Ratushnaya, "Этюды О Колымских Днях [Essays about days in Kolyma]" (1999), www.art.uralinfo.ru/LITERAT/Ural/Ural_7_99/Ural_07_99_08.htm (December 2002).

MS: Michael Solomon, *Magadan* (New York: Vertex, 1971), 84–88 and 92–97.

NS: Nadezhda Surovtseva, " Vladivostok Transit," *Till My Tale Is Told*, ed. Simeon Vilensky (Bloomington: Indiana University Press, 1999), 184.

NV: "Военнопленные [Military prisoners]," *Невское Время* [Neva times], November 5, 1998, www.pressa.spb.ru/newspapers/nevrem/arts/nevrem-1843-art-14.html (December 2002).

ON: Memorial (Kursk), "Сообщение Юстины Николаевны Нагляк [Nikolaevich Naglyak Ustina's message]," www.memorial.krsk.ru/svidet/mnagl.htm (December 2002).

RL: Raul Fumagali, "My Polish Friend: Amazing Life and Adventures," www.thelatinmass.com/lopacki.html (December 2002). This manuscript relays the experiences of Richard Lopacki in the Kolyma camps.

SG: Novokuznetsk City Study of Local Lore Museum, "Сергеев Александр Григорьевич [Sergey Alexander Grigor'evich]" (1995), www.kuzbass.ru/nkz/stalinsk/sergeev.htm (December 2002).

SK: Stanislaw J. Kowalski, "White Auschwitz of Kolyma," www.gulag.hu/white_auschwitz.htm (December 2002).

SL: Marion Sloma, "Lasciate Ogni Speranza," www.najmici.org/kolyma/ksiazka11.htm (December 2002).

SO: Memorial (Kursk), "Сообщение Михаила Николаевича Соболева [Michael Nikolaevicha Soboleva's message]," www.memorial.krsk.ru/svidet/mnsobol.htm (December 2002). This is the biography of Nikolai Fyodorovich Soboleva.

SV: "Биография Нины Владимировны Сароевы (Biography of Nina Vladimirovna Saroeva)," <http://www.sakharov-center.ru/adcs/bio/98.htm> (January 2001).

TL: Zhores A. Medvedev, "Stalin and the Atomic Gulag," *Spokesman Books* (2001): 105, www.spokesmanbooks.com/spokesman/spksmn_69.htm (December 2002).

TS: Thomas Sgovio, *Dear America* (New York, Partners' Press Inc., 1979), 138.

VN: A.G. Kozlov, "Кого Карал НКВД? [Who Punished the NKVD]" <http://www.kolyma.ru/magadan/history/repres.shtml> (January 2002). This citation refers to Vasili Antonovich Noblin and places the date as July 1931. However, this is likely a mistake as the first shipments did not arrive until 1932.

VP: Vladimir Petrov, *Soviet Gold: My Life as a Slave Laborer in the Siberian Mines* (New York: Farrar, Straus, 1949), 148–157, 403–407.

VS: Varlam Shalamov, *Kolyma Tales* (London: Penguin Books, 1994), 175.

YM: Yuri Illarionovich Moiseenko, "Поэзия Каторги [Poetry Katorgi]," www.MTU-NET.ru/rayner/avtorskaja/poes_katorgi11.htm (December 2002).

23. There is some evidence to suggest that both *Kolyma* and *Sovietskaya Gavan* served nonetheless in some capacity with Dal'stroi. Historian John McCannon makes reference to a fleet of seven oceangoing ships operated by Dal'stroi, five of which are those identified by Conquest. For example, at 1,528 gross tons, *Kolyma* was a small ship, only one-sixth the size of *Felix Dzerzhinsky*. Given the relatively large size of the ships in the core Dal'stroi fleet—an average of 6,800 gross tons—the much smaller *Kolyma* seems out of place.

24. Terrance Armstrong, *The Northern Sea Route: Soviet Exploration of the North East Passage* (London: Syndics of the Cambridge University Press, 1952), 24.

25. *Lloyd's Register of Shipping: 1935–36* (London: Lloyd's Register of Shipping, 1936).

26. Peter Horensma, *The Soviet Arctic* (London: Routledge, 1991), 56.

27. Paperno. The captains of *Dalstroi*, *Dzhurma*, and *Felix Dzerzhinsky* were also arrested, and the first two were shot.

28. Conquest, *Kolyma: The Arctic Death Camps*, 47–48.

29. Aleksandr I. Solzhenitsyn, *The Gulag Archipelago: 1918–1956* (Boulder, Colo.: Westview Press, 1998), vol. 1, 535. The individual quoted possibly overestimated the number of prisoners being moved each month.

30. Gakkel, "Арктическая Навигация 1937 Года [Arctic Navigation 1937]," *Проблемы Арктика* [Arctic Problems] *1* (*1938*): 117–34. Given the routing, it is unlikely this specific voyage was in support of Gulag operations.

31. John McCannon, *Red Arctic: Polar Exploration and the Myth of the North in the Soviet Union, 1932–1939* (New York: Oxford University Press, 1998), 172. NarkomVodTrans was also affected by the changes. N.M. Ianson, the former director of NarkomVodTrans and later deputy head of Glavsevmorput, was himself arrested in the 1937 purges and sentenced to death.

32. Dallin and Nicolaevsky, 137. There is potential for confusion of *Komsomolsk* with *Komsomol*, another Soviet merchant ship. *Komsomol* was built in 1932 in the Soviet Union and sunk at sea in December 1936 by Nationalist forces during the Spanish Civil War. It was employed in shipping cargo to Kolyma in the early 1930s, but there are no records of its having carried forced laborers. The *Komsomolsk* was built in 1936 in the United Kingdom as a specialized Arctic timber carrier and is the one referred to here.

33. Paperno, 229–30.

34. The exact number may never be known, but an analysis of Soviet merchant ships operating in 1939 and their subsequent fates indicates that at least sixty of these ships were lost in 1941, another forty in 1942, and about twenty in 1943. The actual number is probably much higher.

35. Material about Lend-Lease in the following paragraphs is from Robert Huhn

Jones, *The Roads to Russia: United States Lend-Lease to the Soviet Union* (Norman: University of Oklahoma Press, 1969).

36. Office of Chief of Naval Operations, *ONI-208R: Russian Merchant Vessels* (Washington, D.C.: Intelligence Division, December 20, 1942). As described in the appendices, *Dekabrist* was sunk by German Ju-88 aircraft of unit I/KG30 on November 4, 1942, during Operation FB, the disastrous attempt to send merchant ships to Russia without escort. *Kiev* was torpedoed and sunk by *U-435* on April 13, 1942, in convoy QP-10.

37. War Shipping Administration, Office of the Russian Shipping Area, *Lend Lease Voyage Ledgers,* National Archives and Records Administration, Record Group 248.3.3, boxes 21–35. The War Shipping Administration maintained handwritten records of each voyage.

38. G. Rudnev, *Огненные Рейсы* [Fiery flights] (Vladivostok: Dal'nevostochnoe Book Publishing House, 1975), 15.

39. While Soviet sources and maritime registers report that *Svirstroi* was sunk, intelligence reports during World War II suggest it was captured. See Office of Chief of Naval Operations, *ONI-208-J (Revised): Japanese Merchant Ships Recognition Manual* (Washington, D.C.: Intelligence Division, 1944), 255.

40. Rudnev, 61.

41. Jürg Meister, *Soviet Warships of the Second World War* (London: Macdonald and Jane's, 1977), 288, and P. Mulder, *De Schepeu v. de KNSM 1856–1981* (Amsterdam: Erato, 1983).

42. Petr Osichanskii, *П.П. Куянцев: Я Бы Снова Выбрал Море . . .* [P.P. Kuyantsev: I would again choose the sea . . .] (Vladivostok: Far Eastern Association of Sea Captains, 1998), 16–23.

43. In addition to the war losses, *Rabochii, Suchan,* and *Indigirka* were lost in accidents before the war, and *Dalstroi* just afterward.

44. Zhores A. Medvedev, "Stalin and the Atomic Gulag," *Spokesman Books* (2001): 105.

45. Elena, Glinka. "The Big Kolyma Streetcar," *Russian Life* 31: 3 (March 1998): 40.

46. Varlam Shalamov, *Kolyma Tales* (London: Penguin Books, 1994), 175.

47. *Nogin* is reported in an unpublished letter cited by Zhores A. Medvedev. *Odessa* is reported by Russell Working, "Odessa Last Breadth of Soviet Liberty," *Moscow Times,* 29 September 2000. The other ships are cited by Okupatsioonide Repressiivpoliitika Uurimise Riikiik Komisjon. There is an opportunity for confusion regarding the ship *Kamenets-Podolsk*—there were two such ships in the Soviet merchant fleet around this time. The first was constructed in 1915 in Britain and was sunk by German bombers off Elkjotshar on August 30, 1941, as documented by Meister, 290. This reference is to the ship constructed in 1944 in the United States and formerly known as the *Robert S. Abbot.*

48. U.S. Department of Defense, Defense Prisoner of War/Missing Personnel Office, *Memoirs* (Washington, D.C.: February 29, 2000), www.dtic.mil/dpmo/special/memoirs.pdf (December 2002). This document contains witness testimony submitted to the U.S. Russia Joint Commission on POWs/MIAs.

49. U.S. Department of Defense, Defense Prisoner of War/Missing Personnel Office, *The Gulag Study* (Washington, D.C.: 2001), www.dtic.mil/dpmo/special/gulag_study.pdf (December 2002). This is a compilation of reports on the poten-

tial presence of U.S. servicemen in Gulag camps, prepared by the Joint Commission Support Directorate of the United States and Russia.

50. D.M. Long, *The Soviet Merchant Fleet: Its Growth, Strategy, Strength and Weaknesses 1920–1999* (London: Lloyd's of London Press, 1986), 11.

51. Horensma, 121.

52. In working condition.

CHAPTER 5: BELOW DECKS:
THE PRISONERS' STORIES

1. Alexander Dolgun, *Alexander Dolgun's Story* (New York: Alfred A. Knopf, 1975), 153, 157.

2. Gustaw Herling, *A World Apart* (Harmondsworth: Penguin Books, 1951), 83.

3. David Nordlander, *Capital of the Gulag: Magadan in the Early Stalin Era, 1929–1941* (Chapel Hill: University of North Carolina, 1997), 150.

4. For example, Sylvester Mora and Piotr Zwierniak, *Sprawiedliwoœæ Sowiecka* [Soviet justice] (Wlochy, 1945). Also *Dark Side of the Moon* (London: Faber and Faber, 1946). For a more recent account, see Robert Conquest, *Kolyma: The Arctic Death Camps* (New York: Viking Press, 1978).

5. This information is available on the original arrangements plan for SS *Childar*, a copy of which is in the author's collection.

6. Stanislaw J. Kowalski "Kolyma: The Land of Gold and Death" (2000), www.personal.psu.edu/users/w/x/wxk116/sjk/kolyma4.htm (December 2002).

7. Michael Solomon, *Magadan* (New York: Vertex, 1971), 85.

8. Evgenia Semyonovna Ginzburg, *Journey into the Whirlwind* (New York: Harcourt, Brace and World, 1967), 353.

9. Thomas Sgovio, *Dear America* (New York: Partners' Press, 1979), 141.

10. Elinor Lipper, *Eleven Years in Soviet Prison Camps* (Chicago: Henry Regnery, 1951), 287–88.

11. *Dark Side of the Moon* (London: Faber and Faber, 1946), 157. Narrative of a prisoner with initials T.L.

12. A.V. Gorbatov, *Years Off My Life* (New York: W.W. Norton, 1964), 125.

13. Ginzburg, 353–54.

14. Lipper, 93.

15. Ibid., 95.

16. Janusz Bardach and Kathleen Gleeson, *Man Is Wolf to Man* (Berkeley: University of California Press, 1999), 191.

17. Solomon, 87–88.

18. Elena Glinka, "The Big Kolyma Streetcar," *Russian Life* 31:3 (March 1998): 39–43

19. Varlam Shalamov, *Kolyma Tales* (London: Penguin Books, 1994), 175–76. Shalamov's book is a series of short stories. Some of these may be a blend of fact and fiction. However, it is known from other sources that *KIM* was in Nagaevo Harbor in December 1947. See G. Rudnev, "Страшные Отголоски Минувшей Войны [Terrible echoes of the last war]," *Zavetniy Krai* 1 (1998), www.vld.ru/ppx/Kraj/Zkr1_pub.htm#Dalstroj (December 2002).

20. Solomon, 141. Here Solomon is relaying a tale told to him by a fellow camp inmate.

21. *Dark Side of the Moon* (London: Faber and Faber, 1946), 114.

22. Nadezhda Mandelstam, *Hope against Hope* (New York: Modern Library, 1999), 387.

23. Deposition of Victor Fedonuk, *Le Procès Kravchenko contre Les Lettres Françaises* (Paris: La Jeune Parque, 1949), 566.

CHAPTER 6: SHIPWRECKS IN THE FAR NORTH

1. Igor Samarin, "Sakhalin Lighthouses" (1999), www.sakhalin.ru/Engl/Region/lighthouses/lighthouses.htm (December 2002).

2. *Lloyd's Confidential Index: Foreign 1938* (London: Corporation of Lloyd's at Lloyd's, 1 June 1939); Jury Vedernikov, "Хроники Кораблекрушений В Российских Водах Дальнего Востока [Chronicle of ship-wrecks in the Russian waters of the Far East]," *Владивосток* [Vladivostok], May 25, 1996, www.vld.ru/ppx/Katastr/Cronics.htm (December 2002).

3. Svetlana Meshchanskaia, *Противостояние Японии и СССР/Бои у озера Хасан (29 июля–11 августа 1938 года)* [*Confrontation of Japan and USSR: fighting at Lake Khasan (July 29 to August 11, 1938)*] (Moscow: BTV-MN, 2002), 40.

4. Vedernikov.

5. Petr Osichanskii, *П.П. Куянцев: Я Бы Снова Выбрал Море . . .* [P.P. Kuyantsev: I would again choose the sea . . .] (Vladivostok: Far Eastern Association of Sea Captains, 1998), 40.

6. Vedernikov.

7. *Lloyd's Confidential Index: Foreign 1935* (London: Corporation of Lloyd's at Lloyd's, 1 June 1936); Sergei Gavrilov, "Трагедия Буксира Кит [Tragedy of the tug *Whale*]," *Новая Камчатская Правда* [New Kamchatka Truth], no. 41 (October 18, 2001), www.iks.ru/~nkp/arhiv/html_arhiv/2001/41/41_4.html (December 2002).

8. Stanislaw J. Kowalski, "White Auschwitz of Kolyma," www.gulag.hu/white_auschwitz.htm (December 2002).

9. Raul Fumagali, "My Polish Friend: Amazing Life and Adventures," www.thelatinmass.com/lopacki.html (December 2002).

10. Igor Samarin, e-mail to the author, February 10, 2002.

11. *Lloyd's Confidential Index: Foreign 1935*.

12. Petr Osichanskii, *П.П. Куянцев: Я Бы Снова Выбрал Море . . .* [P.P. Kuyantsev: I would again choose the sea . . .] (Vladivostok: Far Eastern Association of Sea Captains, 1998), 12.

13. David Nordlander, *Capital of the Gulag: Magadan in the Early Stalin Era, 1929–1941* (Chapel Hill: University of North Carolina, 1997), 256.

14. Osichanskii, 23.

15. Gakkel, "Арктическая Навигация 1937 Года [Arctic navigation 1937]," *Проблемы Арктика* [Arctic problems] 1 (1938): 117–34.

16. "Беспрецедентное Рейс Парохода Рабочий [Unprecedented voyage of the steamship *Rabochii*]," *Арктический Института Бюллетень* [Arctic Institute bulletin] 10 (1935): 342. Conquest claims the ship was carrying prisoners but mistak-

enly gives the year as 1933. Robert Conquest, *Kolyma: The Arctic Death Camps* (New York: Viking Press, 1978), 222.

17. Aleksandr I. Solzhenitsyn, *The Gulag Archipelago: 1918–1956* (Boulder, Colo.: Westview Press, 1998), vol. 1, 581.

18. Fumagali.

19. There are at least five accounts of this incident. Three prisoners in the Kolyma Gulag provide secondhand accounts of the incident as told to them by other prisoners. See Vladimir Petrov, *Soviet Gold: My Life as a Slave Laborer in the Siberian Mines* (New York: Farrar, Straus, 1949), 155. See also Elinor Lipper, *Eleven Years in Soviet Prison Camps* (Chicago: Henry Regnery, 1951), 93; and Evgenia Semyonovna Ginzburg, *Journey into the Whirlwind* (New York: Harcourt, Brace and World, 1967), 355–56. A reference to the incident, though with the year reported as 1938 rather than 1939, is in Solzhenitsyn, 582. The most complete account is from a passenger aboard the ship at the time. See Nadezhda Grankina, "Notes by Your Contemporary," *Till My Tale Is Told*, ed. Simeon Vilensky (Bloomington: Indiana University Press, 1999), 138–39.

20. Grankina, 139.

21. Ginzburg, 355–56.

22. James Oberg writes in *Uncovering Soviet Disasters* (New York: Random House, 1988), www.jamesoberg.com/russian/sub.html (December 2002), that "thousands of political prisoners" were suffocated during this incident. Oberg cites Solzhenitsyn as the source, yet this is not what Solzhenitsyn wrote in the work cited. See Solzhenitsyn, 582.

23. David Cantrill, "Lake Washington Research," 25 October 2001, personal e-mail. Cantrill is the archivist of the Kirkland Heritage Society.

24. There are several accounts of this incident, all from Russian sources. The most complete story, based on interviews with survivor Pavel Kuyantsev, can be found in Osichanskii, 16–23. The incident is also covered in Alla Paperno, *Тайны и История: Ленд-Лез Тихий Океан* [Secrets and history: Lend-Lease Pacific Ocean] (Moscow: Terra-Book Club, 1998), 242–43. Another account appears in G. Rudnev, "Страшные Отголоски Минувшей Войны [Terrible echoes of the last war]," *Zavetniy Krai* 1 (1998), www.vld.ru/ppx/Kraj/Zkr1_pub.htm#Dalstroj (December 2002).

25. Paperno, 241.

26. Lipper, 290–91.

27. Okupatsioonide Repressiivpoliitika Uurimise Riikiik Komisjon, "The Soviet Prison Camps in Extreme North and Estonian Political Prisoners in Kolyma," www.okupatsioon.ee/trykised/oll/oll_kolyma_vang1.html (December 2002).

28. Rudnev, "Страшные Отголоски Минувшей Войны."

29. Leonid Vinogradov, "Ржавые Свидетели Старой Трагедии Найдены [Rusty witnesses of old tragedy are found]," *Ежедневные Новости Владивосток* [Daily news Vladivostok] 183 (1998) novosti.vl.ru/1998/183/hap_01.html (January 2001).

CHAPTER 7: DID TWELVE THOUSAND PEOPLE STARVE TO DEATH ON *DZHURMA*?

1. Epigraph: Alec Brown, trans., *The Voyage of the Chelyuskin* (New York: Macmillan, 1935).

2. Roger W. Jordan, *The World's Merchant Fleets 1939: The Particulars and War-time Fates of 6,000 Ships* (London: Chatham, 1999), 480. The *Wilhelm Gustloff* was a 25,484-ton German passenger liner built in 1938. During the war, it was used by Germany as a hospital ship and U-boat accommodation ship. On January 20, 1945, while transporting refugees, including wounded German soldiers, out of the path of advancing Soviet forces, it was torpedoed and sunk by the Russian submarine *S-13*. Official estimates of those killed range from 5,100 to 5,384. Unofficial estimates are several thousands higher.

3. David Y. Dallin and Boris I. Nicolaevsky, *Forced Labor in Soviet Russia* (New Haven, Conn.: Yale University Press, 1947), 129.

4. Their work does cite a December 1945 interview with a Soviet merchant sailor, published in the journal *Sotsialisticheski Vestnik*. This article mentions the *Dzhurma*, but while this sailor confirms that the *Dzhurma* was used on Gulag routes from 1937 to 1940, it mentions nothing about the reported incident of 1933/34 . See "Кровью Омытое Советское Золото [Blood-washed Soviet gold]," *Социалистический Вестник* [Socialist bulletin] 21–22 (December 10, 1945): 579–80.

5. Robert Conquest, *The Great Terror: A Reassessment* (Oxford: Oxford University Press, 1990), 326. There is at least one mistake in this account. The *Dzhurma* was by no means the first ship to transport prisoners from Vladivostok to Ambarchik. The previous year, a convoy of six ships made the journey, and at least two of them were carrying Gulag prisoners. See William Barr, "First Convoy to the Kolyma: The Soviet Northeast Polar Expedition, 1932–33," *Polar Record* 19:123 (1979): 563–72.

6. John McCannon, *Red Arctic: Polar Exploration and the Myth of the North in the Soviet Union, 1932–1939* (New York: Oxford University Press, 1998), 65. McCannon asserts in a footnote (pp. 191–92) that the casualty figure of twelve thousand is greatly overstated. The depiction of Magadan as the destination rather than Ambarchik is simply an error, as confirmed in discussions between McCannon and this author.

7. Colin Thubron, *In Siberia* (New York: HarperCollins, 1999), 272.

8. Martin Amis, *Koba the Dread: Laughter and the Twenty Million* (New York: Talk Mirimax Boos, 2002). Amis gives no source for this information.

9. Steve Forbes, "Fact and Comment," *Forbes,* February 3, 2003. Forbes, referring to the broad arguments in Amis's book, adds that Amis's "indictment is unchallengeable."

10. In a copy of *Lloyd's Register of Shipping: 1935–36* (London: Lloyd's Register of Shipping, 1936) owned by the author, a new record for *Dzhurma* appears as a hand-pasted update to the 1935–36 edition. The original record for this ship, under the name *Brielle,* also appears in this edition. This update happened after the 1935–36 edition was published, which is consistent with the timing of the transfer to the Soviet Union. This simple hand-pasted update, which was clearly inconsistent with the original accounts of *Dzhurma*'s experiences in 1933–34, is what first caused this author to question those original accounts and subsequently launch this research project. Consequently, this volume occupies a place of special honor in the author's library.

11. See, for example, Aad Schol, *Koninklijke Nederlandsche Stoomboot-Maatschappij* [The Royal Netherlands Steamship Company] (Alkmaar: De Alk bv., 1998), 55. Similar sources include P. Mulder, *De Schepeu v. de KNSM 1856–1981*

(Amsterdam: Erato, 1983). These data are supported by official Dutch records—for example, *Staat der Nederlandsche Zeemat ea Koopvaarelyvloot* (1936).

12. Aleksandr G. Kozlov, "От Истории Колымских Лагерей: 1932–37 [From the history of the Kolyma camps: 1932–37]," *Краеведческие Записки* [Notes of the Museum of Regional History] 17 (1991): 78.

13. Dallin and Nicolaevsky, 129.

14. Terrance Armstrong, *The Northern Sea Route: Soviet Exploration of the North East Passage* (London: Syndics of the Cambridge University Press, 1952), 25–26. Armstrong's data are largely derived from translated Soviet arctic journals in the 1930s, including *Арктический Института Бюллетень* [Arctic Institute bulletin], *Совиетскайа Арктика* [Soviet Arctic], and *Проблемы Арктика* [Arctic problems].

15. Armstrong, 26. Names for the ships in 1931 are obtained from Barr, 563.

16. Barr, 563. Barr bases his account on published Soviet accounts of this voyage and notes, with understatement, that in regard to the one thousand passengers, "one can assume that few of these were volunteers."

17. Yevgenov, "Возвращение Судов Северо-восточной Экспедиции года 132 [The return of the ships of the 1932 northeastern expedition]," *Арктический Института Бюллетень* [Arctic Institute bulletin] 5 (1933): 118–24.

18. Aleksandr I. Solzhenitsyn, *The Gulag Archipelago: 1918–1956* (Boulder, Colo.: Westview Press, 1998), vol. 1, 581–82, explains how provisions were made to hide the nature of the "cargo" on the Gulag ships as they passed through La Perouse Strait, in Japanese waters. It should have been no more difficult to hide this cargo from airborne Western eyes in the Arctic. Clearly, it would have been more difficult to hide the ship's mission should direct contact be made during a *Chelyuskin* rescue operation. Of course, Stalin could have been motivated by reasons that had nothing to do with the potential for accidental discovery of Gulag ships. There are numerous examples of the Soviet Union—and Russia—refusing international help and thereby putting at risk military and civilian shipboard personnel.

19. The earliest known reference is by Eduard Belimov, "Тайна экспедиции Челюскина [Secrets of the Chelyuskin expedition]," *Новая Сибирь* [New Siberia] (March 9, 2000), www.newsib.cis.ru/2000_10/pancl_1.html (December 2002). Also see "Челюскинцы [Chelyuskin]," *Ежедневные Новости Владивосток* [Daily news Vladivostok] (November 17, 2000), novosti.vl.ru/index.php?f=ag&t=001117ag06 (December 2002)

20. Det Statistiske Departement, "Danmarks Vareindførsel og—Udførsel I Aaret 1933," *Statistisk Tabelværk, Femte Række, Litra D, No. 54* (Copenhagen: Det Statistiske Departement, 1934), 176, table 2.

21. Erik Ericksen, *Værftet bag de 1000 skibe: Burmeister & Wain Skibsværft* (Copenhagen: Burmeister and Wain, 1993).

22. *Refrigerator No. 13* was the most famous of this series. As would befit a ship with this number, it was involved in a disastrous collision with Soviet submarine *S-178* in October 1981. A major rescue operation was mounted, but thirty-one or thirty-two crewmen perished.

23. *Soviet Merchant Ships 1945–1968* (Homewell: Kenneth Mason, 1969), 148.

24. *Lloyd's Register of Shipping: 1935–36*. However, it is not axiomatic that a listing in *Lloyd's Register of Shipping* indicates the ship is afloat, especially for Soviet ships at this time, and particularly smaller ships.

25. Office of Chief of Naval Operations, *ONI-208R: Russian Merchant Vessels* (Washington, D.C.: Intelligence Division, December 20, 1942).

CHAPTER 8: QUESTIONS OF NUMBERS

1. Epigraph: Central Intelligence Agency, *The Soviet Forced Labor System: An Update*, F-1990-01720 (November 30, 1985), 4, www.foia.ucia.gov (December 2002). A formerly classified report declassified May 5, 1997.

2. Michael Solomon, *Magadan* (New York: Vertex, 1971), 85.

3. Stanislaw J. Kowalski, "White Auschwitz of Kolyma," www.gulag.hu/white_auschwitz.htm (December 2002).

4. Nadezhda Grankina, "Notes by Your Contemporary," *Till My Tale Is Told*, ed. Simeon Vilensky (Bloomington: Indiana University Press, 1999), 138.

5. David Y. Dallin and Boris I. Nicolaevsky, *Forced Labor in Soviet Russia* (New Haven, Conn.: Yale University Press, 1947), 128.

6. Robert Conquest, *Kolyma: The Arctic Death Camps* (New York: Viking Press, 1978), 224.

7. V.P. Bolotov, ed., "Документы о Гибели Парохода Индигирка в Районе п. Саруфуцу (о.Хоккайдо) в 1939 году [Documents about the destruction of the steamship *Indigirka* in the area of Sarufutsu (off Hokkaido) in 1939]" (1998), www.vld.ru/ppx/Indigir/Docs.htm (December 2002).

8. Varlam Shalamov, *Kolyma Tales* (London: Penguin Books, 1994), 175.

9. Russell Working, "Odessa Last Breadth of Soviet Liberty," *Moscow Times*, September 29, 2000.

10. Zhores A. Medvedev, "Stalin and the Atomic Gulag," *Spokesman Books* (2001): 105, www.spokesmanbooks.com/spokesman/spksmn_69.htm (December 2002).

11. Solomon, 84.

12. *Lloyd's Register of Shipping: 1935–36*. There were a number of 5,000-ton ships built in Scotland in 1939, including *Baron Semple, Barwon, Bhima, Broompark, Bundaleer, Cape Clear, Cefn-Y-Bryn, Dornoch, Hillong, Glenpark, Kaipaki, Saint Bernard, Sangara, Sansu,* and *Seaforth*. All of these ships can be accounted for in 1947, and none were operated by the Soviet Union.

13. Aleksandr I. Solzhenitsyn, *The Gulag Archipelago: 1918–1956* (Boulder, Colo.: Westview Press, 1998), vol. 1, 581.

14. Vladimir Petrov, *Soviet Gold: My Life as a Slave Laborer in the Siberian Mines* (New York: Farrar, Straus, 1949), 154.

15. Solomon, 92–98.

16. Petrov, 243.

17. Elinor Lipper, *Eleven Years in Soviet Prison Camps* (Chicago: Henry Regnery, 1951), 93.

18. Janusz Bardach and Kathleen Gleeson, *Man Is Wolf to Man* (Berkeley: University of California Press, 1999).

19. Alla Paperno, *Тайны и История: Ленд-Лез Тихий Океан* [Secrets and history: Lend-Lease Pacific Ocean] (Moscow: Terra-Book Club, 1998), 237.

20. "Кровью Омытое Советское Золото [Blood-washed Soviet gold]," *Социалистический Вестник* [Socialist bulletin] 21–22 (December 10, 1945): 579–80.

21. I.D. Batsaev, "Колымская Гряда Архипелага Гулаг, Заключенные [Kolyma Range of the Gulag Archipelago]," *Исторические Аспекты Северо-Востока России: Экономика, Образование, Колымский Гулаг* [Historical aspects of Russia's Northeast: Economics, formation of the Kolyma Gulag]" (1996): 50. The Batsaev data are cited in Stephen G. Wheatcroft, "Victims of Stalinism and the Soviet Secret Police: The Comparability and Reliability of the Archival Data—Not the Last Word," *Europe/Asia Studies* 51:2 (1999): 315.

22. Robert Conquest, *The Great Terror: A Reassessment* (Oxford: Oxford University Press, 1990), 325.

23. Conquest, *Kolyma: The Arctic Death Camps*, 227.

24. Central Intelligence Agency, Office of Research and Reports, *Soviet Gold Production, Reserves and Exports through 1954*, CIA/SC/RR 121 (October 17, 1955): 37, www.foia.ucia.gov (December 2002). A formerly classified report declassified January 23, 2001.

25. This table compares estimates of Kolyma camp population from a variety of sources. "Batsaev/Bacon" data represent the average number of prisoners during the year and are from (for 1942) Edwin Bacon, *The Gulag at War: Stalin's Forced Labour System in the Light of the Archives* (New York: New York University Press, 1994), 113, and (for other years) I.D. Batsaev, "Колымская Гряда Архипелага Гулаг, Заключенные [Kolyma Range of the Gulag Archipelago]," *Исторические Аспекты Северо-Востока России: Экономика, Образование, Колымский Гулаг [Historical Aspects of Russia's Northeast: Economics, Formation of the Kolyma Gulag]*" (1996): 50. "Sigachev/Zemskov" estimates are for prisoners as of January 1 of each year and are from S. Sigachev, "History of Magadan Town and Surrounding Territory," <http://www.kolyma.ru/History/dalstroi.htm> (January 2001) and Victor N. Zemskov, "Заключенные в 1930-ых (Демографические аспекты) [Prisoners in the 1930s – demographic aspects]" *Социологические Исследования [Sociological research]* 7 (1996): 6. "Kozlov" data measure the numbers of prisoners at the start of each year and are from A.G. Kozlov, "От Истории Колымских Лагерей: 1932–37 [From the History of the Kolyma Camps: 1932–37]," Краеведческие Записки [Notes of the Museum of Regional History] 17 (1991): 61–91.

"Pohl" data reflect number of prisoners during the month of September and are from Otto J. Pohl, *The Stalinist Penal System: A Statistical History of Soviet Repression and Terror, 1930–1953* (Jefferson: McFarland & Company, Inc., 1997), 43. It is unclear whether the "Pilyasov" data refer to estimates at points in time or annual averages. These data are from A.N. Pilyasov, *Динамика Промышленного Производства в Магаданской Области: 1932–1992 [Dynamics of Industrial Manufacturing in Magadan Area: 1932–1992]*, (Magadan, 1993), 225. The Batsaev, Zemskov, and Pilyasov data values were obtained from Wheatcroft, 315. Wheatcroft is also the source for the Tkachvca data.

26. Conquest, *Kolyma: The Arctic Death Camp*, 227. Conquest estimates shipments of prisoners as fifty thousand per year from 1932 to 1936 and again from 1942 to 1943 (by his calculation, seven years for a total of 350,000); and 200,000–210,000 per year from 1937 to 1941 and again from 1944 and through 1953 (by his calculation, for a total of 3,150,000).

27. Central Intelligence Agency, *The Soviet Forced Labor System: An Update*, F-1990-01720 (November 30, 1985):4, www.foia.ucia.gov (December 2002). A formerly classified report declassified May 5, 1997.

28. Batsaev.

29. Conquest, *Kolyma: The Arctic Death Camp*, 227.

30. Paperno, 232.

31. Conquest, *Kolyma: The Arctic Death Camp*, 223.

32. Bacon, 168.

33. Aleksandr Kozlov, *Исторический Сборник «Дальстрой» и «Севостлаг» ОГПУ НКВД СССР в Цифрах и Документах. 1931–1941 гг. Часть 1* [Historical collection of Dal'stroi and Sevvostlag OGPU/NKVD of the USSR, in figures and documents, 1931–1941, Part 1] Magadan: North-East Interdisciplinary Scientific Research Institute, 2001).

CHAPTER 9: THE NKVD'S SHIPS

1. Epigraph: K.R. Haigh, *Cableships and Submarine Cables* (London: Adlard Coles, 1968), 57.

2. Robert Conquest, *Kolyma: The Arctic Death Camp*s (New York: Viking Press, 1988), 36–48, 220–25, and appendix A.

3. Variations in spelling occur due to the evolution of Russian transliteration protocols and simple cases of human error. In the interest of historical accuracy, the author has repeated past variations in spelling for each ship's name as it has appeared in various publications over time.

4. The exact number is unknown. But *Dzhurma* operated full-time on the Gulag route from 1936 to at least 1950, except for the period 1941 to 1945, when it was mostly used on Lend-Lease supply duties, and in 1938, when it was under repair for at least part of the year. The estimate of 225,000 assumes the ship operated nine years full-time on the Kolyma route, made an average of ten voyages per year, and carried 2,500 people per voyage. These are very conservative estimates.

5. Aad Schol, *Koninklijke Nederlandsche Stoomboot-Maatschappij* [The Royal Netherlands Steamship Company] (Alkmaar: De Alk bv., 1998), 44.

6. Alla Paperno, *Тайны и История: Ленд-Лез Тихий Океан* [Secrets and history: Lend-Lease Pacific Ocean] (Moscow: Terra-Book Club, 1998), 223.

7. Ibid., 223.

8. Schol, 55. See also A.G. Kozlov, "От Истории Колымских Лагерей: 1932–37 [From the history of the Kolyma camps: 1932–37]," *Краеведческие Записки* [Notes of the Museum of Regional History] 17 (1991): 78.

9. For 1936 see Vladimir Petrov, *Soviet Gold: My Life as a Slave Laborer in the Siberian Mines* (New York: Farrar, Straus, 1949), 147–59. Petrov was a passenger on *Dzhurma* in 1936. For 1939 see Evgenia Semyonovna Ginzburg, *Journey into the Whirlwind* (New York: Harcourt, Brace and World, 1967). Ginzburg was a passenger on *Dzhurma* in 1939. See also Nadezhda Grankina, "Notes by Your Contemporary," *Till My Tale Is Told*, ed. Simeon Vilensky (Bloomington: Indiana University Press, 1999), 138–39. Grankina was also a passenger on *Dzhurma*. For 1949 see A.V. Gorbatov, *Years Off My Life* (New York: W.W. Norton, 1964), 124–26. Gorbatov was a passenger on *Dzhurma* in 1939 and 1940. For 1949 see Michael Solomon, *Magadan* (New York: Vertex, 1971), 92–98. Solomon was a passenger on *Dzhurma* in 1949.

10. For 1937 see Memorial (Kursk), "Джафарова Берта Самойловна (Dzhafarova Berta Samoblovna)," www.memorial.krsk.ru/martirol/dj_dl.htm (December 2002).

For 1938 see Yuri Illarionovich Moiseenko, "Поэзия Каторги [Poetry Katorgi]," www.MTU-NET.ru/rayner/avtorskaja/poes_katorgi11.htm (December 2002). For 1941 see Stanislaw J. Kowalski, "Kolyma: The Land of Gold and Death" (2000), www.personal.psu.edu/users/w/x/wxk116/sjk/kolyma4.htm (December 2002). Kowalski was a passenger on the *Dzhurma* in 1941. For 1944 see Memorial (Kursk), "Сообщение Михаила Николаевича Соболева [Michael Nikolaevicha Soboleva's message]," www.memorial.krsk.ru/svidet/mnsobol.htm (December 2002). This is the biography of Nikolai Fyodorovich Soboleva. For 1950 see Larissa Ratushnaya, "Этюды О Колымских Днях [Essays about days in Kolyma]" (1999), www.art.uralinfo.ru/LITERAT/Ural/Ural_7_99/Ural_07_99_08.htm (December 2002).

11. For 1937 see Nadezhda Surovtseva, "Vladivostok Transit," *Till My Tale Is Told*, ed. Simeon Vilensky (Bloomington: Indiana University Press, 1999), 184. For 1938 see Aleksandr I. Solzhenitsyn, *The Gulag Archipelago: 1918–1956* (Boulder, Colo.: Westview Press, 1998), vol. 1, 582. For 1940 see Elinor Lipper, *Eleven Years in Soviet Prison Camps* (Chicago: Henry Regnery, 1951), 93. Lipper relays several stories about the *Dzhurma* as told to her by other Kolyma prisoners. For the period 1937 to 1940 see "Кровью Омытое Советское Золото [Blood-washed Soviet gold]," *Социалистический Вестник* [Socialist bulletin] 21–22 (December 10, 1945): 579–80. An interview with an anonymous sailor in the Soviet Union confirms that *Dzhurma, Dalstroi, Felix Dzerzhinsky*, and *Sovietskaya Latvia* were used on this route at least during 1937 to 1940. This is the first known published account that mentions these ships in the context of Gulag service. For 1949 see Zhores A. Medvedev, "Stalin and the Atomic Gulag," *Spokesman Books* (2001): 105, www.spokesmanbooks.com/spokesman/spksmn_69.htm (December 2002).

12. War Shipping Administration, Office of the Russian Shipping Area, *Lend Lease Voyage Ledgers*. National Archives and Records Administration, Record Group [hereafter RG] 248.3.3, boxes 21–35. The War Shipping Administration maintained handwritten records of each voyage.

13. Records of the War Shipping Administration, Office of the Russian Shipping Area, 1942–46. These records are held by the U.S. National Archives and Records Administration, RG 248.3.3, boxes 21–36.

14. U.S. Department of Defense, Defense Prisoner of War/Missing Personnel Office, "The Gulag Study" (2001), www.dtic.mil/dpmo/special/gulag_study.pdf (December 2002). This is a compilation of reports on the potential presence of U.S. servicemen in Gulag camps, prepared by the Joint Commission Support Directorate of the United States and Russia.

15. Jeffrey Curtis and Ambrose Greenway, *Soviet Merchant Ships* (Homewell, Havant, Hampshire: Kenneth Mason, 1976), 64. As of 2002, the replacement *Dzhurma* was still in service, under the name *Pamela Gold*.

16. *Lloyd's Register of Shipping: 1935–36.*

17. Paperno, 223.

18. Ibid.

19. For the published record from 1939, see Lipper, 92–94. Lipper was a passenger on *Dalstroi* in 1939. Lipper also writes of the explosion aboard *Dalstroi* in 1946, but this incident is unlikely to be linked to a passenger voyage. For the 1938 incident, see Moiseyenko. For the voyage in 1940, see Marion Sloma, "Lasciate Ogni Speranza," www.najmici.org/kolyma/ksiazka11.htm (December 2002). Sloma was

a passenger aboard *Dalstroi* in 1940. For the 1942 record, see Raul Fumagali, "My Polish Friend: Amazing Life and Adventures," www.thelatinmass.com/lopacki.html (December 2002). Richard Lopacki, the subject of this manuscript, was a passenger on *Dalstroi* in 1942.

20. For 1936 and 1939 see Petrov, 157. For 1937 see Surovtseva, 184. For 1940, see Sylvester Mora and Piotr Zwierniak, *Sprawiedliwoœæ Sowiecka* [Soviet justice] (Wlochy, 1945). This book contains a number of anonymous testimonies of Polish prisoners in the Gulag, one of which refers to a voyage on *Dalstroi* in 1940. For the 1937–1940 period, see Социалистический Вестник [Socialist bulletin], 579–80.

21. Е.Е. Starobinskij, "Менеджмент и психология в бизнесе: Королев С.П. [Management and Psychology in Business: Korolev S.P.]" (2001), www.ukrinter.com/ssart_board_view.asp?ID=17&MID=4 (January 2002).

22. *Dalstroi* rescued survivors of the *Nippon Maru*, sunk by submarine USS *Skate* on July 16, 1945, off Sakhalin Island. See Robert J. Cressman, *The Official Chronology of the U.S. Navy in World War II* (Washington, D.C.: Naval Historical Center, 1995).

23. Petr Osichanskii, *П.П. Куянцев: Я Бы Снова Выбрал Море* . . . [P.P. Kuyantsev: I would again choose the sea . . .] (Vladivostok: Far Eastern Association of Sea Captains, 1998), 16–23.

24. Traditional submarine cables had a limited throughput of perhaps two to three hundred characters per minute. By surrounding the cable with a substance that would itself be magnetized by the currents passing through the cable, it was possible to improve the inductance of the cable and boost the transmission rate almost tenfold. The scientists at Western Electric developed such a material, a mixture of 80 percent nickel and 20 percent iron, suitably heat-treated. It was called Permalloy, and submarine cables that included a layer of this material around the transmission wires were said to be "loaded." Engineers at Telegraph Construction and Maintenance Company (Telcon) simultaneously developed a copper-nickel-iron alloy known as Mumetal that had characteristics similar to Permalloy.

25. G.L. Lawford and L.R. Nicholson, *The Telcon Story* (London: Telegraph Construction and Maintenance, 1950), 97. The *Great Eastern,* twice the size of *Dominia*, was used at times as a cable ship but had not been constructed for this purpose. Though half the size of *Great Eastern, Dominia* actually carried more cable.

26. Haigh, 272, 376.

27. Lawford and Nicholson, 107.

28. Haigh, 42.

29. Paperno, 223.

30. Ibid., 235.

31. "Биография Нины Владимировны Сароевы [Biography of Nina Vladimirovna Saroeva]," www.sakharov-center.ru/adcs/bio/98.htm (January 2001).

32. *Социалистический Вестник* [Socialist bulletin], 579–80.

33. Petrov, 406.

34. Grankina, 138–39.

35. G. Rudnev, "Страшные Отголоски Минувшей Войны [Terrible echoes of the last war]," *Zavetniy Krai* 1 (1998), www.vld.ru/ppx/Kraj/Zkr1_pub.htm#Dalstroj (December 2002).

36. Paperno, 239.

37. "Военнопленные [Military prisoners]," *Невское Время* [Neva times], November 5, 1998, www.pressa.spb.ru/newspapers/nevrem/arts/nevrem-1843-art-14.html (December 2002).

38. Conquest, *Kolyma: The Arctic Death Camps*, 25. This author has been unable to obtain independent confirmation of this assertion. It is known that *Kamenets-Podolsk*, a former World War II Liberty ship that carried at least some prisoners to the Gulag, was converted into a mother ship for the Vladivostok fishing fleet.

39. James A. Gibbs, *Pacific Graveyard* (Portland, Ore.: Binfords and Mort, 1950), 91.

40. *Redwing* was not so fortunate. Transferred to the regular U.S. Navy in 1941, it was destroyed by an underwater explosion off Tunisia in 1943. See Navy Department, *Dictionary of American Naval Fighting Ships* (Washington, D.C.: Naval Historical Division, 1963).

41. Ilze Bernsone and Aigars Miklavs, "The Latvians: A Seafaring Nation," *Latvian Institute* (2001), www.latinst.lv/seafaring.htm (December 2002). Aigars Miklavs of the Museum of Riga History and Navigation, e-mail to the author, July 20, 2001.

42. Paperno, 224.

43. For the published account of the 1949 voyage, see Solomon, 84–88. For the record of the 1941 voyage, see Fumagali. For information on the 1946 voyage, see Memorial (Tomsk), "Есть люди нелегкой судьбы . . . [There are people of hard destiny . . .]," www.memorial.tomsk.ru:8100/memo/lud/ade.htm (December 2002). This is a biography of Daniel Egorovich Alina. See also Zhores A. Medvedev, "Stalin and the Atomic Gulag," *Spokesman Books* (2001): 105, www.spokesmanbooks.com/spokesman/spksmn_69.htm (December 2002).

44. *Социалистический Вестник* [Socialist bulletin], 579–80.

45. Rudnev.

46. National Security Agency, *The Venona Documents* (Washington, D.C.: 1998), www.nsa.gov/docs/venona/docs/Nov43/01_Nov_1943_R4_m3_p1.gif (December 2002). Message 451 from San Francisco to Moscow for November 1, 1943.

47. James Meusholt, "Burrard Dry Dock Co. Ltd." Unpublished manuscript, circa 1970.

48. Conquest, *Kolyma: The Arctic Death Camps*, 233, mistakenly lists the name as *Bitoe*.

49. *Lloyd's Register of Shipping: 1935–36.*

50. G.J. de Boer, *The Centenary of the Stoomvaart Maatschappij "Nederland" 1870–1970* (Kendal, England: World Ship Society, 1970).

51. Novokuznetsk City Study of Local Lore Museum, "Сергеев Александр Григорьевич [Sergey Alexander Grigor'evich]" (1995), www.kuzbass.ru/nkz/stalinsk/sergeev.htm (December 2002).

52. For the 1936 voyage see "Восстание троцкистов на Колыме [Troskyite insurrection in Kolyma]," www.gulag.ru/page/zk/v_Trozk/v_trozk.htm (December 2002). This manuscript details the transport of L.I. Girshik to the Kolyma Gulag. For the 1937 record see Surovtseva, 184. See also Solzhenitsyn, 581.

53. Paperno, 223.

54. The use of *Kulu* in the evacuation of wounded soldiers from Lake Khasan is described in G. F. Krivosheeva, ed., *Россия и СССР в Войнах XX Века: Потери*

Вооруженных СИЛ [Russia and the USSR in wars of the 20th century: Losses of armed forces] (Moscow: Olma Press, 2001).

55. *Социалистический Вестник* [Socialist bulletin], 579–80.

56. The 1945 record is from the Office of Chief of Naval Operations, *ONI-208R: Russian Merchant Vessels* (Washington, D.C.: Intelligence Division, December 20, 1942). See also *Lloyd's Register of Shipping: 1935–36*, and E.C. Talbot-Booth, *Merchant Ships 1959* (London: Journal of Commerce, 1959).

57. Oleg Dejev, conversation with the author June 1, 2002. Dejev, who now lives in Chicago, worked as an electrician for Dalmoreprodukt before migrating to the United States. He maintains a keen interest in the Dalmoreprodukt fleet. His father was a mechanic for Dalmoreprodukt and worked aboard *Kulu*.

58. *China Navigation Company Limited: A Pictorial History 1872–1992* (Hong Kong: John Swire and Sons, 1992).

59. H.W. Dick and S.A. Kentwell, *Beancaker to Boxboat: Steamship Companies in Chinese Waters* (Canberra: Nautical Association of Australia, 1958), 81.

60. Dick and Kentwell, 81–82.

61. "Great Lakes Vessels Index, Historical Collections of the Great Lakes," Bowling Green State University, www.bgsu.edu/colleges/library/hcgl/vessel.html (December 2002).

62. Ibid.

63. Thomas Sgovio, *Dear America* (New York: Partners' Press, 1979), 138. Sgovio boarded *Indigirka* on August 2, 1938.

64. Paperno, 223–24.

65. The author has compared photographs of *Ripon* taken in 1919 with photographs of the wreckage of *Indigirka* taken in 1939. It is clearly the same ship, and the wreckage bears no resemblance to the *Tsinan*.

66. Osichanskii.

CHAPTER 10: THE WESTERN CONNECTION

1. Epigraph: request for two-hundred-thousand-dollar overhaul for *Dzhurma* in Portland, Oregon. War Shipping Administration, Office of the Russian Shipping Area, *Memo from J.B. Hutchins, Director of Russian Area for the War Shipping Administration, to H.M. Salisbury of the Foreign Economic Administration* (March 27, 1945). National Archives and Records Administration, Records of the Soviet Far East Region 1942–46, Record Group [hereafter RG], 238, box 26.

2. Information in this section is taken largely from U.S. Shipping Board, Operations Organization, Ship Sales Division, General Records 1919–1936. National Archives and Records Administration, RG 32 B190 069/06/01, box 202, folder S-128-1: "Ship Sales Data."

3. The Eugene Dietzgen Company was a producer of drafting instruments and slide rules, but there is another side to the story. Eugene's father, Joseph Dietzgen, was a well known author of Marxist dialectics in the middle and late 1800s. Eugene, who arrived in the United States in 1885, published papers on his father's political philosophy.

4. Ohsol became a U.S. citizen in Boston in 1913 and was probably living in Washington, D.C., between 1916 and 1919. (His children were born during those years in Washington.) By 1922 he was back in New York, residing at 2074 Mohegan

Avenue in the Bronx. Two years later his address was 880 West 180th Street, New York. He made at least two trips overseas, arriving again at Ellis Island in 1922 (with his wife Klara, son Ernest, daughter Eleanor) and 1924, both times from Southampton, England.

5. "Ohsol Defends Himself," *New York Times*, June 21, 1913, 11:4.

6. "Links Socialists with Beef Inquiry," *New York Times*, October 21, 1919, 19:6.

7. "Soviet Contracts," *New York Times*, September 10, 1922, 10:6.

8. "Amtorg Chief's Right to Enter Country Challenged by Fish," *New York Times*, July 23, 1930, 1:3. (The reference is not to sea life but to Hamilton Fish, a congressman at that time.)

9. United States Shipping Board, "Ship Sales Data" Prices paid were $92,000 for *Chebaulip*, $90,000 for *Aledo*, $82,000 for *Dallas*, $80,000 for *Galesburg*, $69,000 for *Masuda*, $66,000 for *Bellingham*, and $61,000 for *Puget Sound*. These were significant discounts from the original asking prices. For example, the asking price for *Chebaulip* was $141,000.

10. United States Shipping Board, Operations Organization, Ship Sales Division General Records, 1919–1936. National Archives and Records Administration, RG 32 B190 069/06/01, box 1, folder S-101-3 Part 2: "Classification of the Fleet."

11. U.S. Maritime Commission, Division of Operations 1917–1949, *Vessel Movement Cards*. The commission maintained records of ship movements on index cards. These are available at the National Archives and Records Administration, RG 178 B190 079/18/04, boxes 1–24.

12. "Sanctions Sale of 5 Ships," *New York Times*, February 13, 1930, 43:1.

13. A.G. Kozlov, "От Истории Колымских Лагерей: 1932–37 [From the history of the Kolyma camps: 1932–37]," *Краеведческие Записки* [Notes of the Museum of Regional History] 17 (1991): 78.

14. Robert Huhn Jones, *The Roads to Russia: United States Lend-Lease to the Soviet Union* (Norman: University of Oklahoma Press, 1969), 238.

15. Robert E. Sherwood, as quoted by Jones, 113. Sherwood was Director of Overseas Operations in the Office of War Information.

16. Central Intelligence Agency, *Status of Soviet-Held US Lend-Lease Vessels— S-2278* (Washington, D.C.: Office of Research and Reports, April 18, 1967), 2. Formerly classified report declassified January 23, 2001.

17. Central Intelligence Agency, *Current Use and Maintenance of Merchant Ships Acquired by the USSR under Lend Lease* (Washington, D.C.: December 31, 1954), 2. Formerly classified report declassified on January 9, 2001.

18. Russell Working, "Odessa Last Breadth of Soviet Liberty," *Moscow Times*, September 29, 2000. The article cites claims by Nikolai Turkutyukov, a worker on the Lend-Lease program during World War II, that several Liberty ships, including *Odessa*, were employed on Gulag transport duties shortly after their arrival from the United States.

19. Central Intelligence Agency, *Status of Soviet-Held US Lend-Lease Vessels*, 2.

20. George R. Jordan, *From Major Jordan's Diaries* (New York: Harcourt Brace, 1952).

21. James Meusholt, "Burrard Dry Dock Co. Ltd." Unpublished manuscript, circa 1970.

22. Letter to the author from Robert A. Hennig, September 10, 2001.

23. Unless otherwise noted, data in the following section is taken largely from records of the War Shipping Administration, Office of the Russian Shipping Area, 1942–46. These records are held by the U.S. National Archives and Records Administration, RG 248.3.3, boxes 21–36.

24. Memorial (Kursk), "Сообщение Михаила Николаевича Соболева [Michael Nikolaevicha Soboleva's message]," www.memorial.krsk.ru/svidet/mnsobol.htm (December 2002). This is the biography of Nikolai Fyodorovich Soboleva. Additional information about the use of *Dzhurma* on the Kolyma route in 1944 is in Alla Paperno, *Тайны и История: Ленд-Лез Тихий Океан* [Secrets and history: Lend-Lease Pacific Ocean] (Moscow: Terra-Book Club, 1998).

25. National Security Agency, "Report from 'Sergej' on the Suicide in San Francisco of a Seaman," *The Venona Documents* (Washington, D.C.: 1998), www.nsa.gov/docs/venona/docs/Apr45/05_Apr_1945_R4_m1_p1.gif (December 2002). Message 54 from San Francisco to Moscow dated April 5, 1945. The U.S. National Security Agency recently published intercepts of Soviet communications conducted within the United States during World War II. These are known as the "Venona transcripts." It turns out that many of these intra-Soviet communications deal with merchant ship issues; at least three of these mention the *Dzhurma*, including an April 1945 transcript describing the suicide of a boatswain named Aleksej Yanovich Zajchenks while the ship was in Portland, Oregon.

26. Meusholt.

27. Paperno.

28. Roger Dingman, *Ghost of War: The Sinking of Awu Maru and Japanese-American Relations, 1945–1995* (Annapolis, Md.: Naval Institute Press, 1997), 21.

29. Far East Customs Management, "Находкинской таможне 50 лет [Customs house of 50 years]" (May 31, 2001), dvtu.vladivostok.ru/pres3105.htm (December 2002). This article describes the involvement of both *Dalstroi* and *Felix Dzerzhinsky* in the mission. *Kulu* may have also participated, but this is an inference—its schedule of sailing from Portland for Nakhodka matches the profile of some of the other (unnamed) ships in the Gripsholm mission.

30. Dingman, 7.

31. "Военнопленные [Military prisoners]," *Невское Время* [Neva times] 201 (November 5, 1998), www.pressa.spb.ru/newspapers/nevrem/arts/nevrem-1843-art-14.html (December 2002).

32. John Earl Haynes and Harvey Klehr, *Venona: Decoding Soviet Espionage in America* (New Haven, Conn.: Yale University Press, 1999), 32.

33. National Security Agency, "KIM (1945)," *The Venona Documents* (Washington, D.C.: 1998), www.nsa.gov/docs/venona/docs/Sept45/19_Sept_1945_R5_m1_p1.gif (December 2002). See transcript for September 19, 1945, message 100.

CHAPTER 11: WHAT DID THE WEST KNOW, AND WHEN DID IT KNOW IT?

1. Yarnell epigraph: letter, Harry E. Yarnell, commander of the U.S. Asiatic Fleet, to Admiral W.D. Leahy, Chief of Naval Operations, August 1, 1937, President's Secretary's Safe (PSF) Files, Departmental Files/Navy/Oct 36–37, Franklin D. Roosevelt Library. Yarnell's letter was forwarded to President Roosevelt.

Arnold epigraph: Otis Hays Jr., *Home from Siberia: The Secret Odysseys of Interned*

American Airmen in World War II (College Station: Texas A & M University Press, 1990), 145–46. Arnold is describing—forty-four years after the event—his exposure to large numbers of Kolyma Gulag prisoners.

2. Sylvester Mora and Piotr Zwierniak, *Sprawiedliwoœæ Sowiecka* [Soviet justice] (Wlochy, 1945).

3. *Dark Side of the Moon* (London: Faber and Faber, 1946).

4. "Кровью Омытое Советское Золото [Blood-washed Soviet gold]," *Социалистический Вестник* [Socialist bulletin] 21–22 (December 10, 1945): 579–80. An interview with an anonymous sailor in the Soviet Union.

5. David Y. Dallin and Boris I. Nicolaevsky, *Forced Labor in Soviet Russia* (New Haven, Conn.: Yale University Press, 1947), 108–46.

6. Silvester Mora, *Kolyma: Gold and Forced Labor in the USSR* (Washington, D.C.: Foundation for Foreign Affairs, 1949).

7. Vladimir Petrov, *Soviet Gold: My Life as a Slave Laborer in the Siberian Mines* (New York: Farrar, Straus, 1949).

8. Elinor Lipper, *Eleven Years in Soviet Prison Camps* (Chicago: Henry Regnery, 1951).

9. Robert Conquest, *Kolyma: The Arctic Death Camps* (New York: Viking Press, 1978)

10. H.P. Smolka, *40,000 against the Arctic: Russia's Polar Empire* (New York: William Morrow, 1937).

11. John D. Littlepage and Demaree Bess, *In Search of Soviet Gold* (New York: Harcourt, Brace, 1938), 135.

12. Ibid., 134–35. It might also be noted that Littlepage evidently believed in every particular the coerced testimonies from the show trials in the mid-1930s.

13. Timothy A. Taracouzio, *Soviets in the Arctic* (New York: Macmillan, 1938)

14. Terrance Armstrong, *The Northern Sea Route: Soviet Exploration of the North East Passage* (London: Syndics of the Cambridge University Press, 1952), 62.

15. Constantine Krypton, *The Northern Sea Route and the Economy of the Soviet North* (London: Methuen, 1956), 79.

16. Navy Department, *Dictionary of American Naval Fighting Ships* (Washington, D.C.: Naval Historical Division, 1963).

17. Nadezhda Surovtseva, "Vladivostok Transit," *Till My Tale Is Told*, ed. Simeon Vilensky (Bloomington: Indiana University Press, 1999), 184.

18. Steve Kovacs, "1937 Vladivostok Visit" (1999), www.internet-esq.com/_disc1/00000030.htm (December 2002). The contains the transcript of a letter from an officer or crew member of USS *Augusta* during the visit.

19. Yarnell.

20. The ships are silhouetted in the photograph, which makes it relatively easy to establish their outlines and compare them to known ships operating in the Soviet Far East fleets in the late 1930s, based on U.S. Navy ship recognition handbooks prepared for submarine crews. One ship is mostly likely *Svirstroi, Dneprostroi,* or *Volkhovstroi.* The other ship is most likely *Nevastroi, Kashirstroi,* or *Shaturstroi.* All were involved in Gulag operations, but only *Nevastroi* and *Dneprostroi* are confirmed in this operation in the late 1930s.

21. "700 Believed Dead on Russian Vessel," *New York Times,* December 14, 1939, 14.

22. War Department General Staff, Military Intelligence Division (Washington,

D.C., 1942), "Feasibility of Supply Route from Alaska to Irkutsk, Siberia via Lena River." Memo from Col. R.S. Bratton, chief of the division, May 25, 1942.

23. War Department, Office of the Chief of Staff, "Arctic Routes to Russia (Northeast Passage)," August 1, 1942, section 5:2. Map Room file 620, Russia folder: 1942–1944, Franklin D. Roosevelt Library.

24. Robert Huhn Jones, *The Roads to Russia: United States Lend-Lease to the Soviet Union* (Norman: University of Oklahoma Press, 1969), 210.

25. Records of the War Shipping Administration, Office of the Russian Shipping Area, *Lend Lease Voyage Ledgers*. National Archives and Records Administration, Record Group [hereafter RG] 248.3.3, boxes 21–35. The War Shipping Administration maintained handwritten records of each voyage. These records show that the *Dzhurma* in November 1942 sailed directly from Portland to Nagaevo.

26. Jones, 157.

27. Memo, Mr. O'Malley to Mr. Eden, May 31, 1943, President's Secretary's File (PSF) Safe Files: Winston Churchill, 1943, Franklin D. Roosevelt Library Digital Archives. In one of those curiosities that abound in this period, it was on board the same USS *Augusta* that President Roosevelt and Prime Minister Churchill signed the Atlantic Charter in August 1941.

28. Department of the Navy, Office of Naval Intelligence, "Soviet Merships in Pacific—Index of," July 1, 1944. Navy Department Intelligence Report FT-49-441, folder MR450 (7): Location of Russian Ships 1943–1945, Map Room file, Franklin D. Roosevelt Library.

29. Hays, 61.

30. The author learned of this individual's death moments after preparing a letter requesting assistance in this project. The letter was retrieved minutes before it would have been collected by the postman.

31. Joseph P. Kerns in a letter to the author, February 27, 2002. Kearns was a staff sergeant on an aircraft interned in the Soviet Union and encountered the Pottenger crew shortly after that crew was in Magadan. They spent the next several months together and were all released from Soviet internment at the same time.

32. Hays. Table compiled from accounts of individual crews.

33. Ibid., 60, 112, 141.

34. Alla Paperno, *Тайны и История: Ленд-Лез Тихий Океан* [Secrets and history: Lend-Lease Pacific Ocean] (Moscow: Terra-Book Club, 1998).

35. Henry A. Wallace, *Soviet Asia Mission* (New York: Reynal and Hitchcock, 1944), 35.

36. Owen Lattimore, *America and Asia: Problems of Today's War and the Peace of Tomorrow* (Claremont: Claremont Colleges, 1943).

CHAPTER 12: KOLYMA TODAY

1. Epigraph: "Russia's Deep Freeze," *U.S. News & World Report*, January 25, 1999, 35–37.

2. "Western Mining Firms Secure Licenses for Russian Gold Ground," *Northern Miner* 83: 31, 5.

3. Speech given at the Australian Graduate School of Management in Sydney, Australia, in April 2000, attended by the author.

4. "Kolyma Goldfields Private Placement," *Canadian Corporate News*, October 12, 1999.

5. Vladimir Dinets, "Hitchhiking to Oimyakon and Beyond" (1999), www.hotcity.com/~vladimir/kolyma.htm (December 2002).

APPENDIX A: OTHER WESTERN-BUILT SHIPS OF THE GULAG FLEET

1. Epigraph: Constantine Krypton, *The Northern Sea Route and the Economy of the Soviet North* (London: Methuen, 1956), 120.

2. *Lloyd's Register of Shipping: 1935–36* (London: Lloyd's Register of Shipping, 1936).

3. *Lloyd's List*, May 12, 1904. *Lloyd's List* was at the time a biweekly publication of the Corporation of Lloyd's, London.

4. A.E. Tapac, *Warships of the Imperial Russian Fleet, 1892–1917* (Minsk: Kharbast, 2000).

5. Novikov-Priboy, *Tsushima: Grave of a Floating City* (London: George Allen and Unwin, 1973), 351.

6. Sergey S. Berezhnoi, *Военные корабли и Суда Советского Морского Флота, 1917–1927* [The warships and auxiliary vessels of the Soviet Navy, 1917–1927] (Moscow: Military Publishing House of the Ministries of Defense of the USSR, 1981), 160.

7. This explains the incorrect history of the ship as reported in most registries, such as Lloyd's. These registries suggest the ship operated as *Franche-Comte* until 1918, when in fact the ship operated as *Anadyr* in the Russian and then Soviet navies for most of the period from 1904 to 1918.

8. Alexander Mariev, "Воспоминания [Memoirs]," *Уральская Галактика* [Ural galaxy] (1999), www.art.uralinfo.ru/literat/UG/ug3/mar_vosp.htm (December 2002). Mariev describes a trip in 1924 aboard *Dekabrist*.

9. Stanislaw J. Kowalski, "White Auschwitz of Kolyma," www.gulag.hu/white_auschwitz.htm (December 2002).

10. Shafig Amrakhov, "Транспорт: Держать по створ [Transport: To stay the course]" (1999), press.lukoil.ru/text.phtml?result_artic=438&result=66 (December 2002).

11. Mark Llewellyn Evans, *Great World War II Battles in the Arctic* (Westport, Conn.: Greenwood Press, 1999), 100.

12. Bob Ruegg and Arnold Hague, *Convoys to Russia: 1941–1945* (Kendal: World Ship Society, 1992), 45.

13. G. Rudnev, *Огненные Рейсы* [Fiery flights] (Vladivostok: Dal'nevostochnoe, 1975), 39. A detailed description of the survivors' plights can be found in Harry C. Hutson, *Arctic Interlude: Independent to Russia* (Bennington, Vt.: Merriam Press, 1997).

14. "«Декабрист» Приказано Разбомбить [Orders to destroy the *Dekabrist*]," № *Chukotka* 16 (May 2000), www.ropnet.ru/ogonyok/win/200016/16-03-03.html (December 2002).

15. David Y. Dallin and Boris I. Nicolaevsky, *Forced Labor in Soviet Russia* (New Haven, Conn.: Yale University Press, 1947), 137.

16. Ruegg and Hague, 32.

17. Rudnev, 15.

18. *Lloyd's Register of Shipping: 1935–36.*

19. Dallin and Nicolaevsky, 137.

20. Petr Osichanskii, *П.П. Куянцев: Я Бы Снова Выбрал Море . . .* [P.P. Kuyantsev: I would again choose the Sea . . .] (Vladivostok: Far Eastern Association of Sea Captains, 1998), 48.

21. For the 1940 reference, see Sylvester Mora and Piotr Zwierniak, *Sprawiedliwoœæ Sowiecka* [Soviet justice] (Wlochy, 1945). For the 1951 reference, see Elena Glinka, "The Big Kolyma Streetcar," *Russian Life* 31: 3 (March 1998): 40.

22. G. Rudnev, "Страшные Отголоски Минувшей Войны [Terrible echoes of the last war]," *Zavetniy Krai* 1 (1998), www.vld.ru/ppx/Kraj/Zkr1_pub.htm#Dalstroj (December 2002).

23. War Shipping Administration, *Lend Lease Voyage Ledgers.*

24. There is confusion as to where these ships were actually constructed. Gordon Newell, *The H.W. McCurdy Marine History of the Pacific Northwest* (Seattle: Superior, 1966), says that the ship were built in Seattle. Detailed records of the Todd Corporation demonstrate that they were the first three hulls started in the new Tacoma facility. Robert Conquest incorrectly reported these ships to have been constructed in Shooter's Island, New York. See Robert Conquest, *Kolyma: The Arctic Death Camp*s (New York: Viking Press, 1978), 232–33.

25. C. Bradford Mitchell, *Every Kind of Shipwork: A History of Todd Shipyards Corporation* (New York: Todd Shipyards, 1981), 41.

26. Ibid., 40.

27. *Lloyd's Register of Shipping: 1921–22* (London: Lloyd's Register of Shipping, 1922).

28. U.S. Maritime Commission, Division of Operations 1917–1949, *Vessel Movement Cards for Chebaulip*, National Archives and Records Administration, RG 178 B190 079/18/04, box 5.

29. Navy Department, *Dictionary of American Naval Fighting Ships* (Washington, D.C.: Naval Historical Division, 1963).

30. U.S. Maritime Commission, *Vessel Movement Cards for Chebaulip.*

31. *Lloyd's Register of Shipping: 1935–36* (London: Lloyd's Register of Shipping, 1936).

32. David Nordlander, *Capital of the Gulag: Magadan in the Early Stalin Era, 1929–1941* (Chapel Hill: University of North Carolina, 1997), 101.

33. *Lloyd's Register of Shipping: 1921–22* and subsequent years.

34. Navy Department, *Dictionary of American Naval Fighting Ships.*

35. U.S. Maritime Commission, Division of Operations 1917–1949, *Vessel Movement Cards for Bellingham.* National Archives and Records Administration, RG 178 B190 079/18/04, box 3.

36. Jürg Meister, *Soviet Warships of the Second World War* (London: Macdonald and Jane's, 1977), 288.

37. Aleksandr I. Solzhenitsyn, *The Gulag Archipelago: 1918–1956* (Boulder, Colo.: Westview Press, 1998), vol. 1, 581.

38. *Lloyd's Register of Shipping: 1921–22* and subsequent years.

39. U.S. Maritime Commission, Division of Operations 1917–1949, *Vessel Movement Cards for Puget Sound*, National Archives and Records Administration, RG 178 B190 079/18/04, box 19.

40. L.N. Garusova, "Российские-американские Региональные Отношения на Дальнем Востоке: История и Поток [Russian-American regional relations on the Far East: History and present]," abc.vvsu.ru/Books/m_rosamo/page0008.asp (July 2001).

41. Ivan Ivanovich Rodionova, "Хронология [Chronology]," *Russian Air Force* (2001) (www.AIRFORCE.ru/history/chronology/1930.htm [December 2002]).

42. W.H. Mitchell, W.H. Sawyer, and L.A. Sawyer, *British Standard Ships of World War I* (London: Journal of Commerce and Shipping Telegraph, 1968), 10.

43. Victor Kravchenko, *I Choose Justice* (New York: Charles Scribner's Sons, 1950), 291.

44. U.S. Maritime Commission, *Vessel Movement Cards for Puget Sound.*

45. Sergei Gavrilov, "Трагедия Буксира Кит [Tragedy of the tug *Kit*]," *Новая Камчатская Правда* [New Kamchatka truth], October 18, 2001.

46. Jury Vedernikov, "Хроники Кораблекрушений В Российских Водах Дальнего Востока [Chronicle of shipwrecks in the Russian waters of the Far East]," *Владивосток* [Vladivostok], May 25, 1996, www.vld.ru/ppx/Katastr/Cronics.htm (December 2002).

47. Meister, 267.

48. *Lloyd's Register of Shipping: 1921–22* and subsequent years.

49. *Lloyd's Register of Shipping: 1935–36.*

50. For the 1932 reference, see Nordlander, 101. For the 1938 reference, see Solzhenitsyn, 581.

51. War Shipping Administration, Office of the Russian Shipping Area, *Lend Lease Voyage Ledgers,* National Archives and Records Administration, Record Group 248.3.3, boxes 21–35. The War Shipping Administration maintained handwritten records of each voyage.

52. *Lloyd's Register of Shipping: 1921–22* and subsequent years.

53. U.S. Maritime Commission, Division of Operations 1917–1949, *Vessel Movement Cards for Aledo,* National Archives and Records Administration, RG 178 B190 079/18/04, box 1.

54. *Lloyd's Register of Shipping: 1935–36.*

55. Kravchenko, 290–91.

56. Osichanskii, 38.

57. Roger W. Jordan, *The World's Merchant Fleets 1939: The Particulars and Wartime Fates of 6,000 Ships* (London: Chatham, 1999), 577.

58. Syd Heal, e-mail message to the Marine History Information Exchange Group (February 22, 2002).

59. Rudnev, 6–8.

60. General Maltby's dispatches, as cited in Alan Birch and Martin Cole, *Captive Christmas: The Battle for Hong Kong—December 1941* (Hong Kong: Heinemann Asia, 1979), 100.

61. Office of Chief of Naval Operations, *ONI-208-J (Revised): Japanese Merchant Ships Recognition Manual* (Washington, D.C.: Intelligence Division, 1944), 255.

62. Robert J. Cressman, *The Official Chronology of the U.S. Navy in World War II* (Washington, D.C.: Naval Historical Center, 1995). Also available online at www.ibiblio.org/hyperwar/USN/USN-Chron/USN-Chron-1945.html (December 2002).

63. Ibid.

64. Rudnev, 8.

65. U.S. Maritime Commission, Division of Operations 1917–1949, *Vessel Movement Cards for Galesburg,* National Archives and Records Administration, RG 178 B190 079/18/04, box 10.

66. *Lloyd's Register of Shipping: 1935–36.*

67. Kravchenko, 290–91.

68. War Shipping Administration, *Lend Lease Voyage Ledgers.*

69. William L. Worden, *Cargoes: Matson's First Century in the Pacific* (Honolulu: University Press of Hawaii, 1981), 162.

70. *Soviet Merchant Ships 1945–1968,* 219. There is opportunity for confusion here, as another ship by the same name was constructed in Staten Island, New York, in 1918 and acquired by the Soviet Union. That ship was sunk in 1941. For the reference the earlier ship sunk by air attack, see Nikolay Mihin, "Венки на волне: Документальные очерки [Wreaths on a wave: Documentary sketches]" (1998), lib.ru/PROZA/MIHINN/venki.txt (December 2002).

71. Okupatsioonide Repressiivpoliitika Uurimise Riikiik Komisjon, "The Soviet Prison Camps in Extreme North and Estonian Political Prisoners in Kolyma," www.okupatsioon.ee/trykised/oll/oll_kolyma_vang1.html (December 2002).

72. Valery Chymakov, "Кому На Чукотке Жить Хорошо [Who on Chukotka can live well]," *№ Chukotka* (December 1999), www.ropnet.ru/ogonyok/win/199990/90-46-49.html (December 2002).

73. Memorial (Kursk), "Сообщение Антона Иосифовича Миронова [Anton Iosifovicha Mironova's message]" (1990), www.memorial.krsk.ru/svidet/mmiron.htm (December 2002).

74. Sergey S. Berezhnoi, *Советские Суда и Предоставляют Ленд-Лез* [Soviet ships and vessels of Lend-Lease] (St. Petersburg: Velen Publishing House, 1994), 278–79.

75. Berezhnoi, *Soviet Ships and Vessels of Lend Lease,* 278–79, lists the ship as having been broken up in the 1950s. Andrew Toppan reports in "Newport News Shipbuilding & Drydock Production Record" (2001), www.hazegray.org/shipbuilding/nnsb1.htm (December 2002), that the ship was still afloat in 1985.

76. Interview with Oleg Dejev, October 4, 2002. Dejev, a former fleet electrician in Vladivostok, reports seeing the *Balkhash* afloat in the Golden Horn in the mid-1990s prior to his emigration to the United States.

77. *Skinner & Eddy v. United States, 265 U.S. 86, 44 S.Ct. 446 (1924).*

78. Newell, 281.

79. Ibid., 377.

80. Meister, 291.

81. Office of Chief of Naval Operations, Intelligence Division, *ONI-B2: Soviet Merchant Shipping Pacific* (Washington, D.C.: Navy Department, July 1943). Available through National Archives and Records Administration, RG 38 370 13/17/01, boxes 347–48, entry 98A: Intelligence Division, Confidential Reports of Naval Attaches, serial 58–43.

82. Rudnev, 61.

83. Zhores A. Medvedev, "Stalin and the Atomic Gulag," *Spokesman Books* (2001): 105, www.spokesmanbooks.com/spokesman/spksmn_69.htm (December 2002).

84. Okupatsioonide Repressiivpoliitika Uurimise Riikiik Komisjon.

85. Memorial (Kursk), "Сообщение Юстины Николаевны Нагляк [Nikolaevich Naglyak Ustina's message]," www.memorial.krsk.ru/svidet/mnagl.htm (December 2002).

86. U.S. Department of Defense, Defense Prisoner of War/Missing Personnel Office, "The Gulag Study" (2001), www.dtic.mil/dpmo/special/gulag_study.pdf (December 2002). This is a compilation of reports on the potential presence of U.S. servicemen in Gulag camps, prepared by the Joint Commission Support Directorate of the United States and Russia.

87. Berezhnoi, *Soviet Ships and Vessels of Lend Lease*, 289–90.

88. Central Intelligence Agency, Office of Research and Reports, *Status of Soviet-Held U.S. Lend-Lease Vessels—S-2278* (April 18, 1967): 4, www.foia.ucia.gov (December 2002). Formerly classified report declassified January 23, 2001.

89. *Lloyd's Register of Shipping: 1935–36.*

90. Newell, 415.

91. Roger W. Jordan, 408.

92. Berezhnoi, *Soviet Ships and Vessels of Lend Lease*, 268.

93. Okupatsioonide Repressiivpoliitika Uurimise Riikiik Komisjon.

94. Central Intelligence Agency, *Status of Soviet-Held US Lend-Lease Vessels*, 2.

95. Meister, 263.

96. Peter Thompson, "Liberty Ships: Master List of Names," www.andrew. cmu.edu/~pt/liberty/liberty1.html (December 2002).

97. Berezhnoi, *Soviet Ships and Vessels of Lend Lease*, 325–26.

98. Russell Working, "Odessa Last Breadth of Soviet Liberty," *Moscow Times*, September 29, 2000. See also Alla Paperno, *Тайны и История: Ленд-Лез Тихий Океан* [Secrets and history: Lend-Lease Pacific Ocean] (Moscow: Terra-Book Club, 1998),144–45. Paperno's sources include the ship's log.

99. At the time of writing in mid-2002, the fate of *Odessa* is unclear. The owners, Dalmoreprodukt, are in bankruptcy proceedings, and *Odessa* has been listed for sale as scrap.

100. Thompson and *Lloyd's Register of Shipping: 1935–36.*

101. Okupatsioonide Repressiivpoliitika Uurimise Riikiik Komisjon.

102. Berezhnoi, *Soviet Ships and Vessels of Lend Lease*, 310–11.

103. Thompson and *Lloyd's Register of Shipping: 1935–36.*

104. Memorial (Kursk), "Сообщение Михаила Васильевича Иванова [Biography of Ivanov Mikhail Vasilievich]" (2001), www.memorial.krsk.ru/svidet/mmivan.htm (December 2002).

105. Okupatsioonide Repressiivpoliitika Uurimise Riikiik Komisjon.

106. Berezhnoi, *Soviet Ships and Vessels of Lend Lease*, 315–16.

107. Thompson (2001) and *Lloyd's Register of Shipping: 1935–36.*

108. Meister, 290.

109. Okupatsioonide Repressiivpoliitika Uurimise Riikiik Komisjon.

110. Berezhnoi, *Soviet Ships and Vessels of Lend Lease*, 318.

111. *Lloyd's Register of Shipping: 1935–36.*

112. Dallin and Nicolaevsky, 137.

113. War Shipping Administration, *Lend Lease Voyage Ledgers.*

114. *Lloyd's Register of Shipping: 1953–54* (London: Lloyd's Register of Shipping, 1954).

115. War Shipping Administration, *Lend Lease Voyage Ledgers.*

116. *Lloyd's Register of Shipping: 1935–36.*

117. David Woodward, *The Russians at Sea* (London: William Kimber, 1965), 204.

118. Silvester Mora, *Kolyma: Gold and Forced Labor in the USSR* (Washington, D.C.: Foundation for Foreign Affairs, 1949), 15.

119. Roger W. Jordan, 495.

120. Meister, 266.

APPENDIX B: SOVIET-BUILT GULAG SHIPS

1. Epigraph: I.D. Spasskii, ed., История Отечественного Судостроения: в Пяти Томах [History of domestic shipbuilding: In five volumes] (St. Petersburg: Shipbuilding Press, 1996), vol. 4, 68.

2. Aleksandr G. Kozlov, "От Истории Колымских Лагерей: 1932–37 [From the history of the Kolyma camps: 1932–37]," Краеведческие Записки [Notes of the Museum of Regional History] 17 (1991): 61.

3. See for example, Spasskii, 68–69.

4. *Soviet Merchant Ships 1945–1968* (Homewell: Kenneth Mason, 1969), 234.

5. William Barr, "First Convoy to the Kolyma: The Soviet Northeast Polar Expedition, 1932–33," *Polar Record* 19: 123 (1979): 563–72.

6. *Marine News,* July 1974. This is the monthly publication of the World Ship Society.

7. The trips are well documented in the Soviet literature of Arctic voyages of the 1930s.

8. Barr, 564.

9. *Lloyd's Confidential Index—Foreign 1938* (London: Corporation of Lloyd's at Lloyd's, June 1, 1939).

10. David Y. Dallin and Boris I. Nicolaevsky, *Forced Labor in Soviet Russia* (New Haven, Conn.: Yale University Press, 1947), 128.

11. Yevgenov, "Возвращение Судов Северо-восточной Экспедиции года 1932 [The return of the ships of the 1932 northeastern expedition]," Арктический Института Бюллетень [Arctic Institute bulletin] 5 (1933): 118–24.

12. *Soviet Merchant Ships 1945–1968,* 231.

13. Ibid.

14. Ibid.

15. Barr, 563.

16. The trips are well documented in the 1930s Soviet literature on the Northern Sea Route.

17. Dallin and Nicolaevsky, 137.

18. Bob Ruegg and Arnold Hague, Convoys to Russia: 1941–1945 (Kendal: World Ship Society, 1992).

19. *Soviet Merchant Ships 1945–1968,* 231.

20. "Беспрецедентное Рейс Парохода Рабочи [Unprecedented voyage of the steamship *Rabochii*]," Арктический Института Бюллетень [Arctic Institute bulletin] 10 (1935): 342.

21. Robert Conquest, *Kolyma: The Arctic Death Camps* (New York: Viking Press, 1978), 218. Conquest estimates that one-third of the initial batch of prisoners perished.

22. Gakkel', "Арктическая Навигация 1937 Года [Arctic navigation 1937]," *Проблемы Арктика* [Arctic problems] 1 (1938): 117–34.

23. Gerald Howson, *Arms for Spain: The Untold Story of the Spanish Civil War* (New York: St. Martin's Press, 1998), 133.

24. Varlam Shalamov, *Kolyma Tales* (London: Penguin Books, 1994), 175.

Selected Bibliography

GENERAL MERCHANT SHIP DIRECTORIES

Jordan, Roger W. *The World's Merchant Fleets 1939: The Particulars and Wartime Fates of 6,000 Ships.* London: Chatham, 1999.

Lloyd's Register of Shipping: 1921–22. London: Lloyd's Register of Shipping, 1922.

Lloyd's Register of Shipping: 1935–36. London: Lloyd's Register of Shipping, 1936.

Lloyd's Register of Shipping: 1952–53. London: Lloyd's Register of Shipping, 1953.

Talbot-Booth, E.C. *What Ship Is That?* London: Sampson Low, Marston, circa 1941.

———. *Merchant Ships 1943.* London: Macmillan, 1944.

———. *Merchant Ships 1959.* London: Journal of Commerce, 1959.

DIRECTORIES OF SOVIET AND RUSSIAN SHIPS

Berezhnoi, Sergey S. *Советские Суда и Предоставляют Ленд-Лез* [Soviet ships and vessels of Lend-Lease]. St. Petersburg: Velen Publishing House, 1994.

———. *Военные корабли и Суда Советского Морского Флота, 1917–1927* [The warships and auxiliary vessels of the Soviet Navy, 1917–1927]. Moscow: Military Publishing House of the Ministries of Defense of the USSR, 1981.

———. *Военные корабли и Суда Советского Морского Флота, 1928–1945* [The warships and auxiliary vessels of the Soviet Navy, 1928–1945]. Moscow: Military Publishing House of the Ministries of Defense of the USSR, 1988.

Bock, Bruno, and Klaus Bock. *Soviet Bloc Merchant Ships.* Annapolis, Md.: Naval Institute Press, 1981.

Central Intelligence Agency. *Status of Soviet-Held US Lend-Lease Vessels (S-2278).* Washington, D.C.: Office of Research and Reports, 1967. Report prepared April 18, 1967, and declassified January 23, 2001.

Curtis, Jeffery and Ambrose Greenway. *Soviet Merchant Ships.* Homewell, Havant, Hampshire: Kenneth Mason, 1976.

Greenman, David, and E.C. Talbot-Booth. *Warsaw Pact Merchant Ships: Recognition Handbook.* London: Jane's, 1987.

Meister, Jürg. *Soviet Warships of the Second World War.* London: Macdonald and Jane's, 1977.
Office of Chief of Naval Operations. *Russian Merchant Vessels: ONI 208-R.* Washington, D.C.: Intelligence Division, December 20, 1942.
———. *Russian Merchant Ships in the Pacific: ONI 208-R Revised.* Washington, D.C.: Intelligence Division, April 1945.
———. *Soviet Merchant Shipping—Pacific: Intelligence Report 63-43.* Washington, D.C.: Intelligence Division, 1943.
———. *Soviet Merchant Ships in Pacific—Current Listing. Op-16-F-8, ser. 11-41.* Washington, D.C.: Intelligence Division, February 16, 1943.
———. *Sino/Soviet Bloc Merchant Ships: Report ONI 36-1G.* Washington, D.C.: Intelligence Division, June 27, 1963.
Russian Maritime Register of Shipping. St. Petersburg, Russian Maritime Register of Shipping. Archival research of the register provided in personal communication to the author by Victor Volkov, August 2001.
Soviet Merchant Ships 1945–1968. Homewell, Havant, Hampshire: Kenneth Mason, 1969.
Тарас, А.Е. *Военные корабли Императорского Российского Флота, 1892–1917* [Warships of the imperial Russian fleet, 1892–1917]. Minsk: Kharbast, 2000.
Wilson, E.A. *Soviet Passenger Ships, 1917–1977.* Kendal, England: World Ship Society, 1978.

GENERAL HISTORY OF MERCHANT SHIPS

Andrews, Ralph W. and Harry A. Kirwin. *This Was Seafaring.* New York: Bonanza Books, 1955.
Det Statistiske Departement. "Danmarks Vareindførsel og—Udførsel I Aaret 1933." *Statistisk Tabelværk, Femte Række, Litra D, No. 54.* Copenhagen: Det Statistiske Departement, 1934.
Dunn, Laurence. *Merchant Ships of the World 1910–1929.* London: Blandford Press, 1973.
Garnham, S.A., and Robert L. Hadfield. *The Submarine Cable.* London: Sampson Low, Marston, 1934.
Gibbs, James A., Jr. *Pacific Graveyard.* Portland: Binfords and Mort, 1950.
Haigh, K.R. *Cableships and Submarine Cables.* London: Adlard Coles, 1968.
Hardy, A.C. *Merchant Ship Types.* London: Chapman and Hall, 1924.
Mitchell, W.H., and L.A. Sawyer. *British Standard Ships of World War I.* London: Journal of Commerce and Shipping Telegraph, 1968.
Newell, Gordon. *The H.W. McCurdy Marine History of the Pacific Northwest.* Seattle: Superior, 1966.

HISTORY OF SPECIFIC SHIPBUILDERS

Eriksen, Erik. *Værftet bag de 1000 skibe: Burmeister & Wain Skibsværft* [The company that launched a thousand ships: Burmeister & Wain Shipyard]. Copenhagen: Burmeister and Wain, 1993.

Middlemiss, Normal L. *British Shipbuilding Yards.* Vol. 3. Newcastle-upon-Tyne: Shields, 1995.

Mitchell, C. Bradford. *Every Kind of Shipwork: A History of Todd Shipyards Corporation.* New York: Todd Shipyards, 1981.

Nederlandsche Scheepsbouw-Maatschappij. The Hague: J. Hamme, Jr., circa 1985.

Spasskii, I.D., ed. *История Отечественного Судостроения: в Пяти Томах* [History of domestic shipbuilding: In five volumes]. Vol. 4. St. Petersburg: Shipbuilding Press, 1996.

Taylor, Herbert E. *Swan, Hunter, & Wigham Richardson, Limited: A Historical Retrospect.* Wallsend-on-Tyne: Swan, Hunter, 1932.

Two Hundred and Fifty Years of Shipbuilding by the Scotts at Greenock. Glasgow: James Jack Advertising, 1961.

HISTORIES OF SPECIFIC SHIPPING LINES AND OTHER OPERATORS

China Navigation Company Limited: A Pictorial History 1872–1992. Hong Kong: John Swire and Sons, 1992.

Clephane, Lewis P. *History of the Naval Overseas Transportation Service in World War I.* Washington, D.C.: Naval History Division, 1969.

de Boer, G.J. *The Centenary of the Stoomvaart Maatschappij "Nederland" 1870–1970.* Kendal: World Ship Society, 1970.

Dick, H.W. and S.A. Kentwell. *Beancaker to Boxboat: Steamship Companies in Chinese Waters.* Canberra: Nautical Association of Australia, 1988.

Knap, G.H. *Hundert Jahre Seeschiffahrt: Geschichte der Koninklijke Nederlandsche Stoomboot-Maatschappij N.V.* Amsterdam: N.V. Drukkerij En Uitgeverij J.H. De Bussy, 1956.

Lawford, G.L., and L.R. Nicholson. *The Telcon Story.* London: Telegraph Construction and Maintenance, 1950.

McAlister, A.A. and Leonard Gray. *A Short History of H. Hogarth & Sons Limited.* Kendal: World Ship Society, 1976.

Mulder, P. *De Schepeu v. de KNSM 1856–1981.* Amsterdam: Erato, 1983.

Schol, Aad. *Koninklijke Nederlandsche Stoomboot-Maatschappij.* Alkmaar: De Alk bv, 1998.

Torrance, William. *Steamers on the River.* Brisbane Market: W. Torrance, 1986.

Van Popta, W.E. *De Koninklijke Nederlandsche Stoomboot Maatschappij-KNSM.* Alkmaar: Alkenreeks, n.d.

Worden, William L. *Cargoes: Matson's First Century in the Pacific.* Honolulu: Univeristy Press of Hawaii, 1981.

RUSSIAN/SOVIET MARITIME AND NAVAL HISTORY

Fairhall, David. *Russia Looks to the Sea: A Study of the Expansion of Soviet Maritime Power.* London: Andre Deutsch, 1971.

Guzhenko, Т.В. *Морской Транспорт СССР: К 60-Летию Отрасли* [Sea transport of the USSR: To the 60th anniversary of the branch]. Moscow: Transport, 1984.

Hara, Teruyuki. インディギルカ号の悲劇-1930年代のロシア極東 [The *Indigirka* tragedy: The Russian Far East in the 1930s]. Tokyo: Chikuma Shobo, 1993.

Harbron, John D. *Communist Ships and Shipping*. London: Adlard Coles, 1962.

Long, D.M. *The Soviet Merchant Fleet: Its Growth, Strategy, Strength and Weaknesses 1920–1999*. London: Lloyd's of London Press, 1986.

Mitchell, Donald W. A *History of Russian and Soviet Sea Power*. London: André Deutsche, 1974.

Muromov, I. *Сто Великих Кораблекрушений* [A hundred great shipwrecks]. Moscow: Veche, 1999.

Osichanskii, Petr. *П.П. Куянцев: Я Бы Снова Выбрал Море . . .* [P.P. Kuyantsev: I would again choose the sea . . .] Vladivostok: Far Eastern Association of Sea Captains, 1998.

Sovfracht—70 Years. Moscow: Sovfracht, 1999.

The Voyage of the Chelyuskin., Translated by Alec Brown. New York: Macmillan, 1935.

Watson, Derek. *Molotov and Soviet Government: Sovnarkom, 1930–41*. New York: St. Martin's Press, 1996.

Woodward, David. *The Russians at Sea*. London: William Kimber, 1965.

RUSSO-JAPANESE CONFRONTATIONS

Coox, Alvin D. *Nomonhan: Japan Against Russia, 1939*. Stanford: Stanford University Press, 1985.

Hough, Richard. *The Fleet That Had to Die*. London: New English Library, 1957.

Meshchanskaia, Svetlana. *Противостояние Японии и СССР/Бои у озера Хасан (29 июля—11 августа 1938 года)* [*Confrontation of Japan and USSR: fighting at Lake Khasan (July 29 to August 11, 1938)*]. Moscow: BTV-MN, 2002.

Novikov-Priboy. *Tsushima: Grave of a Floating City*. Translated by Eden and Cedar Paul. London: George Allen and Unwin, 1937.

Pleshakov, Constantine. *The Tsar's Last Armada: The Epic Voyage to the Battle of Tsushima*. New York: Basic Books, 2001.

Politovsky, Eugène S. *From Libau to Tsushima*. Translated by Maj. F.R. Godfrey, RMLI. New York: E.P. Dutton, 1908.

SPANISH CIVIL WAR

Howson, Gerald. *Arms for Spain: The Untold Story of the Spanish Civil War*. New York: St. Martin's Press, 1998.

Radosh, Ronald and Mary R. Habeck, eds. *Spain Betrayed: The Soviet Union in the Spanish Civil War*. New Haven, Conn.: Yale University Press, 2001.

WORLD WAR II

Birch, Alan and Martin Cole. *Captive Christmas: The Battle for Hong Kong— December 1941*. Hong Kong: Heinemann Asia, 1979.

Deane, R. John. *The Strange Alliance: The Story of our Efforts at War-Time Co-Operation with Russia*. New York: Viking Press, 1947.

Dingman, Roger. *Ghost of War: The Sinking of Awu Maru and Japanese-American Relations*, 1945–1995. Annapolis, Md.: Naval Institute Press, 1997.

Evans, Mark Llewellyn. *Great World War II Battles in the Arctic*. Westport, Conn.: Greenwood Press, 1999.

Haynes, John Earl, and Harvey Klehr. *Venona: Decoding Soviet Espionage in America*. New Haven, Conn.: Yale University Press, 1999.

Hays, Otis, Jr. *Home from Siberia: The Secret Odysseys of Interned American Airmen in World War II*. College Station: Texas A & M University Press, 1990.

Hutson, Harry C. *Arctic Interlude: Independent to Russia*. Bennington, Vt.: Merriam Press, 1997.

Jones, Robert Huhn. *The Roads to Russia: United States Lend-Lease to the Soviet Union*. Norman: University of Oklahoma Press, 1969.

Jordan, George R. *From Major Jordan's Diaries*. New York: Harcourt, Brace, 1952.

Meusholt, James. "Burrard Dry Dock Co Ltd." Unpublished manuscript, circa 1970.

National Security Agency. *The Venona Documents*. Washington, D.C.: 1998.

Navy Department. *Dictionary of American Naval Fighting Ships*. Washington, D.C.: Naval Historical Division, 1963.

Office of Chief of Naval Operations. *ONI-B2: Soviet Merchant Shipping Pacific*. Washington, D.C.: Intelligence Division, July 1943. Available through National Archives and Records Administration, RG 38 370 13/17/01, boxes 347–348, entry 98A: Intelligence Division, Confidential Reports of Naval Attaches, ser. 58-43.

Paperno, Alla. *Тайны и История: Ленд-Лез Тихий океан* [Secrets and history: Lend-Lease Pacific Ocean]. Moscow: Terra-Book Club, 1998.

Rohwer, Jürgen. *Axis Submarine Successes of World War Two*. London: Greenhill Books, 1999.

Rudnev, Georgi Alekseevich. *Огненные Рейсы* [Fiery flights]. Vladivostok: Dal'nevostochnoe Book Publishing House, 1975.

———. *Огненные Рейсы* [Fiery flights]. Second edition. Vladivostok: Dal'nevostochnoe Book Publishing House, 1990.

———. *На морских дорогах войны* [On the seaways of war]. Vladivostok: Dal'nevostochnogo University Publishing House, 1995.

Ruegg, Bob and Arnold Hague. *Convoys to Russia: 1941–1945*. Kendal: World Ship Society, 1992.

Ruge, Friedrich. *The Soviets as Naval Opponents: 1941–1945*. Annapolis, Md.: Naval Institute Press, 1979.

Stettinius, Edward R. Jr. *Lend-Lease: Weapon for Victory*. New York: Macmillan, 1944.

Wallace, Henry A. *Soviet Asia Mission*. New York: Reynal and Hitchcock, 1944.

Woodman, Richard. *The Arctic Convoys: 1941–1945*. London: John Murray, 1994.

SOVIET ARCTIC SHIPPING OPERATIONS

Armstrong, Terrance. *The Northern Sea Route: Soviet Exploration of the North East Passage*. London: Syndics of the Cambridge University Press, 1952.

Barr, William. "First Convoy to the Kolyma: The Soviet Northeast Polar Expedition, 1932–33." *Polar Record* 19: 123 (1979): 563–72.

Bollinger, Martin J. "Did Twelve Thousand Gulag Prisoners Die on the Dzhurma?" *Russian History/Histoire Russe*, 29, No. 1 (Spring 2002), 65-78.

Brigham, Lawson E. *The Soviet Maritime Arctic*. Annapolis, Md.: Naval Institute Press, 1991.

"Сквозные Груз плавание в Навигация 1935 года [Cargo navigation through the Northern Sea Route in the 1935 season]." *Арктический Института Бюллетень* [Arctic Institute bulletin] 10 (1935): 341.

Gakkel'. "Арктическая Навигация 1936 года [Arctic navigation 1936]." *Арктический Института Бюллетень* [Arctic Institute bulletin] 10/11 (1936): 445–45.

———. "Арктическая Навигация 1937 Года [Arctic navigation 1937]." *Проблемы Арктика* [Arctic problems] 1 (1938): 117–34.

———. "Арктическая Навигация 1938 года [Arctic navigation 1938]." *Проблемы Арктика* [Arctic problems] 1 (1939): 72–77.

Horensma, Peter. *The Soviet Arctic*. London: Routledge, 1991.

Krypton, Constantine. *The Northern Sea Route and the Economy of the Soviet North*. London: Methuen, 1956.

McCannon, John. *Red Arctic: Polar Exploration and the Myth of the North in the Soviet Union, 1932–1939*. New York: Oxford University Press, 1998.

Smolka, H.P. *40,000 against the Arctic: Russia's Polar Empire*. New York: William Morrow, 1937.

Stepaov. "Навигационный 1935 года Законченный [The navigation season of 1935 has ended]." *Sovietskaya Arktika*, no. 5 (1935): 7–10.

"Обзор плавание в водах арктические в 1934 года [Survey of navigation in the Arctic in 1934]." *Арктический Института Бюллетень* [Arctic Institute bulletin] 1–2 (1933): 1–4.

Taracouzio, Timothy A. *Soviets in the Arctic*. New York: Macmillan, 1938.

Trautman, Linda. "The Fall of the Commissariat of Ice 1935–1938." Preliminary working paper presented to the Soviet Industrialization Project Series, University of Birmingham, October 18, 2000.

"Беспрецедентное Рейс Парохода Рабочий [Unprecedented voyage of the steamship *Rabochii*]." *Арктический Института Бюллетень* [Arctic Institute bulletin] 10 (1935): 342.

Yevgenov. "Возвращение Судов Северо-восточной Экспедиции года 1932 [The return of the ships of the 1932 northeastern expedition]." *Арктический Института Бюллетень* [Arctic Institute bulletin] 5 (1933): 118–24.

GULAG HISTORY: NARRATIVES OF LABOR CAMP MANAGERS AND STAFF

"Кровью Омытое Советское Золото [Blood-Washed Soviet Gold]." *Социалистический Вестник* [Socialist bulletin], 21–22 (December 10, 1945): 579–80.

Kozlov, Aleksandr G. "От Истории Колымских Лагерей: 1932–37 [From the history of the Kolyma camps: 1932–37]." Краеведческие Записки [Notes of the Museum of Regional History] 17 (1991): 61–91.

GULAG HISTORY:
PERSONAL NARRATIVES OF PRISONERS

Bardach, Janusz, and Kathleen Gleeson. *Man Is Wolf to Man*. Berkeley: University of California Press, 1999.

Bauer, Josef Martin. *As Far as My Feet Will Carry Me*. Translated by Lawrence Wilson. London: Andre Deutsch, 1957.

Buca, Edward. *Vorkuta*. Translated by Michal Lisinski and Kennedy Wells. London: Constable, 1976.

Ginzburg, Evgenia Semyonovna. *Journey into the Whirlwind*. New York: Harcourt, Brace and World, 1967.

Glinka, Elena. "The Big Kolyma Streetcar." *Russian Life* 31: 3 (March 1998): 40–41.

Gorbatov, A.V. *Years Off My Life*. New York: W.W. Norton, 1964.

Herling, Gustaw. *A World Apart*. Harmondsworth: Penguin Books, 1951.

Lipper, Elinor. *Eleven Years in Soviet Prison Camps*. Chicago: Henry Regnery, 1951.

Mandelstam, Nadezhda. *Hope against Hope*. New York: Modern Library, 1999.

Petrov, Vladimir. *Soviet Gold: My Life as a Slave Laborer in the Siberian Mines*. Translated by Mirra Ginzburg. New York: Farrar, Straus, 1949.

Sgovio, Thomas. *Dear America*. New York: Partners' Press, 1979.

Shalamov, Varlam. *Kolyma Tales*. Translated by John Glad. London: Penguin Books, 1994.

Solomon, Michael. *Magadan*. New York: Vertex, 1971.

Solonevich, Ivan. *Escape from Russian Chains*. Translated by Warran Harrow. London: Williams and Norgate, 1938.

Vilensky, Simeon, ed. *Till My Tale Is Told*. Bloomington: Indiana University Press, 1999.

GULAG HISTORY:
SYNTHESES OF PERSONAL NARRATIVES

Conquest, Robert. *Kolyma: The Arctic Death Camps*. New York: Viking Press, 1978.

Dallin, David J., and Boris I. Nicolaevsky. *Forced Labor in Soviet Russia*. New Haven, Conn.: Yale University Press, 1947.

Dark Side of the Moon. London: Faber and Faber, 1946.

Kravchenko, Victor. *I Choose Justice*. New York: Charles Scribner's Sons, 1950.

Mora, Silvester. *Kolyma: Gold and Forced Labor in the USSR*. Washington, D.C.: Foundation for Foreign Affairs, 1949.

Mora, Sylwester and Piotr Zwierniak. *Sprawiedliwość Sowiecka* [Soviet justice]. Włochy, 1945.

Solzhenitsyn, Aleksandr I. *The Gulag Archipelago: 1918–1956*. Vol. I. Boulder, Colo.: Westview Press, 1998.

U.S. Department of Defense. *Memoirs*. Washington, D.C.: Defense Prisoner of War/Missing Personnel Office, February 29, 2000, www.dtic.mil/dpmo/special/memoirs.pdf (December 2002).

———. *The Gulag Study*. Washington, D.C.: Defense Prisoner of War/Missing Personnel Office, 2001, www.dtic.mil/dpmo/special/gulag_study.pdf (December 2002).

GENERAL GULAG AND "GREAT TERROR" HISTORY

Andrew, Christopher, and Vasili Mitrokhin. *The Mitrokhin Archive: The KGB in Europe and the West.* London: Penguin, 1999.

Applebaum, Anne. *Gulag: A History.* New York: Doubleday, 2003.

Bacon, Edwin. *The Gulag at War: Stalin's Forced Labour System in the Light of the Archives.* New York: New York University Press, 1994.

Batsaev, I.D. "Колымская Гряда Архипелага Гулаг, Заключенные [Kolyma range of the Gulag archipelago]." *Исторические Аспекты Северо-Востока России: Экономика, Образование, Колымский Гулаг* [Historical aspects of Russia's Northeast: Economics, formation of the Kolyma Gulag] (1996): 50.

Central Intelligence Agency. *Recent Developments in The Soviet Arctic.* CIA/SC/RR 82. Washington, D.C.: Office of Research and Reports, October 13, 1954, www.foia.ucia.gov (December 2002).

———. *Soviet Gold Production, Reserves and Exports through 1954.* CIA/SC/RR 121. Washington, D.C.: Office of Research and Reports, October 17, 1955, www.foia.ucia.gov (December 2002).

———. *The Soviet Forced Labor System: An Update.* F-1990-01720. Washington, D.C.: November 30, 1985, 4, www.foia.ucia.gov (December 2002).

Conquest, Robert. *The Harvest of Sorrow: Soviet Collectivization and the Terror-Famine.* New York: Oxford University Press, 1990.

———. *The Great Terror: A Reassessment.* New York: Oxford University Press, 1990.

Fitzpatrick, Sheila. *Everyday Stalinism: Ordinary Life in Extraordinary Times: Soviet Russia in the 1930s.* New York: Oxford University Press, 1999.

Getty, J. Arch, and Oleg V. Naumov. *The Road to Terror: Stalin and the Self-Destruction of the Bolsheviks, 1932–1939.* New Haven, Conn.: Yale University Press, 1999.

Jakobson, Michael. *Origins of the Gulag: The Soviet Prison Camp System, 1917–1934.* Lexington: University of Kentucky Press, 1993.

Khlusov, M.I. *The Economics of the Gulag and Its Part in the Development of the Soviet Union in the 1930s: A Documentary History.* Lewiston, N.Y.: Edwin Mellen Press, 1999.

Medvedev, Roy. *Let History Judge: The Origins and Consequences of Stalinism.* Translated by George Shriver. New York: Columbia University Press, 1989.

Medvedev, Zhores A. "Stalin and the Atomic Gulag." *Spokesman Books* (2001), www.spokesmanbooks.com/spokesman/spksmn_69.htm (December 2002).

Nordlander, David J. *Capital of the Gulag: Magadan in the Early Stalin Era, 1929–1941.* Chapel Hill: University of North Carolina, 1997.

Pilyasov, A.N. *Динамика Промышленного Производства в Магаданской Области: 1932–1992* [Dynamics of industrial manufacturing in Magadan area: 1932–1992]. Magadan: 1993.

Pohl, J. Otto. *Ethnic Cleansing in the Soviet Union, 1937–1949.* Westport, Conn.: Greenwood Press, 1999.

———. *The Stalinist Penal System: A Statistical History of Soviet Repression and Terror, 1930–1953.* Jefferson, N.C.: McFarland, 1997.

Rogovin, Vadim Z. *1937: Stalin's Year of Terror.* Oak Park, MI: Mehring Books, 1998.

Wheatcroft, Stephen G. "Victims of Stalinism and the Soviet Secret Police: The

Comparability and Reliability of the Archival Data—Not the Last Word." *Europe/Asia Studies* 51: 2 (1999).

Zemskov, Victor N. "Заключенные в 1930-ых (Демографические аспекты) [Prisoners in the 1930s (Demographic aspects)]." *Социологические Исследования* [Sociological research] 7 (1996): 6.

INTERNET AND UNPUBLISHED MANUSCRIPTS

Amrakhov, Shafig. "Транспорт: Держать по створ [Transport: To stay the course]." 1999, www.press.lukoil.ru/text.phtml?result_artic=438&result=66 (December 2002).

Bernsone, Ilze and Aigars Miklavs. "The Latvians: A Seafaring Nation." *Latvian Institute* (2001), www.latinst.lv/seafaring.htm (December 2002).

Bolotov, V.P., ed. "Документы о Гибели Парохода Индигирка в Районе п. Саруфуцу (о.Хоккайдо) в 1939 году [Documents about the destruction of the steamship *Indigirka* in the area of Sarufutsu (off Hokkaido) in 1939]." 1998, www.vld.ru/ppx/Indigir/Docs.htm (December 2002).

Chymakov, Valery. "Кому На Чукотке Жить Хорошо [Who on Chukotka can live well]." № Chukotka (December 1999), www.ropnet.ru/ogonyok/win/199990/90-46-49.html (December 2002).

Dinets, Vladimir. "Hitchhiking to Oimyakon and Beyond" (1999), www.hotcity.com/~vladimir/kolyma.htm (December 2002).

Far East Customs Management. "Находкинской таможне 50 лет [Customs house of 50 Years]" (2001), www.bazar2000.ru/custom/custom003.htm (December 2002).

Fumagali, Raul. "My Polish Friend: Amazing Life and Adventures," www.thelatinmass.com/lopacki.html (December 2002).

Garusova, L.N. "Russian-American Regional Relations on the Far East: History and Present," abc.vvsu.ru/Books/m_rosamo/page0008.asp (January 2002).

Gavrilov, Sergei. "Трагедия Буксира Кит [Tragedy of the tug *Whale*]." Новая Камчатская Правда [New Kamchatka truth], no. 41 (October 18, 2001), www.iks.ru/~nkp/arhiv/html_arhiv/2001/41/41_4.html (December 2002).

Kniazev, Lev. *У Врат Блаженства* [At the gates of bliss], www.vld.ru/ppx/Knyazev/Blazh.htm (December 2002).

Kowalski, Stanislaw J. "Kolyma: The Land of Gold and Death" (2000), www.personal.psu.edu/users/w/x/wxk116/sjk/kolyma4.htm (December 2002).

———. "White Auschwitz of Kolyma," www.gulag.hu/white_auschwitz.htm (January 2002).

Kozlov, Aleksandr G. "Кого Карал НКВД? [Who punished the NKVD?]," www.kolyma.ru/magadan/history/repres.shtml (January 2002).

———. "Взрывы в Бухте Нагаева: Правда И Вымысел [Explosions in Nagaevo Bay: Truth and fiction]," www.kolyma.ru/magadan/history/nagaevo.shtml (December 2002).

Mariev, Alexander. "Воспоминания [Memoirs]." *Уральская Галактика* [Ural galaxy] (1999), www.art.uralinfo.ru/literat/UG/ug3/mar_vosp.htm (December 2002).

204

SELECTED BIBLIOGRAPHY

Memorial (Kursk). "Сообщение Антона Иосифовича Миронова [Anton Iosifovicha Mironova's message]" (1990), www.memorial.krsk.ru/svidet/mmiron.htm (December 2002).

———. "Сообщение Михаила Николаевича Соболева [Michael Nikolaevicha Soboleva's message]," www.memorial.krsk.ru/svidet/mnsobol.htm (December 2002).

———. "Джафарова Берта Самойловна (Dzhafarova Berta Samoblovna]," www.memorial.krsk.ru/martirol/dj_dl.htm (December 2002).

———. "Сообщение Юстины Николаевны Нагляк [Nikolaevich Naglyak Ustina's message]," www.memorial.krsk.ru/svidet/mnagl.htm (December 2002).

———. "Сообщение Михаила Васильевича Иванова [Biography of Ivanov Mikhail Vasilievich]" (2001), www.memorial.krsk.ru/svidet/mmivan.htm (December 2002).

Memorial (Tomsk). "Есть люди нелегкой судьбы . . . [There are people of hard destiny . . .]," www.memorial.tomsk.ru:8100/memo/lud/ade.htm (January 2002).

Mihin, Nikolay. "Венки на волне: Документальные очерки [Wreaths on a wave: Documentary sketches]" (1998), lib.ru/PROZA/MIHINN/venki.txt (December 2002).

Moiseyenko, Yuri Illarionovich. "Поэзия Каторги [Poetry katorgi]," www.MTU-NET.ru/rayner/avtorskaja/poes_katorgi11.htm (December 2002).

"Военнопленные [Military prisoners]." Невское Время [Neva times] 201 (November 5, 1998), www.pressa.spb.ru/newspapers/nevrem/arts/nevrem-1843-art-14.html (December 2002).

Novokuznetsk City Study of Local Lore Museum. "Сергеев Александр Григорьевич [Sergey Alexander Grigor'evich]" (1995), www.kuzbass.ru/nkz/stalinsk/sergeev.htm (December 2002).

Okupatsioonide Repressiivpoliitika Uurimise Riikiik Komisjon. "The Soviet Prison Camps in Extreme North and Estonian Political Prisoners in Kolyma," www.okupatsioon.ee/trykised/oll/oll_kolyma_vang1.html (December 2002).

"«Декабрист» Приказано Разбомбить [Orders to destroy the Dekabrist]." № Chukotka 16 (May 2000), www.ropnet.ru/ogonyok/win/200016/16-03-03.html (December 2002).

Ratushnaya, Larissa. "Этюды О Колымских Днях [Essays about days in Kolyma]" (1999), www.art.uralinfo.ru/LITERAT/Ural/Ural_7_99/Ural_07_99_08.htm (December 2002).

Rodionova, Ivan Ivanovich. "Хронология [Chronology]." Russian Air Force (2001), www.AIRFORCE.ru/history/chronology/1930.htm (December 2002).

Rudnev, G. "Страшные Отголоски Минувшей Войны [Terrible echoes of the last war]." Zavetniy Krai 1 (1998), www.vld.ru/ppx/Kraj/Zkr1_pub.htm#Dalstroj (December 2002).

Sakharov Center. "Биография Нины Владимировны Сароевы [Biography of Nina Vladimirovna Saroeva]," www.sakharov-center.ru/adcs/bio/98.htm (January 2001).

———. "Лесниака Бориса Николаевича [Lesnyak Boris Nicolaevich]," www.sakharov-center.ru/adcs/bio/99.htm (July 2001).

Samarin, Igor. "Sakhalin Lighthouses." (1999), www.sakhalin.ru/Engl/Region/lighthouses/lighthouses.htm (December 2002).

Shirokov, A.I. "Первое Десятилетие "Дальстроя" [First decade of Dal'stroi]," www.gulag.ru/page/histori/1ten.htm (December 2002).

Sloma, Marion. "Lasciate Ogni Speranza," www.najmici.org/kolyma/ksiazka11.htm (December 2002).

Sigachev, S. "History of Magadan Town and Surrounding Territory," www.kolyma.ru/magadan/history/dalstroi.shtml (December 2002).

"Восстание троцкистов на Колыме [Troskyite insurrection in Kolyma]," www.gulag.ru/page/zk/v_Trozk/v_trozk.htm (December 2002).

Vedernikov, Jury. "Хроники Кораблекрушений В Российских Водах Дальнего Востока [Chronicle of shipwrecks in the Russian waters of the Far East]." Владивосток [Vladivostok], May 25, 1996, www.vld.ru/ppx/Katastr/Cronics.htm (December 2002).

Vinogradov, Leonid. "Ржавые Свидетели Старой Трагедии Найдены [Rusty witnesses of old tragedy are found]." Ежедневные Новости Владивосток [Daily news Vladivostok] 183 (1998), novosti.vl.ru/1998/183/hap_01.html (January 2001).

Working, Russell. "Odessa Last Breadth of Soviet Liberty." Moscow Times, September 29, 2000.

GENERAL REGIONAL HISTORY

Amis, Martin. Koba the Dread: Laughter and the Twenty Million. New York: Talk Mirimax Books, 2002.

Brooke-Shepard, Gordon. Iron Maze: The Western Secret Services and the Bolsheviks. London: Macmillan, 1998.

Eastern European Section, Foreign Intelligence Branch. Photo Album of the Visit of Henry A. Wallace to China and USSR. National Archives and Record Administration: RG 38, 370 15-5-1, box 61.

Le Procès Kravchenko contre Les Lettres Françaises. Paris: La Jeune Parque, 1949.

Littlepage, John D., and Demaree Bess. In Search of Soviet Gold. New York: Harcourt, Brace, 1938.

Lockhart, R.H. Bruce. British Agent. New York: G.P. Putnam's Sons, 1933.

Oberg, James. Uncovering Soviet Disasters. New York: Random House, 1988.

Spahr, William J. Zhukov: The Rise & Fall of a Great Captain. Novato, Calif.: Presidio Press, 1993.

Thubron, Colin. In Siberia. New York: HarperCollins, 1999.

Index

Ships are designated by the prefix SS and alphabetized accordingly.

About the Author

MARTIN J. BOLLINGER is a senior partner with a leading global management-consulting firm, specializing in business and operations strategy in the aerospace, defense and maritime industries. In his spare time, he researches and write about maritime history. His research related to Soviet maritime history has appeared in *Russian History*, the *International Journal of Maritime History*, and the U.S. *Naval War College Review*. He also serves on the Board of Directors of the U.S. Naval Historical Foundation in Washington, DC. He has lived and worked in the United States and Australia, and currently resides in Great Falls, Virginia.